CERES COLONY CAVALIER

A true account of one man's
twenty year abduction

TONY RODRIGUES

Editing contributions by Andulairah and Jackie Kenner

DEDICATION

I'd like to dedicate this book to the ones that stepped up for me in a time of need. When the memories of my experiences first came back, I was alone. There was no one I could talk to.

Thank you Dr. Salla, Morgan, and Rob Potter for hearing me out.

Tara, Elise, Madison, and Michael for your love and support.

Everyone that has lent me their time and perspective to talk about my memories and connect the dots—Jason Rice, Randy Cramer, Michael Gerloff, Jay Weidner, and many others. Talking about it really has been the best therapy.

Lastly, Andulairah and Jackie Kenner—without your help, this book would not have been completed.

CONTENTS

FOREWARD

Tony Rodrigues first contacted me in August 2015 about his experiences in a secret space program run by a German breakaway civilization. In the subsequent telephone conversations and vetting that occurred, I found Tony to be a sincere and credible witness about his involvement in such a program. We physically met for the first time one year later in Mt Shasta, California, where we did a five-part interview series that publicly presented his story for the first time in video form. Ever since, I have watched Tony share his story on many public forums and have been impressed by the consistency of his memories and his investigations. What impressed me most about Tony was his determination to confirm multiple facts about the time spent in Seattle, Washington, China Lake, California, and Peru prior to him serving in space. His book is no exception; everything in it is consistent with what he has shared with me and subsequent interviewers about his experiences and corroborating information.

One of the things that researchers look for in determining the validity of a witness is their motivation in coming forward. Tony had nothing to gain but everything to lose in sharing his traumatic experiences as a sex slave and a slave in a secret space program. At the time, very little was known about the Dark Fleet (aka 'Nacht Waffen') and how they treated personnel. The first public reference to the "Dark Fleet" was by Corey Goode, who listed it as one of five secret space programs he was familiar with in early 2015. The existence of a Nazi linked secret space program was subsequently confirmed by William Tompkins later that year. Both Goode and Tompkins said that slave labor was used extensively by the Dark Fleet. This was startling confirmation that Albert Speer's book, *Infiltration* (1981), detailing Nazi plans for a post-war Europe in which slavery would be used as a permanent solution to labor shortages, had been secretly implemented in Antarctica and clandestine space operations.

Tony was the first person to emerge with a plausible account of his time with the Dark Fleet, and how slaves were systematically being used and mistreated. Since his public emergence, many others have come forward with remarkable stories of their own involuntary servitude with the Dark Fleet. However, Tony was the first, which makes his testimony especially significant today as we attempt to understand the operations and capabilities of the Dark Fleet.

Tony's story began in 1981 when he was only nine or ten years old and in 4th grade. He was involuntarily recruited into a twenty year program as punishment for something he did to one of his classroom peers. He publicly embarrassed the son of a high-level member of the Illuminati who took it upon himself to punish Tony. Tony says that he was soon after abducted by five aliens. He was then genetically tested to determine what skills he possessed, which could be used in covert 'support' programs and eventually for the secret space programs themselves when he got older.

Tony described that the aliens told him that his consciousness would be borrowed for 20 years, which involved it being transferred into a cloned body. When I first heard this, I tried to reconcile Tony's experiences with what Michael Relfe (1976-1996), Randy Cramer (1987-2007), and Corey Goode (1986-2007) had earlier said about their own SSP experiences. In one of our 2014 interviews, Randy said that he had encountered some of his clones and had to train them. Apparently, it was no big problem to technologically transfer consciousness into a cloned body in case of irreparable injury or death. Cloning, according to William Tompkins, had been first developed by the Antarctic Germans with the help of Draconian extraterrestrials. After the US and the Antarctic Germans had reached agreements in the mid-1950s, it's not surprising that cloning technology was adopted for use in deep black projects, which involved a high incidence of death among super soldiers fighting extraterrestrials. Using clones while preserving the original bodies in stasis chambers meant highly trained and expensive super soldiers could be used again and again in covert space warfare.

Tony describes how he woke up in his cloned body at a medical facility located at Inyokern, California, which is adjacent to the giant China Lake Naval Air Weapons Station. He and eleven other children were joined by hundreds of adults and entered a large triangle-shaped vehicle, likely a TR-3B, which both landed and took off vertically. The inside of the vehicle was arranged like a conventional airplane with seats and aisles. He said that the embroidery on the back of the seat said Douglas, suggesting Douglas Aircraft Company was involved in the manufacturing of the triangle craft. This is not surprising for those that followed the groundbreaking testimony of William Tompkins, who revealed Douglas' earlier role in designing and building anti-gravity spacecraft. Tony said the craft walls could be made transparent so passengers could see outside the craft during the journey and witnessed two Moon bases as they landed about an hour after departure. This matched what Randy Cramer said about his trip to the Moon in early 2014 to a separate lunar facility called Lunar Operations Command, which he was the first to publicly reveal.

Tony's triangle craft landed at a Moon base that had a Pentagon-like trapezoidal shape, which has since been found to be a joint Dark Fleet extraterrestrial facility. After several days of examinations and surgical enhancements by extraterrestrials, he was returned to Earth, ready for use as a psychic. Tony says that he was first forced to work as a psychic for a drug-running operation out of Peru for several years before being recruited as a sex worker in Seattle from age 13. When he turned 16 years old, in 1988, he was taken to the Moon to be tested for any skills he possessed that would benefit the space programs.

After briefly serving on Mars as a slave fighter for a mercenary military force protecting corporate bases from indigenous Martians, corroborating what Randy Cramer said earlier in 2014, Tony says he was taken to Ceres, a planetoid in the asteroid belt. He worked at Ceres for 13 years with a German-led freighter crew that was part of the "Dark Fleet." His detailed account of his time with the Dark Fleet is precious eyewitness testimony of the procedures and operations used by the Antarctic Germans and their collaboration with the US military intelligence community.

Recently, claims have emerged that the Dark Fleet is in disarray and has had to abandon its former Antarctica, Mars, and Ceres bases, and now operates exclusively outside of our solar system. Regardless of the accuracy of such claims, Tony's memories of having served with the Dark Fleet from 1988 to 2001 give us a vital eyewitness account of what historically happened both within and outside of our solar system. His vivid recollections of what happened to him during his time with the Dark Fleet and earlier experiences in Peru and Seattle makes for compelling reading.

Tony's book, *Ceres Colony Cavalier*, gives us an unprecedented look at how the monstrous practice of slavery had been resurrected and extensively used inside covert programs both on Earth and in space. Sadly, there are many that suffered from a life of servitude inside these secret programs who have died or been forgotten. Tony's biographical account of what happened to him will raise awareness of the plight of many that suffered in these clandestine programs and may still be trapped in them. His book will help raise awareness sufficiently to put an end to such practices forever, bring justice to the victims, and a final reckoning for the perpetrators of these crimes against humanity. What you are about to read will both shock and enlighten you of what it means to have been a slave in a secret space program and its support services for 20 years. Tony is to be congratulated for his bravery in coming forward and sharing his traumatic experiences to a world that is finally waking up to the truth of secret space programs and extraterrestrial life.

Michael Salla, Ph.D.
December 20, 2021

INTRODUCTION

My name is Tony Rodrigues.

I don't know where to start really, but I know that I need to get this down. I know that what has happened to me is not something that happens to everybody. And I also know that what has happened to me is a crime.

There was a time when I was on a plateau in life, so to speak. I wasn't happy with it but I knew in my mind that I had been in much worse situations. Then the memories came and I was all alone in knowing the things I'll describe in this book. All at once, I merged with those memories and became a different person. And I believed I was alone. Who was going to even listen to me get half of it out let alone support me?

Sometimes I don't even believe it myself.

One can look back and pick apart every little detail. One can say that it is not possible. That it could never be. Why would I remember now?

It couldn't have happened—it's impossible. There must be some other reason why I am remembering all of these things. Maybe it *is* a dream, or some delusion, or something else I am just not aware of. But the truth of it is, that it *did* happen, and there is no way to *dream up* twenty years worth of dreams.

Not to mention the other testimonies of people coming forward, saying things that perfectly coincide with what I have remembered.

At some point, I had to just admit to myself that what I remembered was the truth. That it did happen, and that it *does* happen—and I am not the only one. And it needs to be talked about.

So here we are.

1

THE NEW BOY

I WAS BORN IN 1972. I grew up in an old farmhouse on thirteen acres in southern Michigan. My older brothers had moved out when I was young, and I lived there with my mom, dad, and my sister, as well as the dog and the cat. We had no farm animals really. My dad was employed with a good job and worked for a big automaker. My mom always told me how lucky we were that he worked so hard. He had given my mom a better life than she expected. They met when she was a single mom of 4 kids. He had been pronounced sterile by several doctors and had always wanted kids. They were married in 1971 and had me one year later.

I was an outstanding student in my early years in school. I was chosen for the Talented and Gifted Program (TAG). As far as I know, this program is still out there, and features something like the top five percent of students in each grade. Our group would meet together on Wednesdays in the school library. Every week, the participants of the program learned new skills such as how to index, or to research subjects, and similar tasks. They were basically teaching us how to do things that were applicable to advanced education pursuits.

It's important to state that the TAG program at my school was only offered for the tenure of one particular student at our school. He and his father were living in town while an important negotiation between Dominos and Coca Cola was being developed, and his father was involved in the negotiations.

There was one particular test that stood out from the rest, and it was the time that I was given an ink blot test by my teacher. On that day, an observer came in to watch the testing. The tester put the ink blot tests away and the observer asked me to simply quiet my mind and tell him if any shapes or symbols came to mind. I was confused and told them but no, nothing came to mind. The observer also said that he didn't get anything either, then left. It was odd, as if they were hoping I could read their mind. This was in the third grade and the TAG program started in the fourth grade.

It was 1981 when I entered the fourth grade. There was a new boy in school. He was weird looking with a long forehead, and he got dropped off each day in a limousine. This was beyond unusual in the sticks. I found him arrogant, and to that point, the most condescending person I'd ever met in my life. I didn't know him but I hated him right out of the gate. He critiqued the teacher and often made comments about flaws in her work. At first she tried to shush him, but over the course of the year, he started to wear her down. He was the student that seemed to have brought the TAG program to our school. It started when he came and was shut down when his family left town.

His presentation from one particular assignment has always stood out for me. We were told to write a report on something we believe that no one else believed. He told the class that he was a reincarnated Pharaoh; that his soul was old and that he had memories of this past life. The story of the Pharaoh was that he commanded an army into battle. When they met the opposing army, rather than all soldiers engaging in a fight, the Pharaoh rode out, shot one arrow, killed the opponent leader, and the battle ended on the spot. This boy could name the Pharaoh and this was apparently a historically documented event, though I can't remember any details, like the name, from his story and haven't been able to find it in my searches.

What I remember most was how visibly upset the boy was getting that our teacher made him say that he *"believed"* he was reincarnated and a Pharaoh. His frustration that he was forced to tell the story this way, as opposed to sharing it as truth, has stuck with me. He really believed what he was saying and didn't think it was fair to have to alter his speech around it.

I remember his name, first and last, but I don't feel compelled to share this information publicly. I have also since found his Facebook Profile to add credence to my story. I've discovered that he currently works in Hollywood in children's animations.

Much like this fellow student, there are many people in my story that I can name, but I won't for the sake of this book. This decision to keep identities anonymous is not about protecting them or enabling them, which I've been accused of. It is about protecting myself, my family, and any affiliations these innocent people have to them. Most people aren't even aware of what certain other individuals are involved with.

One morning, I came into the TAG class and I was a little early. I saw three or four girls sitting on a couch reading area with the new boy there, and they were all laughing. I walked up to them and they all went quiet.

I asked them, "What's going on?"

One of the girls replied, saying, "He can tell you what you're thinking—just think of something, and he can tell it."

The new boy looked at them and said, "No, it's time to stop."

The girls were persistent, and wanted him to keep going.

They turned to me and said, "Do him!"

I joined them, and said, "Yeah, let me try it!"

So, the girls advised me to think about anything. I did and then I waited for the new boy to reveal my thoughts back to me. Of course, I didn't believe any of this, and knew that there was no way that somebody could read my mind. So, as a child of that age, I thought about the cruelest thing that I could possibly think of. The thought I had in my mind was: *You're the ugliest kid I've ever seen, and none of these girls will ever, ever date you when you grow up.*

The new boy looked up at me with total disgust and just sat there in silence.

I was pretty self-assured that he had no idea what I was thinking, and so I said to him, "Go ahead! Tell them all what I thought!"

Instead, he just sat there, not saying a word. The teacher came in and we started our class. I didn't realize it at the time, but the new boy hated me after that. I mean, hated me. I would try to talk to him from time to time and become friends, but it became abundantly obvious that something like that was never going to happen.

He did read my mind. He knew exactly what I thought. It devastated him. I couldn't read his thoughts but I could read his face. And I had told the naked truth. He *was* ugly. His proportions were all wrong.

One morning, a few of the kids and I, along with the new boy, were sitting around talking about what our parents did for a living.

The new boy looked at me, and with a sneering tone he said, "My dad's an Illuminati, what does your dad do?"

I had no idea what the Illuminati was—or did—for that matter, and even to this day, really still don't. But I was proud of what my dad did, and I went on to brag about what a great job he had, and how lucky we were as a family. He was a machine repairman for General Motors. Looking back, that day always stood out in my mind because the new boy asked about my dad and said those words with such anger that it just didn't make sense to me. He never seemed to have gotten over the mind reading day. He stayed pissed at me. I could tell I had hurt him and made attempts to be his friend but he never let it go.

A few months later, we had the school science fair and I overheard my teacher saying that the new boy's father was the most educated person she had ever heard of, and that he had volunteered to be one of the judges of the science fair.

We were setting up our exhibits for the fair in the cafeteria, and I walked by the new boy and his father, to which he quickly turned to his father and said, "There is that boy!"

He pointed to me and said, "He's the one that ruined my confidence."

His father said a few things to him that I found really strange. It was something like:

"Well we can give him to our friends. We'll find use for him in the breakaway. He'll learn humility."

I didn't understand what he was talking about, and I overheard the new boy replying to his father, "I don't think he deserves that."

His father told him that he was going to have to learn how to allocate resources without being emotional. It was a very strange conversation to me. Needless to say, I just walked away from them, and went on with my typical, nine-year-old carefree day.

Not long thereafter, perhaps two or three days after that encounter with the new boy and his father, I had dinner—just like I would any other night— and went to bed.

I remember waking up in the middle of the night to the phone ringing. It was an old-style phone with a bell ringer. No answering machine. No caller ID. There was only one phone in the house and it was downstairs in the kitchen. It rang loud enough to wake up the entire house. It just rang and rang. After about fifteen to twenty rings, it would then suddenly stop. Then, only a few minutes later, it would start ringing again. I remember thinking to myself: *It's probably an emergency, and mom will get up and get it.*

I wanted to get out of bed and get it myself, but for some reason I was really sleepy. I remember laying there, going back to sleep, and then continually waking up because the phone was ringing so loud and for so long. There was another strange thing - that whenever the phone rang, I felt as if I was being enveloped within static electricity. It sounded like the electricity was crackling, and sounded like it was crackling outside of the house too. There was bright light coming down from the sky that seemed to flash on, then disappear for a bit. The phone would ring and then the light would come back.

22

I began perceiving a lot of what I can only describe as weirdness. In the midst of this cycle of waking up and then sleeping again, repeating itself over and over (to which I feel I was only sleeping artificially anyway), something was making me feel unnaturally tired. I really *wanted* to wake up, but my sleepiness was overpowering me.

It is my opinion that all of the loud ringing and bright lights were to ensure that we were all in fact subdued by whatever technology was being used to keep the household asleep.

Then, out of nowhere, a blue orb flew into my room, making the static electricity crackling sound again, until it then whizzed back out into the hallway and went downstairs. There was silence for a few minutes.

My parents, in the next bedroom beside mine, woke up and I heard my mom crying out.

"Oh my God!" I could hear her words, and she said something like, "You're going to take my baby?"

A few minutes of silence ensued, and everything seemingly settled down. I thought whatever was happening was over, and so I closed my eyes to go back to sleep. But it was not so. It was very dark, and I woke up again. When I opened my eyes, there was somebody standing over me.

My dad is the type of guy who is always sneaking up and playing pranks, so at first I thought it was him. "Dad, you have a mask on—you're not funny."

I reached up and touched his face to take the mask off, but to my own horror—it was cold and alive. It felt like what you would imagine a shark out of water to feel like, but there were pores everywhere, like a small, slimy, lotus pod. I suddenly realized that it wasn't a mask. It wasn't my dad. This individual— this being—was smaller. It looked like what most refer to as a grey alien. I was about to succumb to the most incredible shock because whatever it was, it reached out to me and I was immediately paralyzed. It hit me on the back of the right side of my neck, near my ear. I could move my eyes, but nothing else. My body went limp.

I could see out of the corner of my eye that there were three other shorter figures wearing hoods, and they were moving towards me. They looked like reptiles and were about four feet tall. They grabbed me out of my blankets, carried me to the foot of my bed, and then all I remember was melding into a ball of light. I had the feeling that I was going out through my bedroom window, but it felt more like dematerializing than traveling from one point to another as we know it.

I lost consciousness and woke up on a table in some kind of room. I had no sense of where I was. The room was round and it looked like the walls were made of stone. The doorway was also round and opened into a hallway where people or beings were moving about. I was naked and had a sense of embarrassment. I couldn't see what was going on very well because my eyes were bad. Back in those younger years, I needed glasses with severe correction lenses. Despite being in a foreign place, with what appeared to be aliens, half drugged by some kind of drowsiness technology, I was elated beyond words. I was so happy, because to me, I was having first contact. I was going to be the guy that told the whole world that aliens were visiting us, and that we were not alone.

I looked up at them with my outstretched hands and cried, "Yaay! I knew you guys were real! People need you! This is going to be a big deal for us! We were wondering if we were alone or not!"

They didn't respond, and simply continued on with their tasks. They looked as if they were getting some type of equipment ready, as if preparing the room for something. There were two small grays, a white gray, and one small reptilian. At the time, I didn't know about extraterrestrial species or what these beings were -- this was something I learned later in my tour.

I felt the fear beginning to fall over me, and I said to them, "Are you gonna hurt me?"

Telepathically, I could hear one of them reply, saying "No, we are just going to do a few tests on you. You're going to be fine."

At that point, the gray being came and poked my arm with some device. It came from behind me, so I could not see the device. It did hurt, but not that bad. I had developed a child's tolerance for this kind of pain when I had shots and things at the doctor's, so it didn't bother me too much. I was most concerned with maintaining our newly formed relations of first contact with an alien species. So, I told him I was fine.

People ask me if the grays are male or female. While it's really hard to say for certain, I would describe them as more male than female. Certainly no features that we would affiliate with the feminine—soft voices, curves, nurturing—none of that. They were devoid of any kind of emotional response. They were like robots.

I wanted to know more about what was going on and attempted to ask a few questions. But I only received brief and trivial answers. I wanted to know things like where they were from, how old they were, if they were going to contact our president. Again, to me, I was experiencing the first contact for humans. I wanted to know if they would be our friends or not.

The two tall grays left the room. Then a short, reptile-like being came in. He was the same as the ones that wore hoods in my bedroom. The fabric was a chalky charcoal color. He seemed more engaging than the other two, and was willing to answer my questions. To my surprise, he also made me laugh with his good sense of humor. He advised me that they were waiting on the results of a genetic test to see if I 'fit the criteria' for what they were requiring of me.

My curiosity got the better of me, and I kept asking him, "What's that?"

He didn't answer me, so in my haste, I persisted with other questions.

"Where are you from? How long are you staying? Are we in a spaceship?"

He was really short but told me we were in an underground base, that they had been there a while, and that the main message for humankind is that the music sucks. He said he was just like me, here for a job, and that he went home to his planet every night. I asked him what his planet was like and he said way nicer than ours. It was red, had heavier gravity than earth, and the sky was red most of the time.

He said that they were part of a galactic conglomerate and that they were controlled by another intergalactic form of government too. He said that Earth might join the same conglomerate someday and that I could have a job like his. He somehow knew about Bruce

Lee and showed me his impersonation. He was a huge fan.

The two grays eventually returned, advising me that my results were barely passable but still usable.

One of the gray's pulled the short reptile being aside and said, "There is one more thing…"

The reptile being looked at me and said, "That's right, we have to get your permission. Do you want to help us?"

I did not hesitate, "Of course I want to help you with anything I can do."

He said, "We are going to borrow your consciousness."

I was confused. "What does that mean, my consciousness?"

"We are going to take you for 20 years. We need you to help us work."

I quickly replied, "There's no way I can do that. I've got a family, I've got to get back to my mom, my sister, and my dad. I can't be gone for that long."

He quickly stated, "No, no, no. We're going to bring you back in time, and when you're done, you'll have only been gone for a few minutes. You're going to wake up tomorrow morning, and you can tell them about everything you've done."

The reptile being went on and on, explaining that there was nothing to worry about, and that I probably wouldn't remember it all anyway. Considering that I honestly thought I was in a 'first contact situation', and that I was representing the good people of Earth, I truly felt I was helping in some way—and was a part of something bigger than myself—so I agreed.

Then came the "standard" UFO abduction experience —wherein they laid me down on a table, and put a rubber-like sheet over me, something akin to latex. The sheet was dark and I could not see through it. The table somehow sucked all of the air out, so that the sheet was pulled tight around my body, and they then proceeded to take a small, knife-like tool, and cut a hole over my eye and mouth. I was gasping for air and remembered the relief of being able to breathe again when they punctured the area over my mouth.

I glanced up, and noticed a gold colored needle on some sort of a mechanical arm device, hovering over my right eye. The needle then slowly entered just inside the tear duct of my eye. It hurt like hell, and immediately thereafter, I began seeing stars—as if being punched in the eye, and that's all I remember— seeing stars, and feeling like I was getting sucked out of my body. It felt like I was being sucked into the area where the needle went into my head.

2

THE DOCTOR

I WOKE UP TO FIND myself lying on a bed in what looked like a 1950's hospital. It was outdated for the times and felt like something I'd seen in a movie. It was a small room lined with other beds like the one I was in. There were three beds in my row, and seven or eight more around the corner. In each of these beds, there were other kids that all seemed to be around the same age as me. We were all males, except for one female.

A tall skinny man—a white guy—with curly red hair and donning thick glasses, was busily giving me the standard medical exam. He told me that he was a doctor and conducted the reflex test, the flashlight in your pupils, he checked my heart rate, and I gave him some deep breaths. The standard stuff.

He then asked me, "Do you remember your mom?"

I said no.

"Do you remember your dad?"
I said no.

"Do you have any brothers or sisters?"

I said no.

"Do you believe in God?"

I said yes.

He answered me, saying, "Well, we'll take care of that."

I felt awful, like puking, and he advised me to just lay down, as this was going to take a while. He also casually told me that I was brand-new, and that I didn't remember anything because I was a clone.

Waking up the following day, I felt a lot better. The only girl that was there had blonde hair and she seemed familiar to me, though I couldn't remember from where or how. I didn't recognize any of the boys. The doctor ran through a type of orientation where he again informed us that we were all "brand-new." He also told us that we were being trained for jobs that we were to do at a later date. He was bold enough to add that if we could not complete what we were told to do, then we would simply be killed.

"You were made for this," he stated, "And even though it is going to be uncomfortable at times, there are plenty of other people who have successfully completed this program, and you will end up being fine."

He explained that because he claimed to be a doctor, if we were ever injured, he would be able to treat and fix us. For the rest of the day, we continued going through more examinations, such as flashcards and IQ tests. These were simple cards with moons, stars, and things like that on them. He was asking us which one came next in the stack and keeping track of our accuracy. We kept repeating this over and over again.

There were three of four students in the class that were rockstars, meaning that they were psychic as fuck and passed everything with flying colors. I wasn't that psychic, at least not compared to the others, but I did pass some tests. I was in the 30-40% range and it was clear he found me disappointing.

The next day was different.

We were all woken up and were chaperoned out of the little hospital-like building to find that we were in fact, at an airport. There was an active runway somewhere nearby. We could hear the planes but not see them. We were told that we could not go by the windows because there were classified things going on around us. What I realized in hindsight was that *we* were the classified things and that they didn't want the passengers in the planes to see *us*.

It was hot outside. The air was dry. There were a myriad of big warehouse type buildings, and the footpaths were neatly paved as we walked.

We were escorted to a small parking lot area, then into one of several large warehouse buildings. Inside the facility were rows of individual metal cages. We were all designated to our own cage, then three or four men assisted each of us inside. The cages were small, maybe three feet by five feet, and not tall enough for me to stand. I had to crawl in and then sit down. They were stacked one on top of another, and there were wooden bottoms, as if you could lift each cage with a forklift. The outside of the cage looked like steel with metal grating. From the inside, there was a smaller inner grate, which was more like chicken wire sized holes that we were to sit on. There was absolutely nothing inside the cage and we were all stripped down to our underwear.

Once we were all secured within our cages, the men then explained to us that we would be timed, to see how long we could stay inside. We wouldn't be killed, they advised us, but there was a catch—we were to withstand electric shock. Then they turned on the electricity.

The floor, the walls, and the ceiling of the cage were electrified. It was one continuous shock and I don't know how long it went on for, but I do know that it went on for a long time. It was a lot of electricity. I've touched cattle wire in my life and it was minor compared to what they were doing. It was enough that we were all flopping around. I tried to stick my fingers through the inner wire to grab the outer wire. I wanted to lift myself up off the bottom to not get shocked. There was enough voltage going through us that no one could speak.

Eventually, I just gave up. I was the third or fourth to go down. I surrendered myself to the floor, allowing my full body to receive the shock. I remember not caring anymore and resigning myself to death. Something inside you breaks. It wasn't just giving up on the shock; it was giving up entirely. I became almost numb to the pain. There were men calling out things like "nine is down," and then "seven is down." They left the electricity going until all of us were down.

When it finally stopped, I was grateful but dazed. I don't know who went down when, or in what order. I don't know the reason they conducted this test. I can say that in that moment, when I just gave up and resigned to my fate, that moment was the end of my childhood. I was a young boy but something different. My view of life was never the same again. Suddenly, I was aware that I could die.

After what seemed like an eternity, we were all returned to our room, given several tests, and put to bed. The doctor took each of us into his office one by one, asking us what we thought of the activity. This was something that he did almost every day. For this one, he seemed very interested in how I felt. I just remember saying I was happy I didn't die.

The doctor informed us as we awakened the following day that we wouldn't have to go through that electrical experiment again.

Instead, "You will get to have your own chair, and your own helmets," he said, sitting us down on the floor in the middle of the room.

We were now in the middle building of three portable units. One portable we slept in, one seemed to be his office and also the building with the chairs he'd mentioned, and one was more like a hospital. There was surgical equipment and a nurse, but we didn't go there often. We never returned to the shock warehouse again.

The chairs were hanging from the ceiling by chains, almost like a carnival swing ride. The helmets were all sorts of different colors—like the old 70's motorcycle helmets, with the stripe down the middle.

"Go and pick your own," he said.

Everyone wanted the blue one—except for the girl. She wanted the yellow one. I ended up with a yellow one too.

The chairs were suspended at a height that when we sat in them, our feet did not touch the ground. We were all hanging about one foot off the ground. We could get in the chair on our own but none of our feet reached the floor. There was a way the doctor could lock us in too. We were strapped into the chairs with our helmets on, and then he plugged the helmets into wires—wires that also hung from the ceiling.

The doctor sometimes gave us shots, and other times our eyes were forced open by some type of device and we were given eye drops. There was a sort of clamp that lifted your eyelids so that you could not close your eyes. After a while— probably less than two weeks—we didn't need the clamps anymore because we'd become trained to leave our eyes open and pay attention.

Positioned in front us was a standard reel projector and we were shown a sort of movie. These movies would include parts of cartoons that were mixed with scenes from wars and animal mutilations, containing subliminal messages—words flashing by, too much too quick to read. And when the movie was over, it would just rewind and play again. Every day we would get a new movie, and the doctor would play it for half of the day. The one thing that the movies had in common was that they all started with a swirling circle, black and white in color. All throughout the viewing, light electric shock was being administered from the helmet. It was nothing compared to the cages. It was annoying, but not extremely bothersome. The only time the movies stopped was when we would take a break to have a small lunch and go to the bathroom. But straight after lunch, another movie was played on repeat for the rest of the day.

I believe that children have a natural tendency to simply trust any adult that is in charge of them to do the right thing and to take care of them. This doctor wasn't altogether "bad". He was matter-of-fact but it made him like-able. He spoke directly to us. He often bragged of his discoveries in the field of lasers and had received recognition in his industry. Now he wanted to focus on remote viewing.

We assumed that we were in good hands, but really didn't have a choice either way. He was our doctor, teacher, and guardian. Whether he had to hurt us, shock us, or drug us, he treated it all as part of the process, as if it was absolutely normal. I believe it was his calm demeanor that led us to believe we were in good hands.

I remember him complaining that this program was on a shoe-string budget, something he often lamented about.

The doctor came in one morning and explained that he was going to be busy, and that we would have to sit and watch movies without a lunch break that day. He had some meeting to attend, he said, with somebody that was very important. I had no idea what all that meant, and so we just sat and watched another movie again. It would play until the end and then it would rewind and play again. This particular day, the helmet shock was also higher. The volume of the stereo was also turned up before he left. The doctor was right—there was no lunch break that day, and as the afternoon rolled on, we were all desperate to go to the bathroom.

It wasn't long before I heard urine hitting the ground from some of the kids around me. I began feeling tremendous pain, and could no longer hold it in either, so I, too, relieved myself and went right back to watching the movies.

When the doctor finally returned later that evening, he turned off the movie projector and started screaming at us for peeing. He seemed mad when he walked through the door anyway. He dragged us from the confines of our chairs, and then ordered us to lick all the urine up. I looked over my shoulder, and saw one boy had begun to drink his urine off the floor.

I just laid there, unable to move—terrified that I was going to be in trouble, I couldn't drink my own urine, even if I tried. I was shaking with so much agony that it was impossible for me to move. My head was splitting. I felt like it had been cooked in a microwave. The doctor came over and shouted at me to drink it up, but I was unresponsive. Defeated, he eventually ordered us all in line and walked us back to our sleeping portable. There was no debriefing that day. Typically when we went to bed each night, there was a nurse type woman that helped us change our clothes. But that day, she was not there.

These same movie-watching experiences continued day after day, but something different happened several days later. We were strapped into our designated chairs once more, and I heard the doctor doing something to the girl beside me. My head was fixed forward in my helmet, unable to focus anywhere but in front of me. My eyes were trained open and I slowly succumbed to the psychedelic effect of the drugs I'd just been given. The chairs that we were restrained in were held up by chains fastened to the ceiling. And the chains of that girl's chair were moving rapidly, muffling her tormented cries. The doctor was raping her. I didn't even know what that was at the time. But I could feel it was bad. She was hysterical. She could not have been any older than me, and I was ten at the time.

When the doctor had finished with her, he seemed very happy with himself and returned to his office.

He said something like, "I don't mind this part of the job."

The girl just remained there, crying hysterically in her chair. A few minutes later, he came back out, trying his best to console her.

"You're in a cocoon now, and are going to be a beautiful Monarch butterfly."

It did nothing to help her and she continued to cry inconsolably. Losing his patience, the doctor got mad and sounded as if he was hitting her.

"Shut up!" He told her.

"Quit crying!"

Frustrated, he stormed to his office for a brief moment and then came back, drugged the girl, at which point she just passed out. We watched movies for the remainder of the day, like usual.

On one of these repetitive days, we were separated as we watched our movies and every so often, the doctor would call one of us into his office, do something, and then put us back into our chairs. I couldn't see what was happening with the other kids, but I could hear them yelling out in pain in the office.

When it was finally my turn, the doctor brought me into his office and said, "What I am about to do is part of the process, and this needs to happen. Don't worry about your arm—I am a doctor! I will fix it without any permanent damage."

He then took out an antiquated looking device made of wood, fitted it over my arm, and fastened it on. The device had big screws in it, and seemed more suited for a carpenter's workshop, rather than a doctor's office.

I asked him, "What are you doing to me?"

He replied, "Your arm has to be dislocated or possibly broken. But don't worry, I will fix it for you. You will be fine. I assure you that this is a vital step in completing the program you are a part of."

He began turning the screws until my arm was dislocated at the shoulder. Not only that, he left it dislocated, and did not pop it back into its socket. I was in so much pain, but he simply put my arm into a sling and then sent me back to watch my movies again. Only at the end of the day did he put my arm back into place. I was crying. Most kids were crying. I believe my arm reset itself sometime during the day, because the pain lessened. There were other kids, however, who had fully broken arms and cried for the rest of the day. The next day, some kids had casts and some kids had slings.

Things like this happened continually. Every day presented new and different methods of inducing trauma to us all. I suspect we were given different drugs on different days because they had very different effects. There seemed to be some kind of rotation. Looking back, I suspect it was LSD, or something similar. I tried LSD in my late teens, which gives me some idea that he was using similar drugs.

It is difficult for me to think about this period of my tour. I mostly felt like an exhausted zombie, and the memory of this time is hazy and hard to talk about. There were times when we were sleep deprived, going for long stretches without any sleep or rest, and it got to the point that when the doctor did painful things to me, it didn't matter so much—I was that numb to it all.

The sleep deprivation was conducted through an alarm that went off in the night. There was a loud sound and a strobe light. We were told to stand at the side of our bed when we heard it. A large soldier-looking man would walk through and open-handed-hit us in the face. We were then told to go back to sleep. This repeated again in what seemed like twenty minute intervals, all night long. Eventually the hitting transitioned to shocking with a cattle-prod looking device.

After a long time, probably many weeks, we were allowed to sleep. After a while of sleep deprivation, you lose the ability to track linear time. It's hard to say how long some of this went one.

One day, we were taken into the third portable, the one that looked like a medical unit. There were oxygen tents on cots. We each went onto our own cot. They hooked up EEG equipment onto our heads and onto our fingers. We were told to relax. I could hear a machine that sounded like a breathing support machine. What it was actually doing was removing the oxygen or replacing it with an inert gas. We were being suffocated.

When we eventually passed out, a bell would ring. It sounded just like the little metal bells you push for service. When it rang, oxygen would re-enter the tent. I would wake up and be able to breathe for a minute, then the cycle would happen again. We were strapped down with leather straps and we could not move. I didn't even try to fight it. No one did. There was no screaming, no struggle. We had all accepted this exercise, this existence. When it started, I didn't have fear of dying. By the end, I wanted to die. I could feel the other side, and it was good. When I woke up, I was suffering and in pain. Each time I went to the other side, I wanted to stay.

After hours and hours of this oxygen deprivation cycle, the time near death got longer and longer. At first it was only a second or two, by the end, I was edging death for longer. I remember thinking like an adult when the death cycle got longer.

I spoke out loud and said, from what seemed like an adult voice within, "Hey, let this kid die."

It felt like me, like my voice, but as a fearless adult. This voice from within is hard to describe. I was pissed. I was me, but not.

The nurse came over and said, "Hey, this one's talking."

They stopped the exercise on me after that.

On a day not long after that, the doctor called me into his office to congratulate me. "You have all passed the program," he said.

He referred to our program with the Greek Alphabet, stipulating that each program was called either Alpha, Beta, Theta, and so on.

"I thought this group didn't have what it took," he stated.

"I thought you were all going to become Monarch sex slaves."

But our group did pass, and we would be used for a much higher purpose. Apparently we were qualified for the "Theta Class," which meant we were going into psychic service. From that point forward, I was allowed to sleep, and that was the end of the movies and the torture.

There were exercises given to us for the next few days that felt similar to the initial index card exercises. I was still terrible at them. I wanted to do well and I wanted to perform, but it was just not my thing.

3

THE MOON

IN THE MIDDLE OF THE night a few nights later, the doctor woke all of us up, and we were escorted out onto a runway that was within walking distance from the hospital building. We climbed a staircase to what appeared to be a huge airplane. There were only ten or twelve of us kids and there were also what seemed like hundreds of people boarding the plane. It felt weird to see other people, like the first day of school. We were apprehensive. But seeing all the other people gave me a sense that nothing bad was going to happen to me because they were all willingly going to the same place we were going. They felt professional to me, as if they were there for work.

It wasn't really a plane. It didn't look aerodynamic in the slightest. It was a triangle that had vertical slits all the way around the edge. Much like how you would envision shark gills. We actually watched it land and everyone was cheering when it did. It came straight down at us, vertical out of the sky. It was silent. There was no wind. It landed with precision by the stairway that had been wheeled out.

We waited in line with everyone else, then went up the stairs. The doctor did not join us, but instead handed us off to a type of chaperone on the runway. There were two or three of them and one was female. They were wearing office type clothes, but nerdy. Imagine a crew that would wear pocket protectors.

When we got on, I noticed how wide the rows and aisles were. There were maybe twenty seats in each row. It was otherwise the same furnishings as an airplane with overhead bins and all. The seat embroidery on the back of the chair in front of me read Douglas. There were small fold down trays and common barf bags.

We were ushered to our seats and strapped in, and once the craft took off, it was silent. It was a short trip, maybe only thirty minutes to an hour long ride. The most surprising feature of the trip was that the walls of the plane could become transparent. The pilot could activate the technology that turned the walls clear. It happened immediately. I listened to other people sitting on the plane, talking about what they saw beyond the walls of the plane.

But I stayed in my seat and didn't look. I was feeling sick. Not from the flight, but from what I had endured, and all I really wanted to do was to lay down and not pay attention to anything.

The pilot spoke over the intercom, "To your right-hand side is the moon base."

He had the stereotypical pilot voice, American accent. The moon! There was something both exciting but also so routine about it. Plus, I had just had my brain fucked up. I wasn't myself and certainly wasn't computing the way I normally would.

We had only been flying for another ten or fifteen minutes when the pilot came over the intercom again.

"On your left-hand side, is another moon base, and the base that we are going to land on."

He said the actual name of the bases, but in all honesty, I don't remember them.

I was seated on the left-hand side, and as the wall of the plane became transparent once more, I glimpsed a triangular-type building coming into view. It was just like the photos that you see of the moon's gray surface. It was lit up, and we were flying downward, right at it. I could not see the sky, just the gray surface of the moon.

People talking nearby said, "It looks just like the Pentagon but in a trapezoidal shape."

The pilot explained that when it was built, they reused the blueprints from the original Pentagon plans because it was designed to withstand being bombed and was easy to convert to a vacuum rated building. It saved a lot of design time and money and construction could be completed much quicker.

Eventually we landed. We disembarked as you would expect from a commercial plane, but the umbilical was airtight. We walked for a good while, and then came into a crowded room. It felt similar to a waiting gate at an airport as well. The people around were in plain clothes aside from a few in military uniforms. If I had to guess, based on what I know of American military uniforms, I would describe them as most similar to the Air Force formals.

I was taken to a small room that had a pillow and blanket on the floor. The room was probably four by six feet and all of us children were separated into our own rooms. There were two doors leading into the small room, one that was like a metal gate and then a standard door behind it. When the main door was closed, I could not hear anything. It was very cold in the room — uncomfortable—   but I was out like a light. For years after my experiences, I could easily fall asleep. I lived feeling totally exhausted. As I reflect back on this experience now, ironically, I dreamt a lot about that tiny room in my younger years.

One time, when I was ten years old, I went to sleep in my home in Michigan, and I woke up in that room. It's as if the two experiences were happening at the same time. I was sore and in pain when I woke up in the room. I looked around and felt confused that I could physically move my blanket because to me the only thing that made sense was that this was a dream. Then I would see myself sort of astral travel through the roof of my house and land back in my body. When I woke up next, I was in my Michigan life again.

The memories of being at this secret moon base are vague to say the least, because I was sedated most of the time. What I do remember however, was being constantly wheeled down never ending hallways on a gurney by a typical gray alien—from one surgery to the next. Every now and then, the gray would stop and liaise with some humans in a type of uniform— but that was it. It was a blurry time. The bits of the surgery that I do remember were things being done through the back of my neck and behind my ears. The grays were performing the surgeries and they would have telepathic conversations with each other during them. They didn't speak of anything too compelling, just their everyday lives. They were talking about being late and over scheduled, simple things like that. They talked about what time they would get to go home, like they were on a rotation.

The final procedure was just a gold colored needle with a huge hole, that came down on a robotic arm and pointed to the center of my forehead. I remember being terrified that this thing was going to drill into my head. Instead it would just vibrate a little distance from my head and didn't hurt at all—it actually felt relaxing. I was thrilled to not be tormented by the pain from this needle. It's funny what can feel exciting, or induce happiness, after so much torture.

I was told we were heading back to Earth and it was all over. My guess is that I was only there a matter of days. They had done something to us that let them easily put us in a dissociated state. I remember when it would start I would kind of take a back seat in my mind and start to feel sickly. I would just walk where I was directed and then suddenly wake up not remembering walking from point A to point B. This was the case for the entire ride back to Earth. I had no real memory of the journey. I woke up in my cot back at Inyokern. It all felt like it was a dream.

The morning after we arrived back, the Dr. gathered us all together as usual, and explained that each of us would be sent off to our assignments. He was disgusted that after the procedures we had on our trip, he wouldn't be allowed to test the measurable difference in our abilities. He was being ordered to ship us off.

We went through our morning routine. Wake, shower, brush our teeth, eat a packed breakfast that the nurse woman carried in with a cooler. But this time it was so much better. I had slept, and something about what was happening today felt like we were being set free. A bus—just like an old yellow school bus, but painted dark green—pulled up and we all got on. The Dr. came with us this time and told us that we were heading to China Lake. The other kids were in high spirits as well, asking questions about where we were and got excited when we would see planes or aircraft on pedestals at some of the intersections. It appeared to be an air force town. I remember being upset when everyone stood up looking out the windows at a jet plane or something because they were blocking the view and I couldn't see out. I wasn't motivated to try and see, or even to leave my seat for that matter.

When we arrived at the building that was our destination, there was a propeller plane on a pedestal in the parking lot and I got a good look at it so I didn't feel left out.

The building was modern looking with a big glass front and big glass doors that we were walked in through. It was a busy area, and we were rushed straight through to the elevator. There was a military man talking to the Dr. the whole time. Two other men in uniform ran and caught the elevator just before the doors had closed. The man with the Dr. tried to tell them the ride was full and to get the next one. They both pleaded to squeeze in with us because they were late and only going two floors down. The man with us gave them permission to ride and gave them a small speech about running late and how they need to remember that they aren't on some backwoods post. They both just stood and looked forward as if they wanted the conversation to end. The man looked at the Dr. behind them and motioned for him to not say a word. When they got off and the door closed he took out a key and put it in a slot on the panel where you selected what floor to go to and he hit two of the floor selections. I could feel that the elevator moved faster than it had originally.

The Dr. asked, "How far down does it go?"

The man gave some distance like five thousand feet and said that we could travel faster to get there because there weren't floors the whole way—that the elevator speeds through the distance where there are no floors.

When the elevator doors opened, we walked out into what looked like a train station. There were dozens of people waiting, and also people walking through passageways from one side to the other. It was obviously a big place. The Dr. stopped right outside the elevator and signed a clipboard—then he just walked away. No goodbye or good luck kids, he just walked away.

The man turned to us and said, "Go with this man and do what he says," and a younger man in uniform motioned for us to follow him.

His uniform was a pale blue shirt, worn with a tie, and no jacket. We walked down a flight of concrete steps and into a waiting cue for the next train. While standing in the line, I heard people talking. One of them was there for the first time and he was asking questions about how fast the train went and if there had ever been an emergency on one. I realized that it wasn't a normal train and I was looking forward to the ride. As we walked on board, the man that was riding for the first time looked at us and told us that we were all lucky to be able to experience this.

The seats were all blue and pretty tall. When we sat down, we were told to buckle into a harness that was over our shoulders and came down into the center of the seat. There was an emblem that read something like "Super Sub Trac". The man that led us there came by and made sure my harness was on correctly and gave me a piece of paper that had my destination on it. He stressed to me that whatever I did, I could not lose this paper. It was my ticket to getting off of this train. He told me that there was a stop near San Francisco and then we would go on to my stop in Montana directly after. I was to make sure that I showed my papers if someone asked me to get off the train at the stop outside of San Francisco.

It was a couple of hours of riding altogether. About an hour to somewhere in California, half an hour waiting there, and then about an hour more to Montana. To me, It seemed like a long ride. But looking back at it now, the train would have had to be moving over five hundred miles an hour. But I wasn't paying attention to time. I was happy that I was able to nod off for a bit. Sleep was still everything to me.

When I departed the train in Montana, it was just me. The station was tiny by comparison to the one where we boarded. Just a small platform, more dimly lit, in a smaller room with an elevator. Two men escorted me onto the elevator and out of a warehouse looking building to the front gate. It didn't look like a military facility at all. It was more like a farm than anything, but industrial looking. On the outside of the gate was a fancy looking light blue car unlike any I had ever seen. A petite woman stepped out to greet them and to sign some papers. Then away we went. She was smoking a cigarette and gave me a juice to drink and told me to take some pills. I did as I was told and fell asleep.

I woke up on the road feeling sick to my stomach. I asked her where we were going and who she was and she didn't answer me. The second time I asked, she said to shut up or I'd regret it. That she would speak to me if she wanted and otherwise, I was to remain silent. I tried to do as ordered, but I had to use the bathroom and I eventually broke my silence to ask her to stop. She did nothing bad to me and stopped the car. I asked if I could use the bathroom and she said I had to sit tight while she made a phone call on a payphone. Then a while later, I was allowed to use the bathroom in the gas station. We stayed one night in a motel. I slept on the floor. The whole time she acted worried, as if I would try to run or do something along those lines. But I had no such thing in mind. I knew quite well that she was my meal ticket, and I was hungry.

She had diverted the drive to our destination from the route that she was directed to take because she wanted to see Mount Rainier from the direction we were driving from. She explained to me that she could see it from her house, and she has always wondered what the other side looked like. And she wanted to know what it was like up close. She seemed to open up to me a bit over the course of the drive when she realized that I was cooperative.

4

THE FARM

WE EVENTUALLY ARRIVED AT home. We had taken a ferry to get to the small island. She was noticeably in a worse mood the closer we got to her home.

There was a gate that she put a code into and once it opened, there was a moderate drive until we came pulled up to a decent sized house. It looked more like a home from the sixties than a farmhouse, even though it had "Farm" in the name on the gate.

She got an attitude with me all of the sudden, and took me around the back of the house next to the laundry room, where she locked me in a dog kennel. She began asking me things about myself.

"How do you feel?" she questioned.

"Are you sick? Do you need to use the bathroom?"

She went off for a while and then returned with a sandwich, and then left me alone for the rest of the day. It was literally a wire cage dog kennel. I had a small pillow and laid directly on the kennel pan.

This became my new routine every day. She would come check on me in the late morning, let me out of the cage to use the bathroom that was adjacent to the laundry room, and then she would make me a sandwich and then leave me alone again. I never heard anyone else in the house; no visitors or housekeepers that I could sense.

"This cage is not very strong," I boldly said to her one day.

"And if I want, I could break it."

She turned and looked down at me.

"You are on an island surrounded by freezing water," she responded coldly, "and if you are found, you will be punished. You will get shocked if you don't do what I say. I have a shocker upstairs! Should I go and get it?"

I bit my tongue from that point on. And anyways, I didn't have much in me to rebel after all that I had been through. I figured that if these people went to so much trouble to give me all of these surgeries, as well as fly me to the moon and back, well then, I must be of some kind of value to them.

A few days later, she came in during lunchtime with the usual sandwich.

"I'm going to teach you a lesson," she said, handing me the sandwich.
"People like you don't know how to act when bad things happen. I'm going on a trip today and I might be gone longer than I've planned."

She then walked out and left me alone. And as she had hinted, the next day, she didn't come. The afternoon dragged on and I was busting for the bathroom.

"Hey!" I yelled out.

"Anyone there? I have to pee! Help me!"

I realized that I was really left alone. The thought did cross my mind to try and escape, but I had so little information about where I was and who I was with, that I gave up on that idea quickly. And at that point, hell, I didn't even know who I was, let alone know who everyone else was.

But desperation can make one do desperate things, and my impulsiveness got the better of me. I tried breaking the cage. I kicked and kicked as hard as I could, but it was useless—I was just too exhausted from no food and no sleep for such a long time. My energy was zapped from me. I gave up trying, succumbing to my bodily urges, and peed out through the cage and onto the floor. It felt like I was shriveling up from starvation.

The following morning, I heard a car pull up and my blood turned cold. I was terrified of what was going to happen to me when she saw the puddle of pee next to the cage.

Hearing her footsteps, she finally walked in and glanced down at the pee. And to my utter surprise, she wasn't angry! I couldn't believe it. I guess she had expected worse.

"I was starving!" I looked up at her.

"Why didn't you leave me extra food?"

"Well why did you eat the entire sandwich I gave to you?" she snapped back.

"You should have saved some in case something happened!"

That was my lesson learned, I suppose. She eventually fed me, cleaned up my mess and wandered upstairs, to where I heard other people talking. There seemed to be a little commotion going on for an hour or so, and I even heard some children talking up there as well. I got excited. *"Maybe I will get to meet them,"* I thought to myself.

Later that night, a woman—probably in her late twenties—came in and said hello to me. I will call her Nelly. Up until that moment, Nelly was the most polite person that I had met throughout this entire abduction ordeal. She was the kind of woman that ended her sentences with things like, "Ok sweetie."

"I'm a nurse," Nelly said to me warmly, "And you're going to be taken care of—you have nothing to be afraid of." Then she left me alone. Something about her made me feel okay, that I was being taken care of.

Quite some time after, the older lady walked in and got me out of the cage.

"You need to shower," she said, and gave me a set of pajamas to wear.

I showered and cleaned up for the first time in ages. The old lady then chaperoned me upstairs, where I was surprised to meet two other children my age. One was a boy that I had never seen before, and just by the look of him, he was just as mentally broken as I was. The other was the blonde girl that I had gone through all the mind programming at Inyokern with.

She, too, wasn't much better off than the boy. They were wearing the same pajamas as me.

We were then taken into the downstairs area of the house. It was an odd looking area—a strong nineteen seventies vibe with dark stained wood, and the carpet and countertops were an aqua pastel color. We sat down on chairs in a living room area. We waited outside of sliding pocket doors that took us into what looked like a storage room. We were given I.V. drips in our arms, and then given the signal to move.

There we were—an I.V. bag attached to each of us on a rolling stand, now sitting down just outside of the living—again, being told to wait. After another twenty minutes or so, the boy heard muffled sounds coming from inside the living room and stood to his feet.

"Now," I heard a man's voice command from the other room.

The two women immediately took off all their clothes, stark naked, and put masks over their heads.
Strangely enough, these masks were animal's heads—one was a white porcelain mask with feathers and the other had horse characteristics.

They lined us up, and the young woman wearing the bird-like feather mask opened the door. We were led into the living room one at a time. First the boy, then the girl, and finally me.

I walked into the tri-level area, pushing my own I.V. bag on its stand. Through the dim light and musty smells, I glimpsed a man at an altar, donning an elaborate goat head mask, and also totally naked.

When I got close enough, I noticed a dead boy laying on the altar. He was similar age to me, possibly slightly older. I was utterly shocked—his chest cavity had been opened up, and beside him there was a small burner, some books, and a pan. Horrified, I stood beside him, while two women stood on the other side of the altar, with both the boy and the girl.

The goat head man behind the altar turned and looked down at me. "Hello," he said, "I'm Richard."

I couldn't even speak, as I was so terrified by what I was seeing. I was in shock realizing that the boy on the altar had been murdered.

"Do you have any questions?" Richard pressed on. "Do not be afraid to say what you feel.

"Why is that boy dead?" I asked him, mustering up some courage. "Did you kill him?"

"I did," Richard said, without a hint of remorse. "Why?" I demanded.

"He is one of the dead," Richard answered.

"Like you, and like them."

He pointed at the two other children standing there, nursing their I.V. bags. I was a nine year old boy at the time, and I was feeling insulted by a murderer.

"I am definitely not dead!" I snapped back to him.

What I really wanted to do was to tell him how crazy he was, but I was afraid to insult him.

"Why do you have such a problem?" Richard wondered.

"Are you afraid of sinning? Is that what it is? Do you believe in God?"

"Yes," I shook my head.

"Well, then pray to your God for help and for the boy to come back to life."

Feeling defeated, I just stood there silent. I knew at that point that I was not educated enough to have an argument with an adult—especially a crazy one—and I really started to become an intense combination of angry and afraid.

Richard continued on with more of a sickening ritual and began to say things that were strange to me. He then held up the pan beside the dead boy, which had some pieces of his flesh on it.

"I saved you some," Richard said, offering it to me.

"It's cold, but at least it's been cooked."

Mortified, I couldn't believe what I was hearing. He then handed me the cup of the boy's blood.

"You need to eat this meat, and drink from the cup."

"No!" I refused adamantly.

Richard lowered his head and shot me a darkened eye.

"You have a choice," he said firmly.

"You can eat and drink, or you can join the dead boy on the table."

I stood there silent in denial. Richard repeated what he said.

"I have no problem killing you right here and now," he added, showing me a fancy knife.

"I don't believe in God, or any of this," the blonde girl spoke up.

Then she turned to me and said, "Just eat it and be done with it. Nothing bad is going to happen to you. I did it and so did he," she said, looking at the boy next to her.

"We are fine. Just do it."

With all my heart and soul, I wanted to tell this Richard guy to fuck off, and that I was going to kick his ass. But I was a nine year old boy that had just completed a brutal MK-Ultra style programming. I knew that if I didn't do what he said, he would kill me, without a problem. So, I ate the piece of flesh meat and drank the boy's blood from the cup.

Things then seemed to reach a climactic part of this crazy ritual. Richard with his goat's head was muttering some prayer type invocations, and asked for 'Baphomet', or someone like that, to grant him knowledge along with a few other things. I shied away from whatever else he did to the poor boy's body, and tried my best not to look.

He then had each of us three children lie down on table height folding cots and gave additional instructions to the women. It almost seemed as if they hadn't done this before. They began drugging us with different solutions. First the boy. It wasn't long until he started grunting and groaning slurred words.

Next was the girl, and almost immediately she started rambling too. "I'm Pepper Potts!" she yelled over and over.

The women were holding papers full of questions in their hands, ready to record responses as they spoke with the children. Richard had instructed them to be ready as he wanted to make the most of the time. Then it was my turn. Richard stood over me and added something to my I.V. line, and soon after, I lost consciousness.

I awoke just before dawn the following morning in a sleeping bag on the floor outside of the storage room. It was dark and I felt a sense of clarity for the first time since my MK-ultra training. I began to plot my escape. It seemed easy to me and I realized that it was possible for me to escape. I remembered the ferry ride in, the gate, the distances traveled, what I needed to get over the wall. But by the time the sun came up, my mental precision had completely faded. I went back to being a mentally damaged child. And I wanted the feeling back. I felt a craving, a withdrawal.

The next few days after the horrid ritual, I was kept in the downstairs area of the house, along with the other boy and girl this time. The area we were kept in was much different than the cage—there were three bedrooms, as well as a living room. We even had a few games to play and could use coloring books. Yet despite our upgraded living environment, the three of us were physically sick after the ritual and couldn't make use of our new privileges.

One night during the week, a group of people came to the house. We could hear them all talking and laughing jovially upstairs. A few hours later that night, the same two women that were with us in the ritual came downstairs and started getting us ready for something again. We were all dreading it as they put us in hospital-looking gowns made with leather. They then smeared a thick wax onto our faces.

"Don't mess with this," one of them said, wiping it over my skin.

Then came more drugs. They used needles and shot us up with something. I felt scared; things were becoming surreal around me. They took us upstairs, one by one. First the boy went, then me, followed by the girl. A dog collar was fastened around my neck and I was guided up the steps on a leash. As I entered the area, all of the participants were wearing masks again. But their attire was different—they seemed to be of a higher quality. Long white robes and porcelain type masks. The mood was light, and a formal ambience was exuded into the night air.

The woman escorted me in front of the fireplace, where every participant was standing in a circle. Richard, 'the sacrificial priest', who conducted the previous ritual, was again leading the ceremony.

"What is your name?" he asked me.

Truthfully, I do not remember the name I was given, as I think back. I knew enough to know that the name they had given me was not my real name, and on top of this, they had also assigned me a numerical name. I told Richard both.

"That will not do!" Richard replied irritated. "You are not strong enough to live and must die!"

He muttered a few other things of a strange tongue, and then grabbed me, thrusting my face into the scorching heat of the fire. The flickering flames terrified me, and I had no choice but to inhale them, and as I did, I felt my nose hairs singeing, burning down to my skin and suffocating my breath.

I became stricken with panic and knew that I would fry any second. When I thought I was about to die, Richard pulled me back out.

"Look at what's become of your face!" he cried.

"Your face is your identity, and it's not strong enough to withstand the fire!"

He pushed me in front of a mirror. Looking at the reflection, I could see wax dripping from my skin. I was terrified by what I saw staring back at me. And whether the terror was drug-induced or not, the whole experience was horrifying. I actually felt like my face had burned and was melting off.

"Do you swear upon your life to serve me?" Richard stared down at me with harrowing eyes.

"Yes," I nodded.

"That is no answer!" Richard bellowed, and before I knew it, he thrust me back into the flames of that burning fire again.

This time around I was so stricken with fear, that I didn't fear, but instead *knew* that I was going to die. I desperately tried to escape his strong grasp but it was no use. Fortunately, he yanked me out of the flames much sooner than the first time around.

"Do you solemnly swear to pledge yourself to me?" Richard cried again.

"Yes," I answered quickly and with grit.

The two women brought over a porcelain mask and pushed it onto the melted wax on my face. Richard grabbed me and pushed me in front of the mirror again. I was tripping balls to be frank. I thought I was being disfigured in this process. When they showed me myself with the mask, I realized I was safe. I felt relieved this time. He pushed my face back into the fire. It was beginning to feel never ending. I held my breath as the flames licked around my face. This time however, I couldn't feel anything.

"Now you must serve me!" Richard proclaimed, pulling me out of the fire.

"You are much stronger! You are more worthy now!"

The night was kind of a blur from that point on. I remember there being roughly twenty people there, with a mostly equal split of men and women. Some of them were in costumes, which looked like they belonged in a Robin Hood play. The others were in tuxedos and formal gowns. I remember the other two kids going next after me with the fire ritual. It didn't feel like very long before the remainder of the ritual was over, and I was taken downstairs to be cleaned up.

The following night, the three of us children were taken back upstairs again, near the same fireplace. There were fewer people this time and I don't remember the number but it needed to be exact, like exactly nine or exactly twelve. They were all men this time. They were wearing white masks, white robes, and white shoes. Richard was instructing people, as if it were their first time for this ritual. They were talking about meeting an ET, but I don't recall much more.

One man brought out a mortar and pestle, where he proceeded to grind up dried flowers. The powder then was added to a goblet of red wine. Each of us three kids drank a couple gulps. They began lighting incense, watching a timer closely. After a few minutes, they asked questions about how we felt. When we responded, seemingly unfazed by the potion, they started to doubt that it would work. Richard was concerned about getting the timing exactly right, as there was only a short period of time that it would "work".

We sat for a few minutes. It was really awkward at first. I just felt like I was being watched but I also knew that something bad was coming. Then the blonde girl said that we were starting to look shiny.

"Here we go," Richard stated. "It's about to happen."

Two men came with the big incense bells, swinging from a chain. The three of us kids were made to sit in a circle. The group of men encircled us and began chanting in what I guessed was Latin, as they swung the incense above us. It created a huge ball of smoke above our heads. I started to trip the fuck out. I was seeing lights everywhere and I was terrified.

The three of us children started talking to each other. It felt like they could hear us, but they didn't understand what we were saying to each other.

The other boy told the girl, "This is what I was telling you about. This is why I came here. Because of him."

Then he told me to concentrate on making the light brighter. I had no idea what was going on or what he was talking about. I felt angry that he had obviously prepared her for this and had left me out of the conversation. I felt unprepared.
"I waited my whole life for this," he emphasized.

We looked up at the smoke. The boy became a bright white light. Through the smoke, I could see the blue sky. I experienced something like a pulsing in and out of two worlds. I would, within milliseconds, be in the cloud world, then drop back down into the earth world. This only happened for a second or two but I had many back-and-forths in that short time. Then a green being appeared. He looked like he was made out of thick green glass, with a hideous face. But it wasn't a typical *face* that you would see on a human. It was almost like he was faceless. He was the size of a larger grown man.

"Do you remember me?" the boy asked, turning himself into a bright light. "I've come back for you. Because of what you did."

Then his light became focused and shot up at the green being. It was like an attack. It was like the purpose of the boy's entire incarnation was to come back and avenge this entity. And he did. You could tell that what he had done had severely rocked the being.

The green being looked like he'd just realized he was caught in a prank. Like he'd been had.

"How dare they summon me for this. They're going to regret this."

Then he put his hands together and the opening in the cloud of smoke disappeared. My hallucination peaked at that moment, then quickly began to wear off. The men around us kept asking us if we were seeing anything. The girl and I said the same thing, that we'd seen a green man. The boy insisted that he saw nothing.

The men that were there for the first time were impressed that the girl and I saw the same thing. Richard was upset and embarrassed that there was no dialogue with the green being. They were hoping to communicate with him through us. Richard blamed our caliber on the faulty connection and said we must be inadequate for the task.

We were then escorted downstairs to cots with sleeping bags. I was sweaty and felt like utter shit. It wasn't hard to go to sleep. I had a splitting headache but I felt exhausted by it all.

5

THE CAPTAIN

THE MORNING AFTER THE GLASS man ritual, we were woken up and given breakfast downstairs in a game room with board games like Shoots and Ladders and Othello. The three of us children were feeling so sick that we didn't care about the games or trying to have any kind of fun. Richard came down the stairs, showered and dressed. It was as if he was walking on air; he was so happy. He and the woman were talking amongst themselves about the next place the three of us little ones would go.

"Well where are they going to go?" the woman asked.

"I need to know."

Then the little blonde girl spoke up. "Where am I going next?"

"You're going to go somewhere important," Richard turned to her.

"You're very valuable."

Then the boy looked up at Richard. "And what about me?" he wondered.

"Where am I going next?"

"Don't worry," Richard assured, "We make sure that everyone goes wherever their abilities are suited best, so that everything works together like a perfect symphony."

I wanted to know where I was going too, but I was too scared to ask after what I had already seen and experienced. So instead, I just stared down at a game. We were so broken mentally that nothing seemed to matter.

The following Monday morning, I was dressed and loaded into a car. This property would have been hundreds of acres in size. I was driven by people I had never seen before to a grassy airfield, where waiting for us was a twin-engine propeller plane. Bewildered by the situation I had found myself in, I was taken onboard and buckled into a beautiful white leather seat—a seat much wider than the standard seat in an aircraft. The pilot got in, fiddled with his gadgets, and before I knew it, we took off. We flew for maybe six or so hours, eventually landing at a regular busy airport in the desert, only we had landed on the private side of the airport. You could see the larger, commercial planes coming and going on the other end of the airport. Where we landed, it was all small, private planes like ours.

There was one stewardess onboard, as well as a few men in sharp suits, one of them with a gun. I was so tired. All I wanted to do was go to sleep. The stewardess gave me water and coloring books.

"Go to sleep," she looked down at me.

As the other people disembarked from the plane, the man with the gun told the others leaving that he was going to sleep on board the plane with me on the airstrip. We stayed on the plane overnight. There was one seat that folded out like a sofa and he took that. I was uncomfortable in a smaller seat for the night.

Early the next morning, the flight crew came onboard the plane. Something was going on with the crew and the Captain of the plane was mad. I watched him wandering off the tarmac, back into the airport, until finally he came back onboard taking up a seat beside me.

"How are you?" he asked me.

"I'm fine," I replied, looking up at him.

"Is there anything you need?"

"I was told to be quiet and not to ask anything."

The Captain looked firmly at me. "Do you know where you are?"

I shook my head. Then the Captain said something that has stayed with me ever since.

"Listen to me," he began, turning to face me, "no matter what you are in life, or what people tell you— no matter *what*, you have the right as a living person to know where you are and to be able to ask questions."

Something struck a chord about the way the Captain said this to me. It was a lot deeper than a normal conversation, and I could tell this just by the look within his eyes.

"You are a sovereign human being," he continued solemnly, "and it is *your* right to know where you are in your life's journey."

"Well, where am I?" I asked him.

The Captain gave me a big smile. "You're in Dallas, Texas, and we are on our way to a place in Peru, in South America."

The Captain then got up, and walked to the front of the plane. I was allowed to sit in that beautiful, big, folding seat, where the man with the gun had been overnight. I slept for most of the trip.

I woke up when we made a stop. I was told that we were in Colombia, where we stayed for a few hours. Shortly after taking flight again, we started passing over jungles and huge rivers. The Captain began the plane's descent, and we landed on a small grassy runway in the middle of thick, wild jungle.

When I got off the plane, I learned where we had landed. We were in Puerto Tahuantinsuyo, Peru.

There were dozens of people waiting there for us. They were tanned, Meso-American looking, and most of them donned machine guns or other firearms. Surrounding them were several big trucks, resembling the old style military trucks from the T.V. show *Mash*.

I was escorted to a younger man that felt like he was a local. He looked to be in his twenties with dark eyes, dark skin, and medium length curly black hair.

"Hello," he gruffed, glancing down at me.

He was not at all happy to see me.

We loaded into one of the big military trucks and rode for about a mile down a dirty road into a town. It wasn't like a regular town that I was used to seeing. It looked a lot like a third world type of town, all dirt roads, some buildings wide open with no windows or doors. I began to feel concerned because I didn't know what to expect. We came upon something blocking the road and we had to stop. After a short while, we got moving again and as we passed, I saw why we had been stopped for just a moment. On the side of the road, there was an older woman crying hysterically flanked with children crying beside her. In front of her there were about six men with guns. I didn't know what was going on, but it was at this moment that I had the sudden realization of how much my situation had dramatically changed. I knew there would be no flying high in white leather seats any time soon.

We arrived at a small warehouse or some place of storage as there was mail and boxes and all sorts of stuff piled up. I was grabbed from behind.

"Come on, you're coming with me," said the young impatient guy, pulling me along to an office.
Inside was an old man engulfed in piles of paperwork on the desk. It was a mess. I was seated and the two of them spoke in Spanish to each other at length. Eventually, they both turned to me.

"What's your name?" the young guy said to me.

I stared at him blankly. I had no idea what my name was.

"Don't worry—we'll find a name for you. I'm Manuel. I'm the only one that speaks English, so I'm stuck with you. Do you remember that old lady that you saw on the side of the road?"

"Yes," I answered.

"That woman's son got caught stealing. He was in a place he shouldn't have been, so we fed him to the piranhas," Manuel said.

"And if you act up and don't do what you're told, we'll feed you to the piranhas too, do you understand me?"

I felt the fear spread over me like a rash.

Manuel unpacked a suitcase that I had been sent with all the way from Montana. I thought there was going to be a bunch of clothes for me in there, but there weren't. Instead, there was one pair of pants and a shirt, with the rest of the space taken up by a bunch of IV bags. There was a book in there too.

"I have to read this whole book because of you," Manuel spat.

He was not happy about it. In fact, he had a chip on his shoulder from the moment he saw me.

My first few nights there were uncomfortable. I slept on the floor in a sleeping bag in some ramshackle kind of place. Manuel was forced to stay with me and he made sure that I knew how inconvenient I was to him.

"I hate this," he would sputter to me in frustration.

"I'm stuck with you only because I speak English— what a curse! And if you try to run away and cross the water, the piranhas will get you. And if you try to run into the jungle, *everything* will get you!"

It was absurd because I had no intention of running away—I was scared out of my mind. The Latin lands were so foreign, it was as if I was in another world. The people were foreign. No one spoke a lick of English, except Manuel. I wasn't going to leave his side.

A few days later, Manuel came to my room and took me to an office. An old man was in there again, amongst all the piles of paper. A conversation in Spanish started between the two of them. Then they turned to me.

"His name is Ricardo. He's the boss," Manuel said.

"He wants to know what they did to you that makes you able to have these abilities."

"I don't know what you mean," I looked up at him blankly.

"Did they train you?" Manuel pressed on.

"Is it a drug-induced thing only? What did they do to you?"

"Well, they put us through classes and then took us to a base on the moon where I had surgery," I responded.

Manuel was dumbfounded. He turned to Ricardo and explained to him in Spanish. Ricardo broke out in laughter and appeared to be elated. He lifted his arms above his head, chuckling in Spanish.

"What is he saying?" I asked, perplexed.

"He's saying 'those Gringos did it! After those Gringos went to the moon, they didn't just quit goin back…"

The two of them kept asking me questions until the conversation was exhausted, and ironically, that's how they came up with my nickname *los locos pequeño de la luna*, meaning, the crazy boy from the moon.

A few days later, I was taken to a shed in between several houses all compacted together in a field of grass along the edge of the jungle. It was like a village with dirt roads and everything was old and not well constructed. Most of the buildings were painted with bright colors and I wondered if that meant something, but it didn't. Inside the shed was a couch and black and white TV. There was a bathroom that had no water and a hole in the floor where the toilet should have been that had a bucket stuffed into it.

"Stay here and don't move," Manuel said.

He went on to try and sell me the idea that I had it made there.

"Look, you have TV you can watch until the power goes out at night. No one can hear so you can play it loud all you want. You have a nice couch, no more sleeping on the floor. I know you're a spoiled gringo but this is more than you deserve. You're lucky, so don't do anything stupid and end up piranha lunch," he laughed.

He stressed over and over that I was not to set foot outside the door and that if I did, people were watching and I would get punished.

And this is how it was for quite some time. Everything was pretty uneventful for days with Manuel occasionally bringing me food. Until one day, something different happened. Manuel took me to an airstrip where I saw an airplane on the runway. He took me up beside the plane and turned to me.

"This is our plane."

He was all smiles. For the first time since I'd known him, he actually appeared happy. I'm not sure if this was because I was going on board to do 'my thing' or because it was a C-46 Commando. He went on and on wanting to name his gun "Commando" or change his own name to it as well.

He seemed to be in love with the word commando and that projected to the plane. He seemed to love the plane because of its name as well as its value. He was like a kid with a toy when he looked at the plane.

The pilot and his people worked on the plane for a few days. One morning, not long after our first visit to the Commando, Manuel and I were picked up in a truck. We returned to the airstrip to find the plane loaded up. There were several people standing around, ready to load it.

"Hope this thing works!" Manuel joked with the pilot.

I had no idea what they were talking about. We all boarded and after the plane took off, I was able to take a look around. It was loaded with wrapped blocks.

Manuel opened the big book that had been delivered in my suitcase.

"I've been up all night reading this thing," he grunted, opening my suitcase and setting up the IV bag and stand.

"I'm freezing," I chattered through my teeth.

"Here—lay down," Manuel said, covering me with a blanket.

He got the IV needle and tried to find a vein in my arm. He kept missing because of the air turbulence.

"It's okay—I'm okay," I reassured him.

He was frustrated and yelled at me to stay still. He took time to think about it and tried again.

"There," he looked pleased, "think I got it!"

He adjusted the drip and hung up the saline bag, then added something else into the solution.

"This better work," he looked at me, "or you know we're gonna feed you to the piranhas."

Pretty soon thereafter, I lost consciousness. When I woke up later, I was disorientated.

"Where are we?" I asked, looking over at Manuel. He didn't answer me.

"Well, did I work? Did I do what you needed?"

"I don't know," Manuel sighed. "You know, I—I really don't. I'm kinda scared for you."

His response made me chill to the bone.

The plane landed and for days, I sat in anxiety. I didn't hear anything from anyone, but people around the place started to know about me.

When Manuel brought me food one day, I asked, "Am I going to be okay? Because I didn't do what you wanted? Are you gonna feed me to the piranhas?"

"Who knows—we might." Manuel's response was short.

Despite the growing sense of anxiety, I was happy to stay in the old shed. I was content at doing absolutely nothing. There were three or four channels on a black and white TV—soccer, news, and I even got to watch Bugs Bunny in Spanish.

After what was probably a few weeks, I was taken back to the airstrip and boarded the C-46 Commando again. Manuel jabbed me with that IV, this time before taking off.

"What?" I looked at him confused as he shuffled me around onboard.

"Are we going again? I thought I didn't work before?" I wondered as I sat on the cot.

"We contacted your owner," Manuel answered.

"He said that there was interference from the electrical instruments of the plane and we were given a pure silver blanket." He looked impressed.

"Your owners must be so rich! This is your silver blanket."

He then wrapped me in a silver mesh blanket, tucking me in tightly.

"If you don't work this time," he peered down at me, "then we're probably going to send you back to the US."

I liked watching the takeoff on that C-46 as we climbed high over the endless primal jungles down below. After about a half hour, Manuel put the drug solution into my IV and I went black.

This time, when I came to, everything had changed. It was as if Manuel was a completely different person. He looked at me strangely.

"Well? Did I work?" I asked anxiously. "What happened?"

"*Brujo*! You are brujo!" Manuel answered excitedly. "I cannot wait to get back and tell everybody what happened."

Manuel was totally blown away by whatever had happened on board the C-46 Commando. I later learned that his dead grandmother came through me and spoke to him in fluent Spanish, talking of things that only he would know. There were other people that came through me also. And now, instead of being stuck in the old shed on my own all day, he paraded me around to everyone in the village town. One day, he took me to a cafeteria type of place and I remember all eyes were glued on me. No one was allowed near me, but they looked at me all the same.

The next time we went up, Manuel had a long list of questions in a notebook that he wanted to ask when I was 'under'. Questions not only from him, but from other people in the village that wanted answers, in particular, the old boss Ricardo. I found out this was the name of the man from the office with all the paper. He looked strikingly similar to Pablo Escobar, but it wasn't him.

"So where do we actually fly to?" I wondered.

This time Manuel opened up about things.

"Well, right now we're flying over the state of Acre," he said, "and then we'll continue on to Colombia. We aren't sure where our last plane went down. Probably in the mountains of Colombia due to a bad storm. And that's why we need you—to see if there's a storm or if there's policia."

"Is Colombia a nice place?"

Manuel gave me a scornful look.

"Pffft, no! I hate Colombia, and I hate Colombians! Their soccer team cheated in a championship game years ago! Always thinking they're better than everyone else! If you knew what I know about Columbians you would hate them too!"

To say he was completely racist against Colombians, would be a huge understatement. After the second flight, Manuel took me from my shed to a big plaza of a couple of acres, nestled in the middle of town. There were several bulldozers parked. They had grubbed the area and it was a big square of flattened dirt.

"This is what the money from your second flight paid for," Manuel said.

"We are building ourselves a town plaza. We've wanted one forever."

As Manuel was talking, I found myself distracted by a bunch of kids playing soccer and having a great time kicking the ball in this plaza area. It was muddy and dirty, but they didn't care, and it looked like a lot of fun.

"You would be the best one out there," Manuel joked.

"You would get out there with your IV bag, and you would know where the ball would be about to go and score every time."

I wanted to play with them.

"Can I play with those kids?"

"No," Manuel shook his head quickly, "You can't play. You can never play with the kids here."

His words triggered something inside of me that set me off. I cried and cried and cried. To have friends as a kid is a big deal, and at that moment, I realized I was never going to have any friends my age while I was in Puerto Tahuantinsuyo. Manuel got frustrated by my outburst and shuffled me back to my shed.

This went on for months, these flights. In fact, it was a monthly air flight, and Manuel was always excited about putting me under. He couldn't wait to speak to all the personalities coming through, and he had even made friends with some of them. But all I remember was feeling sick upon waking. It usually lasted for about a half hour after, and then it would gradually wear off as the plane would descend.

He told me that he had asked about a girl in the village and I told him that she would get pregnant. She did shortly after. He would also tell me when I had channeled assholes that day, or when he liked the people he was able to talk to through me instead. I don't remember any of it.

After a few months of this, at Ricardo's behest, they tried to stretch my dosage of whatever it was that they were giving me to half. Their reason for doing this was to maximize the experiences these people could have with me, and to give themselves a type of 'personal session' with me. My owners only gave them a certain amount of drugs to administer per flight. But after trying this new technique, I began lucid dreaming upon awakening, and I found that I could still give Manuel 'clairvoyant tips' of where we were or where we were going.

"I know we're gonna land in Santa Marta," I blurted out. Or one time when we were flying in a storm and we were lost. "There's some mountains —8000!"

Manuel told me when I woke up what I had said, and that the pilot was flying blindly in a storm and some instrument wasn't working and he needed to hear 8000. He said it probably saved us.

Everyone seemed to be comfortable with my presence around Puerto Tahuantinsuyo—and I never thought it possible, but Manuel started to become my friend. He eased with me and his grudge seemed to disappear. He would take me to ponds and teach me how to fish —but we never went to the rivers.

"No, we don't go to the rivers," he would say.

"They're dangerous. Alligators, piranhas, you name it. And the people that live along the east side of the river don't want anything to do with you. You could get killed if you go there, or worse. So don't ever go there."

I understood.

But one time Manuel did take me along the east side of the river, where he told me about its history.

"Tahuantinsuyo means "where the two rivers meet." And the rivers here have spirits in them. When I was a kid, there used to be an old gold mine up along this river about twenty miles up, that was started in the seventies," he said.

"Both rivers were beautiful and clean. The best fishing in all the area. Everyone came to fish in Tahuantinsuyo," he reminisced fondly.

"But after this gold mine began, one river was polluted. All muddied up and destroyed. It died. And so we had one beautiful flowing river, and then there was this dirty dead river. It was a disaster. Our people cried endlessly. It was awful."

When the rainy season ended, all the birds would flock around the village, and Manuel and I would spend time talking about the birds. There were many beautiful birds. There was a yellow parrot that would come outside of my shed often. When I told Manuel about the birds I saw by my shed, he agreed that they were beautiful. But he taught me that the most impressive and beautiful bird by far was the Scarlet Winged Macaw.

"We love this bird," Manuel would say.

"Everybody in South America cherishes this bird. It's the most beautiful. Keep a lookout for this one."

After a few months, Manuel started taking me to his mother's house, which was towards the east side of town. She had a cozy, colorful home, bright red walls and teal cabinets. I found it very inviting. She was an interesting woman, Manuel's mother. With her long dark hair, she had no front teeth and all of her clothes were covered in bright colorful patches—so much so, that the patches covered the entirety of her clothing. That was her livelihood among other things. She would patch clothing for people, so her clothes were an advertisement as well. People could point to a patch design she had on her and she would take their garment home and patch it. Literally her nickname was "Parches" - which means patches in Spanish.

She was a nice woman, a bright soul as I would say like a grandmother to me, and I came to learn that she was the one who had been sending me food the entire time I was in Puerto Tahuantinsuyo. She was always looking out for me—bringing me things like coloring books and crayons. When I finished all of those, she gave me paper and more crayons. I would watch her stare at me, and then she would say something to Manuel in Spanish.

"What is she saying?" I wondered.

"She says you have the most beautiful green eyes. She says it is very rare here for anyone to have green eyes."

Another time, Manuel had found himself in trouble. He was always in trouble—trouble with other young guys around the village, mainly because of girls.

"I send their girlfriend's flowers. Things like that," Manuel would say.

"They don't like that. But they can't touch me, I'll beat them up!"

But one day as we were loading up in the truck, ready to go on another flight, when one young guy— smaller than Manuel, came right at him—fearless, and ripped him to shred with his words, and for the first time, Manuel, ever the macho brutish kind of guy, was struck with a fear that I had never seen before. Later on that plane ride, I asked Manuel what happened.

"What's going on? Why didn't you just beat that kid up?" I asked curiously.

"I can't, because that kid is blessed. He has a blessed life."

I was confused. "Well, what does that mean?"

"He's always lucky," Manuel replied. "Everything he does he has good luck. He is blessed."

"Well, does that mean that some people have cursed lives?"

"Oh yeah," he answered quickly. "For sure. We believe that people have either blessed lives or cursed lives, and people can weave between the two of them."

"Well then, my life is definitely cursed," I said. "Do you think I can have a blessed life one day?"

"I don't know, it is up to you!" Manuel shrugged.

"Well I've never seen the red wing Macaw, so I must have a cursed life!"

"You'll see one," Manuel assured. "And if that's the case, you will have a blessed life. Just keep your eyes open."

Towards the end of my time in Peru, I began having problems when Manuel would try to put me under on the flights. Instead of giving him the prophetic insights he had now become accustomed to, I started talking gibberish more and more as they were trying to stretch my drug dosage so that they could have some dosage for their own personal sessions with me. Not only was I talking gibberish, but I also started waking up mid session.

One time, I woke up when they were unloading the cargo at Santa Marta, Colombia. I remember saying "the police, we need to get out of here, we need to leave now." I told them not to unload, but they did it anyway and then we took off in a panic.

I remember being at that airport several times. It was always tense. We were carrying two tons of cocaine and we were an unregistered aircraft. Leaving Santa

Marta felt like relief; we were safe when we left that airport.

Manuel didn't know all the details, but from what I came to learn in the following months was that there was some kind of problem with the production in the jungle and the supply chain broke down for a while. What this meant for us was that Manuel had an extra dosage of the drug that was used to put me under, because we wouldn't be making flights.

"Apparently, they have unearthed some ancient ruins in Chan Chan," Manuel said one day while watching the news, sitting in the office with Ricardo and I.

This was around 1984 and for whatever reason, this topic was making headlines.

"They don't know who built them. We could take brujo up there and see who built them. I have a cousin up near the city."

Ricardo agreed and let us go. We took a plane to Chan Chan, and were picked up at sunset by a van full of guys—the dangerous looking sort, and I did not have an easy feeling about them or this situation at all.

It was hot and we drove for what felt like hours along a road filled with lights in the middle of nowhere, until we reached an apartment. It was filthy and decrepit. I was given a couch.

Lots of cocaine was being handed around, and they even gave me a beer. The next morning, I woke up feeling sick, but we got in the van and drove about fifteen minutes to the Chan Chan ruins. It had been fenced off and was closed for the day. Everyone was so disappointed. Manuel stuck an IV drip in me anyway and hoped to retrieve some information about the ruins. Adding to his disappointment, however, no more information was given.

This was a time that stood out for me because for the first time since I had been in Peru, nothing followed a strict protocol. I always had a handler, and I always had a regimented schedule. These few days of randomness were unprecedented and it scared the hell out of me.

From this trip on, things went from bad to worse. Manuel would try to stretch out the dosage of the drugs given for every flight that was scheduled. I became sicker and sicker. It started off with me being sick for a few days, then a week, and by the time I had finished another flight, I was sick for almost the entire month until the next scheduled flight. This was creating more than a few headaches for those in charge of me. Manuel's mother got wind of this, and became angry that they were responsible for my sickness. She thought they would kill me if they kept going.

The boss Ricardo didn't like this interference from her, and she was kept away from me. I could no longer see her. But every now and then, she would sneak out to come and see me and sneak me food like muffins, but mainly just to check on me.

But the sickness wore on. It got to the point where Ricardo and Manuel thought I would die, so a call was made to my owner back in the US, and my contract was cancelled.

A couple of weeks before I left, there was a huge monsoonal rain that fell over Puerto Tahuantinsuyo and went on constantly for weeks. It was impossible to wear shoes because your feet would sink so deeply in the mud. I was in the central plaza of Puerto Tahuantinsuyo after the big rain, and it was here that I saw my first red wing Macaw.

The big rain had impacted their standard migration pattern and it was then that I experienced my chance encounter with one of these beautiful, big birds.

"I'm going to have a blessed life," I said to myself.

I felt I was going to have a lucky life.

Before I left, Ricardo did let me visit Manuel's mother 'Patches' once more to say a final goodbye. Patches was crying and gave me a big hug. I looked up at her.

"What is my real name?" I asked her.

She smiled and clapped her hands together "los locos pequeños de la luna" she cried, "La familia!"

I was shocked. She said I was family to her? I looked at Manuel who was busily zipping me up in some clothes.

"Are we family?" I asked quickly, "Am I family to you?"

"No," Manuel answered. "Amigos."

Well I knew what that was. We were friends, and that was more than enough for me. That was a huge moment for me to hear something like that from him. I remember how much that affected me. He had never said anything like that before. It was the first and only time that he said we were friends, and I had asked him many times in the past.

I was taken to a big truck in the central plaza where I saw all the village people from the town had gathered in a line to send me off. I couldn't believe it, I thought I was hated. As the truck pulled away, everyone cried out "adios!" The kids screamed excitedly and ran after the truck. All along that road, there were people —families and small groups of people littered along the roadway as we drove on, waving and giving their good wishes. I was shocked and deeply moved.

"You know, they don't want you to leave," Manuel said sitting in the back of the truck with me.

"They want you to stay. In fact, we even tried to gather enough money to buy you from your owner in the US, but their price for you was outrageous and we didn't have enough."

I was floored.

"Really?"

"Yes."

I piled onto the plane amongst all the cargo and sat down on the floor. Out of the entire twenty year abduction program that I came to be a part of, it was the Peru experience that I remembered most and longed to go back to. I felt loved. I felt like I had a family and a home.

6

SEATTLE

FROM PERU, I WAS FLOWN out on what seemed to me to be a United States Military cargo plane. It was green, unmarked, and there were men in uniforms on board the plane. I sat in the cargo area, on the floor, with giant cardboard boxes all around me. It was cold and I cried the entire flight back. I felt like I was being ripped away from my home.

We made a couple of stops en route. Once we unloaded a few items, but otherwise I would assume we were getting gas as no one came on or off, nor was any cargo transferred on or off of the plane. We landed in California in the dark of the early morning hours on a small airstrip on what seemed to be a military base. Peggy was parked there, in her Jaguar Saloon. Peggy, the woman from Seattle.

She loaded me into her car and we drove for what seemed like hours up through the middle of California. Later, we pulled into a hotel to sleep for what remained of the night. I asked her why she trusted me this time and why she spent the extra money for me to have my own bed. She said that they had received reports of how I behaved in Peru and it was obvious that I wasn't some kind of dangerous child. And that I wasn't going to run.

We got up early the next morning and kept driving.

"I wish we were driving up along the coast," she told me as she held the wheel.

"It's so much more scenic."

Every bit of her journey was already budgeted and planned. He knew her mileage and how much gas she would need to take that route. Her food and cigarettes were also budgeted. She had to follow his plans or pay a price.

Eventually we arrived in the Seattle area. I had been napping in the car and I woke up just in time to see the Tacoma Bridge before we made our way out to the massive private island in the bay.

She made it known that she hated having to take the route that we took. Just like the last time that I had been driven there, we couldn't use the Fauntleroy ferry because sometimes they asked for identification from every passenger and made note of the children. The South Worth ferry didn't make any records of children. So we made the trip around and across the Tacoma Bridge to take the South Worth Ferry. I know that she had paperwork that I was a foster child on her farm. I had the most uneasy feeling when I laid eyes on it. Like I was still sleeping and having a nightmare at the same time. I knew what I had seen last time at the farm and that chances were high that I would see something very bad again. I wanted to disappear. I couldn't imagine going back there.

Things at the house looked different to me than when I was first there a few years prior, back in 1982. It was now 1985, and the house had been remodeled and there were three or four other boys living there. It wasn't long after arriving that the feeling of total dread swept over me again. The memories of my past at the house flooded back into my mind.

"Am I going to be sleeping in a dog kennel again?" I asked Peggy.

"No," Peggy quickly answered.

"You will have a room now. You'll be sharing with another boy, but you will have your own bed."

When we got downstairs, there were boys spread out across the floor, playing the very same board games that I had played there before, like Othello and Chutes and Ladders. The main difference was that the carpet had been changed and additional rooms had been added. One of the rooms even had a reel to reel camera. I felt excited.

"You make movies with those?" I asked Peggy, noticing it was pointing to a sofa.

"Yes, we do," she answered. "You may be able to be in one later."

One of the boys walked over to me, sizing me up.

"Who is this?" he said looking at me, with a hint of attitude in his voice. "My name is Jeremy—and just so you know, I'm the alpha here."

Jeremy would've been no more than sixteen or seventeen years old.

"Jeremy is in charge here," Peggy said. "He looks after things when I'm not around."

I was tired, and Peggy took me to my room so I could settle in. I only had a bag of clothes with me.

"You won't be needing those," she said. "We have new clothes for you. You can sleep for a little while if you like."

I was exhausted and did not protest. When I woke up later that night, there was a dinner put on for all the boys. As I sat down at the table, they all looked at me with curiosity.

"Who is this?" they wondered. "What's his name going to be?"

I also shared their curiosity. I had no idea what my name was.

"What is my name?" I looked at Peggy.

"We're going to give you a new name here," she said.

"Well, can I be called Manuel?" I asked eagerly.

"No," Peggy answered quickly. "No Spanish names here. You're not in Peru anymore, and please don't speak in any Spanish while you are here. The closest name to Manuel in English would be Michael perhaps, or Michele."

This comment was funny to me as I didn't speak any Spanish, despite the two plus years I had spent in Peru.

"Call him Michael," Jeremy offered from across the table.

"No, all the new boys are going to get girls names," Peggy advised.

My heart sank. Girls' names?

And after about five minutes Peggy had come up with my new name. "We're going to call him Shelly."

Shelly!!? I couldn't believe it. I hated it. I hated it so much that I wanted to puke. I kept trying to think of ways to protest—excuses to change my name—but nothing worked. I pleaded until I made her angry. She made it very clear to me there was no appeal to be had. And so that became my name on that farm— Shelly.

I didn't integrate into the new group, but I wanted to. I was unwelcome and ignored most of the time. I felt very unsettled in the first few days there. None of the other boys wanted to be friends with me. It was as if I was something *dangerous* to them. It was weird. A week or so later, we were all sitting outside doing our own thing, which was strange because there was always a routine the days before. But now, there was none. One of the boys struck up a conversation with me when we were playing games.

"So, what was it like there? What did they call you?" the boy wondered.

"Los locos pequeños de la luna."

"Gee, Peru sounds awful," he answered.

"No, it wasn't," I replied. "It was wonderful there—they loved me."

"So what does los locos pequeños de la luna mean?"

"Means *the crazy boy from the moon*...because I've been to the moon before. There's a base on the back of it—actually there are a few bases," I answered him.

"Getta outta here!" another boy scoffed.

"You're crazy. There's no bases on the backside of the moon!"

"No!" I argued. "There are!"

One of the boys eventually went to Peggy and asked her if there were any bases on the back of the moon. Peggy, inevitably, pulled me aside later that day.

"You are never to speak about the moon to the boys again," Peggy warned me.

"They don't know about it—and they don't need to know. Can anything be proven about the moon?"

I agreed with her. "No, there can't be."

"So say nothing more about it!"

These boys were actual foster children, from adoption agencies. Some of their parents had died, then they got lost in the system—shuffled from place to place. They remembered who they were and pieces of the background they had, unlike me. But most of them were taken young and had accepted their fate. They didn't seem to question who they were or how they got here, because they couldn't remember anything to compare it to. The families that owned them, like the one we were with on the island farm, were untouchable. They were beyond wealthy and no one questioned them.

So life went on at the island. It was like a boyzone, and it was the same thing day in, day out. We would get up, eat breakfast—but we were never allowed to overeat—and then we just basically wasted our day. None of us got along, and Jeremy was the only one that had access to the entire house. We were limited to the pool, the deck, and around the house area. There was a pond beyond the lawn area, but we weren't allowed to go to that. Jeremy was well suited for his role. Not only was he obnoxious, but he was homosexual, so he enjoyed being around all the boys and doing whatever else he was made to do.

"You're cute," he would say to me. "I'm gonna get to you."

I never knew what he meant by that. One day, we

were having lunch around the table, downstairs when Jeremy looked at Peggy.

"So when is it going to be time for him?"

"When he gets an erection," Peggy answered.

After lunch, Jeremy followed me into another room, and he proceeded to put a video into the VHS machine. It was one of those dirty aerobics workout videos from the 80's. You know, the tight spandex type. The video was full of close ups of girls in their stretched postures, it was like a soft porn movie.

"You watch this," Jeremy said.

"No!" I protested, "I don't wanna watch this. Put something else on."

"No, you watch this."

And then, I was made to sit and watch this video. Sure enough, after watching this video several times, I got an erection from what I was seeing.

"Shelley's got a boner!" Jeremy went shouting through the house.

"Shelley's finally got a boner!"

I could feel my cheeks burning with embarrassment. Later that afternoon, Peggy came to me.

"Would you like to help us make a movie?" she asked.

"Yes," I told her. I was excited.

"Well, it's a scene where you are a prisoner," she said. "You have to strip to your underwear and wear handcuffs."

And they did exactly that. When they had me as they wanted me, Peggy finished setting up the movie camera.

"Lay down on the couch face down," she said, "and Jeremy will come in."

I did what she asked and Jeremy wasted no time in getting into character. He quickly pulled down my underwear and started to rape me. It was very forced, to say the least. It was the most painful thing I had ever endured, and I began to get hysterical. I couldn't understand what was going on.

"Be quiet!" Jeremy cussed at me, hitting me. That just made me worse, and I began resisting him.

"Why!" I screamed. "*Whhyyyyyyyy!*"

I became livid and tried to get out of it any way I could. I was smaller than him but strong enough to roll over and deny him. Eventually Peggy stepped in.

"Okay you can stop now Jeremy." She turned off the projector.

I went out into the living room where the other boys were playing board games and I just curled up and cried. I felt so violated.

"You little fucker!" Jeremy stormed out angry. "I'll get you! You should've let me finish!"

Later on that night, Peggy came over to me on the couch.

"I'm going to give you something that will make you forget about what happened."

"Okay."

Peggy pulled out a needle and injected me. I woke up in the dark around 3:00am the following morning in even more pain. At breakfast later on, Jeremy came up to me.

"We were able to finish filming with you last night," he said very much at ease.

"Huh?"

"Yeah, I was able to finish what I started and we filmed it. Otherwise I was gonna beat the shit out of you."

They were selling these bootleg movies with all of us boys in them. Jeremy told me that people came to the farm and bought the films. He said they were a hot commodity. Sometimes other people would come and we weren't even allowed downstairs when they were filming, except for the ones being used in the film. It was then I garnered a firm understanding of how much of a dangerous place I was in, and that my wellbeing was of absolutely zero concern to them.

The reel to reel only stayed for a few weeks. It was then turned into another bedroom so that we could board two more boys. It felt like they weren't trying to work out protocols as they went. This had long been planned. And they made it clear that they weren't the only homes in America doing what they were doing. They were a network, and were very sure of themselves. Peggy often spoke of it, as did the people who came and went from the house.

A few weeks after being raped on film, I was basically in shock. I became skeptical of anything I was told. I felt a constant underlying disappointment because I thought the other boys there would want to be friends with me and they didn't. Only a couple of the new boys, David and Paul, made any attempt to be nice.

Paul eventually became 'Paula' because of Peggy's rule of new boys getting girls' names.

I also began noticing a sort of strain and sadness in Peggy. It was obvious to me that she was not a happy woman. One day, I saw the gardener of the property —who was perhaps in his 60's—talking with her at the table having a coffee and a cigarette, where Peggy was seemingly venting to him about her husband. She was incredibly protective of her cigarettes and wasn't allowed to smoke as many as she would have liked. Richard chose her daily ration, and she complained about it often.

"Good morning," I wandered past them.

"You know I'm a slave like you," she muttered, inhaling her cigarette.

"I can't do anything. I don't have any money to do anything. Everything is so perfectly budgeted. I don't even have money to buy one cigarette!"

I tried to be uplifting. "Well, at least you can drive around."

But it fell on deaf ears.

Whenever she would talk about being a slave or would start complaining about her life, she'd proclaim that one day she would burn this whole thing down. I always had the sense that she didn't know what was really coming when she married him. Richard had told her exactly what life would be like together, and she didn't believe it could *actually* be this way.

I once heard Jeremy say, "He told you it would be like this. What do you expect?"

So she must have talked about it with him.

By the fall, a couple of new boys had arrived, and every now and then, some men in office-like trench coats would come, donning military style trousers. They looked official. We would have to line up for them and they would observe us.

They would say things like "We're going to have a pizza party, or a hot dog party..." and at the time, I didn't really know what that meant, but judging by what had already happened to me, I knew it wasn't going to be good. Sometimes they didn't like the line-up of boys and wanted to see more.

It turned out that these parties did happen, but the men had made a 'pass' on me to be present for them. Meaning I wasn't choses in the lineup. I wasn't trained in oral service, so I wasn't desirable. So thankfully, I was locked in my room until the party was over. At first I felt bummed out, because I didn't know what I was missing. I couldn't have been more relieved because I would wake up the following morning and would see the boys who were present at these parties. They were beaten—physically and mentally. Some would come with black eyes, scratch marks and bruises, it was terrible. I dreaded to think what had happened to them.

When I asked them about what happened, they told me that they didn't want to talk about it. Jeremy joked and said that it had been a rough night for them. Jeremy had freedom at the parties. He danced around and offered services, and often bragged about how much he loved it.

These parties were happening in the house, upstairs. I never saw them, but I could hear it. There were males and females, and it felt like a good size crowd.

As the summer season ended, the parties calmed down and it became like groundhog day—super boring— just wasting time. David and Paul, the two boys I got along with the most, were taken to a party and they never came back.

"Where are they?" I asked Peggy one day.

"They were purchased," she said, "They've got new homes."

In the winter, the younger kids were taken off site for the parties. Sometimes they would come back and sometimes they wouldn't. I was always afraid I would go, but I never did. I was too old. They made it sound like it was good luck to be chosen and I sometimes felt left out.

When fall came around, and the days were constantly cold, two new boys came. One was called Timothy. Timothy was different from any of the other boys that came through the house. He had been abducted off the street, not taken from the foster system. He told me that a few men rode up in a car and grabbed him in broad daylight. It had been about a year since his abduction and he had tried to escape multiple times.

"I'm gonna escape," he told me one day.

"I'm not gonna stay here."

"Look, you're on an island surrounded by freezing water!" I said to him, "That's crazy. You got nothing—what are you gonna do for money? You got no money!"

"I've got my mom and dad, I'm gonna find them again." Timothy's eyes lit up.

"You wanna come with me? I'm gonna go in the morning."

Turns out that both he and the other new boy went into the kitchen with their pillow cases the next morning and raided the fridge, and then made a dash for it. They walked straight through the back garden and over the fence. They were gone.

Panic ensued later that morning when they discovered their absence. We were made to search the house. We couldn't find them anywhere. What's worse is that it started snowing that morning. They had picked the day of the first snow to try their escape. I knew they were going to fail. I hoped they wouldn't freeze to death.

The old gardener came into the house.

"I found them," he said.

"Where?" Peggy asked.

"In a pond, freezing to death," he said without any remorse.

"I'm keeping them in the barn."

That old gardener was one of the coldest people I had ever met. When you would look into his eyes you felt your blood turn cold—one of those types.

We later learned that those boys were taken away and shipped off somewhere else. We never knew where and we never saw them again.

The night of the first party that I was to participate in was chaotic. A crew arrived early to start setting up things like tents, tables, and all the preparatory stages for a big elaborate event. We weren't allowed outside and later in the day, Peggy took us into the bathroom and gave each of us an enema.

"Your outfit just came for tonight," she said.

"Well, can I see it?" I asked.

"No—you'll see it tonight," she answered, "Go and wait in your room."

Around 9:00pm, she came in with that outfit.

"Time to put this on now."

She handed it to me. It was basically a thong, but it had a pocket for our packages. It was black and hideous. I reluctantly put it on and waited in the room again until about 11:30pm. I knew what was coming.

Peggy came and got us all, then sat us down in the living room. She pulled out a batch of syringes and started injecting each of us. I watched as she was shooting one of the boys and the needle broke. I was last in the line-up and she looked at me.

"There won't be any for you. I don't have enough dosage."

At the time, I didn't know what this would mean for me and didn't feel all too concerned about what was going to happen. I didn't realize how much of an impact the events that were to follow would have on me.

She put us all in handcuffs, with a type of Velcro fastener around our necks that was connected to a chain. Our costumes were basically, giving a "slave-like" vibe, and we were escorted outside into the field down towards the end of the island where the party was. My only instructions were to do whatever I was told.

The area where we stopped was set up with red carpet and large, red, square pillows and a few of us were taken onto the 'pit'. I noticed a really big red headed guy in khakis and loafers with a buttoned up shirt.

"He's going to take care of you," Peggy said and she left us with him.

I would guess he was around six foot five and over three hundred pounds. He walked up to us and gave me a hard, aggressive face.

"Do what I say or I'm gonna beat your fucking ass!" he seethed.

Another guy walked up beside him and had us sit down.

"Look, there are rules tonight," the other guy said.

"Number one, you always stay on your back, or on your hands and knees, but you're never going to fully stand up. If you need to move around, you need to stay bent over—never stand."

He went on, "Keep your mouth open—never shut your mouth. The only time you can close it is when you are off this carpet. And if you don't do what you are told tonight, this one here will take you and beat the living shit out of you."

The two of them left and it was just us three boys.

"We can just lay here for a while," one of them said.

We did just that and watched the party unfold. I saw about a hundred people or so, mingling, listening to the music. Some were even taking drugs. There was a bar on wheels that went around with a mixture of options, from cocaine to pills, to probably more but I didn't know what it was. My time in Peru had exposed me to cocaine, so I knew it was bad.

There was also an alcohol bar, and beyond that was a stage of some sort. But every now and then, people would come by and look at us. They were all well dressed. *Well this isn't too bad...*I thought to myself. But not long after, a few guys came up and took their pants off and proceeded to put their penis in my mouth. Then the sex followed. They were grown men, in their early twenties and up. For whatever reason, the younger guys came first and as the night progressed, the older men would come. The older men usually just wanted a blowjob. The younger ones wanted sex. Sometimes there was lube and some men used condoms. Most didn't use either.

At that point, I had no reference to what an orgasm was or any way to make sense of anything that was happening. I started crying.

"Quit your fucking crying!" one of the guys said, hitting me in the face as he raped me.

The other two boys with me were more tolerant of what was happening, but unbeknownst to me, they were sufficiently drugged to a point of bearable oblivion. They were the ones that got the injection—I didn't. And as the night wore on, I was getting more and more resentful, and the party guests were complaining about me and my 'services'.

I was later pulled aside by one of those party organizer guys who gave me a jab with his fist.

"Look, you have to at least *try*—otherwise your ass is going to be beat!"

There must've been between twenty to thirty guys that came through our pit that night to have sex with us. Sometimes there was a line and I would lose count of the rapes. At other times we'd just lay there, cold and waiting.

The next day, we were given feedback on our services. I was told that I was "all teeth" and that I needed to work on my oral services. I was given no instruction, just to "do better next time."

On the days after the parties, we were allowed to pig out on leftover food. This was the only time that we could overeat and not do our daily workout. We were all incredibly sore, depressed, but also relieved. We tried to make light of it and were calmed by knowing that it would be at least a few weeks before it happened again.

As time wore on and there were more parties every three to four weeks, I don't want to say that I ever became used to them, but I grew more tolerant. Everyone tried to normalize it, and there was nothing normal about it. The only one who really enjoyed it all was Jeremy.

I hated every second of it. I remember seeing the joy that Manuel had when he was with women, and I remember feeling that I had that to aspire to. I was never into the homosexual thing. It was just that, or get beaten. The only time I felt anything positive, was the relief I would experience when the sun would come up at dawn the next morning. That was when the parties were over. We were then allowed to rest and recuperate in our beds for a couple of days thereafter. I definitely needed it because we were sore, bruised, and often bloody.

A few days after one of these parties, Peggy called me downstairs. I came in from the pool.

"Shelly, I've seen all the boys today," she said, handing me a towel.

"This is for later."

"Are you gonna hurt me?" I asked her, feeling concerned.

"No, no," she assured me, making me take off my pants.

She had baby oil and I wondered what she was going to do with it. She was smoking a cigarette. She pulled down my pants and started playing with me until she gave me an erection. It was the first time I had had any sexual encounter with a woman as a teenage boy. What she was actually doing was measuring my erected penis size for specific requests that would come up for another party. She used a tailor's tape measurer. The request was actually for boys with smaller penises for whatever reason.

"Right, well you can finish yourself off," she said as a matter of fact, then tossed the towel at me.

I remember feeling let down. It was all business, and no pleasure. I had a lot of weird feelings as a teenager and I just wanted to be loved. I didn't want to be rich, I didn't want a house, all I wanted was a girlfriend, or some kind of loving relationship. Like Patches. Or like Manuel had with his ladies.

The next party was much, much bigger. There were a lot more people and it went on during the day. And whatever drug she was giving us, Peggy made sure she had a lot of it and it did its job—because us boys were totally out of it. It was basically the same routine but a different costume—this time a hospital outfit, but still chained and cuffed together. And for the first time, I could see the girls, girls like us, except they were in Mardi Gras type costumes with big feathers and sequins. The girls were our counterparts. I never got a close look at them, but they didn't seem developed. They were likely younger than us. The girls had their own house nearby, but a lot of effort was put into keeping them separate and secret from us.

For the first three hours of being in the pit, I didn't feel a thing. There were a lot of new people and one in particular was a doctor. He came right up to me and glared at me deep into my eyes.

"I know what this kid's on," he said looking at my arm, and he went on to mention the name of the drug.

I don't remember what he called it, it was the medical terminology. This doctor was shocked and disturbed by what he was seeing. You could tell it was his first party. The new people tended to participate in the pit. The repeat guests often just watched.

Another time a bunch of women came into our pit. They didn't really participate, but they wanted us to do things with each other.

"Can we do anything we want with these boys?" one asked with intrigue.

The bouncer looked down at her. "Anything you want. They're yours to do as you wish."

They made us have sex with each other, and they wanted us to do it in a chain. It didn't work very well, logistically. We couldn't keep a rhythm for more than a few seconds before the chain broke down. They got bored with it and walked off.

Some time passed before the next party, and in a way, I sort of became acclimatized to them. But in between these parties, the complaints kept rolling in about me. Me not being a good performer when it comes to oral sex. One day, Peggy sat me down with Jeremy listening in.

"Listen," she said with all seriousness, "You are going to have to up your game with this, or you leave me no choice but to sell you off to the military."

She glanced at me, "In the military, you don't have any rights and you'll most likely get really badly injured, or will probably die in combat. You will be like fodder to them."

I just glared at her. I didn't know what to say.

"You have to get better at oral sex," she shrugged, "Or else!"

"You can practice on me," Jeremy offered.

"No way," I shook my head.

"Okay fine," Peggy said, "Go back downstairs then."

So I did. I returned back to the pool.

The next day was gorgeous outside. Sun blazing, blue skies, and all of us boys were swimming out in the pool while Jeremy was sitting at the ladder.

"You sit right here," Jeremy instructed.

"What are we playing now?" I said.

In my naivety, I thought I had managed to make a few friends in the boys, but little did I know how wrong I was. Before I knew it, they had ganged up on me and handcuffed me and pushed me under the water. I couldn't swim. After my struggle, they finally let me back above water, gasping for air.

"What are you doing to me?"

"We're gonna keep you under, until you can learn how to suck a dick," Jeremy said.

Great, I thought to myself reluctantly. I succumbed to the pressure. And truth be told, it wasn't any kind of "proper practice." I think it was more of a dominance thing Jeremy had going over me. I will say that I forever remained a disappointment in dick sucking. I hated it. I wasn't into it, or anything bisexual at that stage, so I was always a let down in this department. Up until the day I left Seattle and the parties, I was known for being deficient in that department.

The next party was the biggest, and the set up was a huge event. In preparation for this party, Peggy kept us starving for weeks. We got one egg and one piece of toast in the morning, a light tofu salad at lunch, and for dinner, something random but small. We literally did nothing all day except a calisthenics routine in the morning and starved out near the pool for the rest of the day. I remember the day of the party seeing how much setting up there was. We were going to be at a "public showing" for the first time—meaning, thousands of people were going to be seeing us.

We went out to this party just before midnight—after the 'main' party crowd had left. It was the same routine, on with the costumes, in with the injections, and out we were paraded. But this time it was a little different, because *women,* for the first time, were sexually participating in our pit with us. I remember this one woman, dressed very smartly in a business, dress-type suit, and she watched at first, encouraging the men to have their way with us, but then one of the boys grabbed her leg and she lowered herself down onto the carpet. Eventually, one of the boys lured her into having sex with him, and before we knew it, there were nine of us having an orgy and I remember how exciting it was for me to be so close to a woman. I dreamed of having sex with her—but then it happened. Her husband stormed into the tent and went ballistic.

"What the hell are you doing!" he screamed at her, slapping her endlessly, shocked at what he was seeing.

Then he started laying into us, punching us left, right, and center. He was beyond mad.

"He was the one trying to have sex with your wife!" my pit boy counterparts pointed at me.

They did this in order to please the husband, knowing that one of us had to be punished, and the pit boys decided it would be me. The husband threw a big fit and really spat it, and before I knew it, I was being chaperoned back into the house. This was a different crowd of people—well to do and classy, sipping on champagne and cocktails—and I was totally out of my depth. I had no shoes, shirt, or pants to speak of, and they left me inside in a tiny thong that barely covered my bits, in front of all these people. I was finally taken to the kitchen and Peggy came up to me.

"What happened?" she asked flustered.

"He misbehaved, so we took him out," the pit man said.

"Take him down to the wine cellar with them," she pointed to the staff.

The wine cellar was no ordinary wine cellar. It was a secret one. A collapsible dining table folded out over the entrance in the kitchen nook and in order to gain entry, one had to push the table back and the floor parted away, revealing a long spiral staircase.

The guard turned to me with a hardened face. "You stand down there and don't move!"

So, I was taken down into this covert wine cellar where I found myself amongst what looked like secret service agents. Three of them actually. They were dressed exactly how they would be if they were guarding someone in an extremely sensitive position —the sharp dark suits, the earpieces, guns, the whole kit basically. They were working for a man down there, who didn't wait to introduce himself to me.

"Hi—I'm Dick," he said cordially, his bald head catching the dim light.

"Look, this kid's been kicked out of the party for bad behavior," the guard chipped in over my shoulder, "He's gotta stay down here until the party's over."

Dick nodded.

"I'll do anything you want me to do," I offered to Dick. "Would you like me to do anything for you?"

"No, no son," Dick answered quickly, brushing off my advances. "I'm not into all of that. The only reason I'm down here is because this wine cellar is the only secure place for me to *talk*, and to make a phone call to Washington."

As I stood there at attention, Dick drew closer, looking at me, with his curiosity eventually getting the better of him. "Is this kid one of the clones?"

Clones? I thought to myself.

"Yeah, this kid is a *LH1203 (or something like that)*," one of the secret service agents answered. One of the '82 models."

Dick leaned in taking a closer look at my face.

"Do they enhance his eyes to make his eyes look like that?"
"Nope—as far as I know they're exactly how they're supposed to be."

At this point, I did not understand the conversation happening between Dick and the secret service agent.

Dick smiled at me.

"You know, you're lucky," he patted me on the shoulder affectionately.

"You might well be able to go into space when you're a little older!"

And that was the last time I saw Dick. He walked back up and out of the cellar and that was that. I knew I had already been to the moon, but I wasn't allowed to tell anyone about that. Dick's words shocked me, and I never forgot them. Little did I know at the time just how deep into space this program went.

After standing at attention for so long, I eventually sat on the floor and passed out asleep. Peggy came and got me in the morning and took me to my room, and in a way I felt lucky, getting 'off the hook' from my working shift that night.

The following party, they gave us a drink with a drug that would prevent us from getting an erection. I remember the guests being so disappointed because they wanted to see us boys around our pit, erect, all night. This would be the last party for the summer, and next came the cold winter.

It was a pretty low key last party. But there was a new group of guys there that turned out to be soldiers—a type of special forces group. They had a rule amongst themselves that whatever one soldier did, the others had to do also. So that meant that if one of them wanted to have sex with a boy, the others would be obligated to do so also—even if they were straight men. It was bad luck for me that night, because one of those soldiers had sex with me, and in the heat of the moment before he ejaculated, he punched me hard in the right eye. Then they *all* had sex with me, and *all* thumped me in my right eye. One soldier even tried to just give me a slap across the head, obviously feeling a little sorry for me, but another soldier stepped in and thumped me for him. And all the while this is playing out amongst them, they are talking to each other.

"The main house is forty yards to the left," one would say.

"There's a barn and a runway," another said.

"They have no idea we're even infiltrating them!" another joked. "They have no idea of what we are."

"Well what about these guys?" another soldier said, referring to us. "They're hearing us talk."

"—Don't worry about these guys," a soldier reassured, "They probably won't even live long enough to talk about us."

The soldiers were definitely there on a mission. They would gather near us boys to talk with each other because our pit was on the outskirts of the party. Then they would go into or around the party to gather info, before returning to the area to speak with each other. I don't know whatever came of their mission. Nothing that night or during the remainder of my time on the island.

So that was the last party and then winter came around. It was a really nice time because we all got new clothes. I actually had accumulated three pairs of jeans! Not only that, but we could eat more—our dietary intake was increased, which was great. Don't get me wrong, we were still kept hungry, but Peggy would bring home pies and give us more to eat, so that was nice about this time of year also.

During the Winter of '86-'87, a lot of the boys left—we were told they were being sent off to bigger parties at other properties, and at one point, it got down to only three boys. We felt like we could relax. But as soon as the weather started warming, a new group of boys came, and we would have to take our morning pills, eat our one egg on one piece of toast with orange juice, and start doing calisthenics again.

As the spring was well under way, someone would come by and tell us our upcoming schedule, meaning the parties that we would be 'working' at. By now, I was a seasoned veteran and I was one of the older boys of the group. I was 'upgraded' to a different role. Not only was I in the pit, but for the first time, I was going to be able to walk around with the others at parties. I was told to offer my services to anyone who wanted them but when I did, mostly people said no. It was a much easier task than the pit.

One day we went out on the patio for our morning calisthenics. Normally, we were given a glass of water and a small plastic container full of pills to swallow. I don't really know what they were. Maybe steroids, and some painkillers, diet pills, vitamins, who knows. But on this day, there was a change in our formula. And the pills that we were given made me sick. I complained about feeling sick to my stomach, finished the workout, and went on about my day. The next day I was even more sick to my stomach. I asked if there was any way we could change back to the old pills. I learned that Peggy had made inquiries about it and the answer was no. The third day I was so sick from the pills that I began to vomit and I couldn't do the workout. It was decided that the formula would not be changed and that if I couldn't continue with my duties where I was, I would go off to the military.

Peggy made a phone call. I could hear some of it from the other room.

"Can't we just put him back on the old medication?" she asked the receiver.

Eventually, she got off the phone, upset.

"What happened?" I asked.

"You're going," she said with disdain. "You're going to get sold off to the military."

Of all the time I had spent with Peggy, we had formed somewhat of what I felt was a special bond. She was nice to me during my time there. She looked hurt and sad about hearing this information. Her face turned and she looked terrible. Because of the 'hyper-sexualized' environment that I was existing within, I had become a form of 'attracted' to Peggy. I would be sad to leave her too. But after learning this, she ignored me for two weeks. I was a dead man walking so to speak. I would say good morning or hello to her —nothing. It was like I was a ghost.

It wasn't long after that, maybe a week to ten days later, that I was told goodbye unceremoniously by the boys there. Many of them said they wouldn't miss me and good riddance. Some of them said they would miss me. I asked Peggy if she was going to miss me. I told them I was going to miss all of them. She said she wouldn't miss me, that I was just a possession and that even though she had played a mother role for me, she didn't love me. I had asked her.

There was a debate over someone riding along with us, to which she decided no one else would come along. She piled me in the car and I knew it was the day I was leaving. I felt elated to be leaving this loveless and cold life, and couldn't wait to be going to the military—I believed that anything had to be better than this.

Peggy and I drove away. I remember being so happy as I looked out the window that I was not going to come back to this place. The soulless gardener was building a circular garden as we drove by. It was seeing him that made me realize that there was no love, ever, in my entire experience on the island. It just didn't seem real to me that a place could function with everyone being so emotionally cold and withdrawn.

When Peggy stopped speaking to me, it became unbearable there. Despite looking forward to leaving, I was also very afraid of what was coming next. We had been deeply conditioned to be afraid of being taken to the military. We were programmed to remember that with it, came the very real chance of death. But I knew that ultimately I was better off anywhere but where I was. My time there, although mixed with abuse and a strange form of stability, was more spiritually damaging than anything. In Peru, they loved me. Patches showed me affection and kindness. Here, it was a place that existed and ran efficiently with absolutely no joy. There was no comfort, ever.

We drove for a few hours. It began to get dark and we turned into a parking lot behind a big box store. We were met by some men driving a cargo van. I got out of the car, possessionless, and Peggy had a conversation with them. Then they took me into the back of the van. They had me lie down and gave me an injection. That was my last memory of being a permanent resident on the earth during what I would come to learn is called a "Career Return Program".

7

THE ARENA

I REMEMBER WAKING UP on basically the same ship that had taken me to the moon the first time. We were already in flight when I woke up. I was laying in the seat and saw across the wide aisles that there were a handful of other teens, probably sixteen or seventeen years old, as well as adults in uniforms. I then remembered hearing officers talk about my age when I went through various checkpoints, concerned that my documents didn't show my age. When asked, any handler would say that I was seventeen, though I knew I wasn't.

This flight, in contrast to other flights to the moon, was packed. Sitting beside me was a man in a military uniform. It was a formal, Air Force looking uniform.

He was putting something away into the bag at his feet and he said to me, "I carried you on here, but you can walk off by yourself."

He told me there was a bag in the seat in front of me if I felt like I was going to be sick. I looked at the seat and it had an embroidered logo on it. I commented that the plane was pretty old.

"Well it's not a plane, but yes, it's quite old."

I sat there for a minute and got my bearings about me. I felt the urge to brag.

"I have been on one of these before, a long time ago. Probably when they started flying them."

He looked at me and laughed. I was feeling the logo embroidery with my hand.

"Last time this wasn't this nice. Are we going to the moon?"

He said, "That logo is obsolete. Now it's McDonnell Douglas, but they will probably never change it to the new one. Do you know what that logo means? Or what does that represent?"

He pointed at the rocket flying up away from the planet. I shook my head no.

He told me to take a guess. I was at a loss.

I guessed, "Was it a missile they shot at the moon?"

He looked a little frustrated and reached for his bag.

"No. I have the old logo in here somewhere."

He took forever to find the paper he was looking for. Like he was possessed, he must have gone through the whole bag twice. Finally he pulled out some document that looked boring to me, and at the top of it was a version of the same logo but with planes— one of them flying upwards away from the earth.

"Here this is a very old logo, from before you were even born. What do you think that means? It's symbolic."

I guessed again, "They were flying to the moon way back before I was ever alive?"

"Yes that's right, there's hope for you yet. We have been going to the moon for a long, long time."

About a half an hour passed. I did nothing, just sat in my seat, not feeling very well. I thought I was being drafted into the military. I had asked the man if I would be in combat or even die. He had told me that there was a possibility of both of those scenarios happening. I asked him my name and he told me that I would have a number and that in time, most guys got a nickname. There were no ladies that I was aware of in our military group.

The walls of the craft went transparent and it seemed that I had missed the pilot's comments this time about where we were. I saw that we were flying near the building on the moon, shaped like a trapezoid. We were close so that I couldn't see much of the building this time.

We flew into a hangar that was inside a crater off to the side of the trapezoid base and slowly taxied up to an attached umbilical hallway. Even though we were inside a hangar bay, it was still a vacuum, meaning there was no air. People walking about were in fully sealed suits with helmets.

The umbilical that was attached to our plane had oxygen and gravity, so we were able to de-board and walk directly into the base. I was disappointed because now that I was older, I wanted to see the ship we were on in better detail. But that didn't happen because the umbilical ramp had no openings to see through.

I was led in, and immediately separated from the rest of the passengers and taken to a medical area.It looked like the inside of a hospital for the most part. I remember long halls with windows to the rooms on each side. I was put through a medical exam. It was the standard blood pressure, temperature, cough type exam. Within an hour, I was put on a table where they performed some kind of surgery on me. I was strapped down for some surgeries, possibly immobilized but not anesthetized. I could feel everything and if I told them it hurt, they would just carry on and say it didn't matter, and that I wouldn't remember anything anyways.

I would wake up in a hospital gurney type bed and lay there for hours. Then there would be another surgery. This went on for the first two or three days. Most of the surgeries were around the back of my head and my chest, and sometimes on or in my back. They would open me up and put things in my body. It was beyond painful, an excruciating nightmare. Tall white aliens were doing the operation. They look like the standard gray but they were bigger. There were also shorter grays in the operations. They were all rude—abusive. They didn't care about me in the slightest. They treated me the way I would imagine animals used for product testing are treated. I had no human rights. I was replaceable.

I was eventually given a small room with a bed, like a cell. There was a concrete floor and a two foot by three foot blanket on the floor. I was fed something like dog food from a metal bowl. Every few days, a tall white alien would come in and take me to a room to be hosed off with cold water. There was a urinal nearby; more like a basin that you could pee and poop in. Between each trip to surgeries or the hose down room, I was allowed to use the bathroom.

Eventually I was taken into a room with what looked like computer stations lined up. It looked like the computer lab on a college campus. The main difference was that it was staffed solely with the taller whitish grey alien, and the lights were different somehow. They would only shine on the area that the light was pointed towards and it would remain dark in the area around it. It wasn't a spotlight though. They were nothing like the way lights work that I was used to. The computer station had a place to rest your head in front of the monitor. There was a shelf for your chin and a device to press your forehead against, most similar to visiting the optometrist. I was strapped in and there were speakers near my ears. They gave me some sort of drug. It was mild compared to other drugs I'd been given and only produced a slight buzz.

After I was fastened in, the speakers played a binaural sound for a few minutes. Then the screen would display movies for fighting motivation. It would show scenarios like a group of boys walking down the street and then bullies approaching. The bullies would target your friend and then ask you, in multiple choice videos, what you should do to help. Scene A might be you all walking away. Scene B might be you pleading for peace. And so on. You got to choose what was best, using your eyes to select the best multiple choice answer. Any answer that was not aggressive confrontation was wrong. They were testing our fight or flight response and simultaneously training me to choose a fight—to not run from danger.

The scenarios became more violent over time. After a while, there were guns and combat situations— hopeless scenarios. In these, they wanted you to sacrifice your life to save your friend (which I was trained to believe was anyone with authority over me). And then people would celebrate your sacrifice. Then it would cut to a scene of a festival or parade type environment, very cheesy, but over time, it did have the desired effect. I felt eager to have a situation arise so that I could sacrifice myself and be celebrated.

This occurred over and over, for days. Sometimes the movie was about a tactic, like how to get close to someone without looking like I was approaching them. I would get a day or two of the movies and then a surgery. Then back to the movies. The whole process didn't last long as it felt at the time, however I was drugged much of the time. If I had to guess, I would estimate about a month in total. The video training room was large, and there were sometimes others doing the same training, but not near me.

My wound sites from the surgery were mostly all on the backside of my body, so I couldn't really see them. I know there was a type of medical grade tape that they used to seal the incision sites. There was also a medically advanced salve that they would put on the wounds that caused them to heal in record time.

There was a machine they put me in to measure my strength and range of motion. The only reason I remember it is because it was the only procedure I went through that whole time that was fun in a way. Imagine the DaVinci drawing with resistance rings at my hands and feet that had a hold of each arm and leg individually and moved them in all directions. There used to be contraptions like it at carnivals that you could get strapped into and they would twirl and circle you in all directions. The device would tug and I needed to resist. From this, they were able to measure my strength and range of motion. The technicians could read my data in real time. If I asked them how I did, if I was strong, they just said nope.

One day myself and ten or twelve others from my "class" were loaded up into the hangar and taken on a smaller ship out and over the surface of the moon. The flight was maybe fifteen minutes long. This craft or plane felt like a cargo plane and we couldn't see anything. We de-boarded straight into a gymnasium looking room. It was very well lit, contrary to the other building on the moon. I remember being amazed by the size of the area. I thought that this time I would get a chance to see what I was flying in, but we were rushed off into a hallway.

The group of us were all kept together and lined up in the small hallway for a long time. Finally an officer, I assume based on the way he gave orders, came and collected us and walked us through a network of more tiny hallways. We were told to keep our heads down, our sight on our shoes, and walk single file. We got into an elevator where we were all made to face the wall. We exited the elevator to another long hallway and walked until we reached double metal doors. There was a lower ranking man there, in camo pants and a beret. He made us stand at attention and seemed pissed off.

We waited there for what felt like an hour, and another man came up to us and handed us each a canister that looked like a half-sized can of spray paint. It had a big button on the top of it.

The officer told us, "Do not push the button! Here, where you are standing, NOTHING will happen. But when you walk through those doors these cans will be armed, in which case when you push the button you will immediately be blown to pieces. If you should encounter something beyond those doors that should be blown to pieces, you cannot throw these at them, you must be close enough to destroy whatever it is AND yourself. Think about your friends here and saving their lives by giving your own."

That was the sum of our combat instruction. He had us line up against the wall at attention and he stood at attention behind us staring at the door we had been marched to. A few of us talked between ourselves and he allowed it but when we all began to talk and it got loud, he made us stand silent. After a few minutes, the doors opened. I was towards the back of the line to go inside and I was afraid but I was confident that nothing really bad was going to happen. I told myself that this was another scare-trip that I was going to go through like the fire thing with the mask years before, and that I was going to be fine. The boys in the front were obviously scared. The officer in the back had to yell at us to go inside.

Once we all went through the door, it slammed shut behind us. We walked into a large concrete room with a layer of sand on top of a concrete floor. It was the size of a middle school basketball court maybe. There were bright lights shining straight down from the ceiling so that you couldn't look up without your eyes straining and watering. I could hear that there were spectators, but could not see them from the brightness of the lights. They were probably twenty five feet above the arena.

There was huge chain link fencing hanging from the ceiling with wires and cables holding it up. It looked like it could be dropped down to seal the area off from up where the spectators were. At first the spectators were laughing mostly, and talking among themselves. We had spread out close to the door we'd come in through. Then there was a buzzer sound and there was a door on the other end of the room that opened. A few seconds later, a huge insect came crawling out slowly. It had to be four-hundred to five-hundred pounds. Five feet tall and about ten feet long. It looked like an ant for the most part. It had a striped pattern on it almost like tiger stripes but more spotted, and the markings were mostly on the rear of it. It was an otherwise beige color. It had more than one set of pinchers on its huge round head and many eyes. The pinchers were near the mouth and scissor-like.

I never got very close but I remember it being terrifying. It moved in a very slow way, like it was intimidated too. All of us huddled together in a ball of scared shitless little boys. We would volley to not be in front. I was in the middle for only a minute and then others pushed me forward. I was stuck out front and I pressed my back up against the wall of boys behind me. The bug was a good distance away and it wasn't moving towards us.

The crowd began to yell, "You're all gonna die, you faggots! Don't pussy out, now let's see some blood!"

I couldn't believe what I was hearing. I thought to myself are we really all supposed to die now? The bug started to act like it figured out where it was. At first it only inspected its immediate area. But now it had its eyes on us and started creeping towards us. It moved along the wall towards our huddle and we began to press up against the other corner of the room and start to move along the wall away from the bug and towards the door it had come out. We were attempting to stay as far away from it as we could. It began to move in a more direct way to us and I remember doing the math in my head on what was going to happen if I ran up and pressed the button and blew myself up and it as well. I was afraid it would be able to keep its distance from me with its front legs and I would die for nothing.

In the next moment, one of the boys ran at it full speed with the bomb in his hands like a football and he dove on it and blew himself in half and the head of the bug into pieces. It shook for a few seconds and dropped to the ground. The boy was in two halves on the ground, split at the waist, in a bloody pile of parts. The crowd cheered and went crazy. The door we came in opened and people started rushing in. We were taken out in a single file line and people with medical coats ran over to the boy on the ground and started working on him.

We were taken back to a room set up with twenty or so medical beds, and they fed us. an officer came in, followed by his staff, and they deliberated amongst themselves as if we were not even in the facility with them. They were excited, speaking about how the Project was going to be a huge success and they went on about progressive plans to be implemented from this point forward.

We each had a minor medical exam taken—pulse, temperature, blood pressure—then a nurse walked in with bags of clothes for us. We were wearing dark blue jumpsuits and she had given us dark blue fatigue looking pants and white cotton t-shirt to put on. Our shoes were slips with rubber soles. My clothes fit me.

"You can change right there," she said and quickly left us to our own devices.

So we changed, and then we slept.

We were told that the suicide boy lived. They had the technology on the moon to restore his body, despite it being blown off at the hips. He was going to be assigned to an easier job than us in reward for his actions.

8

MARS COLONY CORP

THE NEXT DAY, WE WERE walked out onto a ship with the wide rows of seating. This one seemed like the same model as the one we took from the earth to the moon, but not as new, or at the very least, not as plush. It was also bigger. On every third row of seating, there were chrome bars that went up from the floor to the ceiling. It also had the same layout as the moon-bound ship before, but the walls were different colors as was the fabric on the seats. Our chairs were not as soft as the other one I had flown on. And for this flight, there were mostly empty seats.

There were all the boys that I had been in the same program with sitting on one side. On the other side of the cabin were fifteen or twenty other boys that were older than us but similar in age to each other. They seemed to be at home with the whole experience. By that I mean that they seemed to be aware of where we were going and what they would be doing. My group, on the other hand, had not been given any briefing or information other than a few orders to follow. This caused a general feeling of fear about what we were going to be doing.

The other boys were joking that the chrome poles between the seats were stripper poles, but at that time I didn't know what that was. We later learned that the poles were positioned beside the seats so that should there be an emergency or a zero-gravity situation unfolded, the occupants would be able to orient themselves and have something to hold onto.

Other than the two groups of guys, the craft was basically empty. About a dozen or so of us, a few officers, and those other soldiers who sat by the windows, and who had obviously spent a lot of time together as they shared a camaraderie with each other. They were even boisterous.

The captain of the craft came over the speaker.

"We are about to embark on our journey to Mars. Our journey will not take long, and we are all clear to go with no delays."

The ship took off quickly and the windows became transparent, but unluckily for me, I still couldn't see anything outside except for blackness. I don't remember if there was a time distortion because I didn't feel it, but we arrived in the orbit of Mars no later than fifteen minutes after taking off.

I looked out the window and there it was—the redness, the sparseness of the place. It was Mars. The younger soldier boys were thrilled.

Within a few moments, the captain came over the speaker system.

"We are currently within the orbit of Mars. Unfortunately, there is going to be a little delay, as we are awaiting clearance to land, so therefore we will remain in orbit until given the all clear."

After sitting in our seats for at least two hours, A man in uniform walked up to us and told us that it was going to be awhile, and that we could get up and walk to the bathroom and change seats if we wanted to. Most boys moved towards the walls of the plane, where they could see out. I remember feeling afraid of everything and I didn't have much courage on a social level. I wanted to get up and socialize with the other boys but I was terrified to make friends. I remember sitting there trying to talk myself into getting up and just walking around. In my mind, I went over the possibilities. I was afraid someone wouldn't like me and something bad would happen. Just the day before they were all trying to feed me to a giant bug. So I had no reason to believe I was going to be treated better. I concluded it was safest and best to remain in my seat.

The captain came on over the speaker again.

"Now because we have been forced to delay our landing on Mars and because you have been all very patient with it, I'm going to give you all a little treat!" he said. "I'm about to turn off the artificial gravity so that you may experience some zero G's. Weightlessness! You'll get five minutes of it, and I will inform you when I am going to turn the gravity back on."

I had been sleeping with my seat belt on. This was the exact situation and feelings as before. I wanted to unbuckle and try to do a flip, but that same inner fear that crippled me took over. I remember watching, paralyzed, as the older boys flew around on the other side of the cabin. They did cartwheels and flips and pushed each other from one chrome bar to the other. It looked like they were having the time of their lives. But I was too scared. Before I knew it, the five minutes was up. For years after, I regretted not taking off my seat belt. Later in my tour, I would serve on a ship that had a gravity distortion on one of the ladders in between decks and I would take it every morning down to my station. I would do trick drops through the field of one-third gravity on the ladder and I would always think back to the time around Mars that was my only chance for zero G. I guess that's why the memory sticks out so much.

When we finally landed, we pulled into an open air hangar and walked down steps into another umbilical hallway off to the side. We were approaching two officers.

"Woah, woah," one put his hand up.

"Stop here."

They separated the older boys out from our unit and we became concerned about what was going on. Then they threw bags over our heads.

"Now hold each other's hands and keep walking," they ordered.

"Oh come on!" I protested.

"Do we really have to have bags over our heads?"

No answer.

We were taken aboard a smaller shuttle and flown to something called a forward base, meaning that it was closer, or more forward, to danger. It had been abandoned on Mars. I could feel that we were in a tiny ship, despite my head being covered. I could also detect the movement of the craft, much like the difference in a commuter plane versus a jet.

The craft was flown or taxied underground, which is where the base was. The hangar and the entire base were beneath the surface. We walked straight off the plane and could breathe the atmosphere in the base. It was here that the bags were taken off, and I saw that my guys and I were lined up inside a building, at attention. There were Marines—men in uniform, and they were taking a roll call of us and all the gear we each had. They themselves told us that they were Marines.

"Welcome," the Marine in charge said, "You are now at a Forward Base. You are here as part of our program and you are known as the Orbit Troop."

He turned to his younger colleague.

"Chuck here will give you an orientation, and will escort you to your accommodation."

The Marine then left us, and Chuck, who appeared much more relaxed than his counterpart, gave us a small nod.

"Come with me," he said.

We followed Chuck, and he began a tour of the facility.

"Okay, so we're currently on the second level of this

facility—there are five in total that you will be associated with."

Chuck turned to us.

"Look, I'm gonna sum this whole tour up very quickly for you right now," he advised.

"The top two levels have all the good stuff, and the bottom three levels are boring as hell and you guys are going to be on the very bottom level."

Well, that's just great.

We walked on a little, and one of the other guys next to me looked curious.

"So what's on the top two levels?" he asked Chuck.

"Well there's the flight hangar, where we keep all of our vehicles and craft," Chuck began. "Then you also got the hospital, and then the armory where you suit up and everything. Then the bottom three levels are administration and lodging."

This facility was a strange place. Everything was color coded in, frankly, ugly colors. Blue, orange, yellow, red. With lines that went along the floors and brick walls, as well as the furniture and doors to other wings and various rooms on each level. They were used as a guide to take you from one wing to the next.

You would follow the color of the line that matched your designation; it gave me the vibe of a system that an elementary school would implement. It looked like the place was built to accommodate a lot more people than there were.

Chuck continued.

"We use Latin abbreviations to name each level. So the bottom is alpha or A, followed by beta…"

I remember how confusing we always found it and it was always a topic of conversation between us—how stupid the layout of this facility was.

"This is just dumb" one of the guys I was with would say. "Why not start with alpha at the top level of this facility instead of echo?"

This would become one of many things that did seem dumb to me too.

We took an elevator down to the cafeteria where there were a bunch of soldiers and officers already eating.

"Whoooooah!" They hollered and screamed. "Look at these girls!"

They immediately started in with the hazing.

"Don't pay attention to those guys," Chuck quickly said.

"Come on. Just keep walking."

So we did, and he led us up a slight ramp into a large room that looked like an old office, cubicles and all, except that the desks had been taken out, and military cots put in instead.

"Okay you guys," Chuck said.

"Relax, put your bags down and settle in. Someone will be here shortly to take you to dinner."

In our bags were sets of clothes, socks, granola bar type things. No toiletries. We did not unpack them.

It was late in the day and we settled in quickly. About twenty minutes later, someone came by our room to take us to dinner. The cafeteria was a standard one—a typical line along a counter, which was a self service buffet—with one guy manning it. We could help ourselves to a small meal, one scoop of this, one scoop of that kind of thing. The food was much like what you'd expect at a school cafeteria. Salisbury steak type things, cubed carrots, mashed potatoes, stuff like that. A lot of the buffet was empty, indicating again that this place was made for more people.

The guys and I found a table and sat down. Immediately, we were reprimanded.

"No, no!" our officer said. "You can't sit at that table. You have to sit at the yellow table. Over there."

Really? Even the cafeteria was color coded? Sure enough, there were colored lines on the floor that took you to your matching colored table.

"Why do we gotta sit at the yellow table when that other one is closer?" One of the guys with me asked.

"Because there isn't a *pink* one," a soldier said.

Everyone broke out in laughter and thought it was hilarious. Then three soldiers in t-shirts and fatigues came over and knocked all of our food off the table.

"Now pick it up!" the third soldier ordered.

I just stood there glaring at them. I was pissed.

"Ohhhh, well now! What have we got here?" One of them sneered at me.

I still just glared at him. Quickly, another soldier with a slightly higher rank than this third soldier, intervened.

"Come on, look," he said.

"Just pick your plate up, this happens to everyone new here. You still got food you can eat."

I sure as hell wasn't going to eat off the floor. Luckily, I managed to grab one bite of food before it was knocked off. I also refused to pick my food off the floor. One of my more relenting guys picked mine up for me and handed me my plate. I just threw it in the trash. I wasn't having any of it.

Eventually, we all went back to our room where we were shown the showers and toilets. The toilets had no toilet paper. Instead, a bidet system was in place.

"Is there any toilet paper here?" I heard one of the guys call out.

"Well son, you're on Mars," I heard the officer reply.

"We got plenty of water, but there are no trees here." One could even see where the toilet paper would go in the empty toilet roll holder. A few days later, someone actually did bring us some toilet paper—one roll. What a luxury.

There were stalls for the toilets and a communal shower with four or five shower heads. There was hot water, lots of it. Water was never a problem on Mars.

For the first several days, our group of guys did nothing. We sat around doing nothing at all. We had no phones and nothing to read. I believe we were all somewhat mind fractured to have been able to endure the long periods of inactivity like we did.

Then things began to happen. We started preparing for a hiking mission. An officer started coming and instructing us through our workout in the morning. We ran circles through the hallway. They told us that we were preparing for combat missions. One day they took three of the guys for the day. When they returned, we asked them what happened and they said they went hiking on the surface. They said it was warm, sunny, and beautiful.

I was given a bright white rubbery suit that had a 'belt unit' fastened to it, that applied three injections. It had a switch that had to be turned on in order to fire the injection buttons. These injections would be administered into our hip and they would rid the body of any pain, while simultaneously giving you an incredible boost of energy. In addition to our personal three, the other soldiers had more injections on their belts.

"These injections are armed now," one of our superiors informed us.

You couldn't just hit the injections and make them active. Both the shots and the oxygen, and probably many other features in the suit, were remote controlled. Many functions of the suit had to be "turned on" or "armed" by our superiors to work as needed on the surface.

We also had an auto tourniquet positioned in a pocket on the left thigh area, the size of a cigarette packet with a black cord attached. In the event that we needed to use it, we could pull the cord with our teeth, apply the tourniquet to the limb area that was required, then simply push a button and it would tourniquet. The suit was literally the most comfortable outfit of clothing I have ever worn in my life, boots and all. At some point unknown to me, I had been measured exactly for it to fit me perfectly, and it did. There was a backpack that had some equipment in it and a small oxygen tank. We were told to not touch the backpacks at all and that they were automated.

I was told that we were simply going for a hike, and at the time, even all of the combat-oriented suit features were not enough to alarm me. The marines had suits that looked like Iron Man. They were armored and hid their faces. Their suits were also reddish in color and had the ability to shift colors to better camouflage themselves. They had small guns that they carried as well as massive guns attached to the arms of their suits. The guns were electric rail guns that shot a kinetic round.

"The bugs here on Mars prefer to dismember you, as opposed to killing you," they told us.

"As soon as those sliding doors open, they will come for you, and will try to rip or bite off limbs before any killing takes place. Your auto-tourniquet is vital for you to stay alive."

We each had radios with a 'group leader' having a stronger signal than the rest of the group. We also each had a digital wrist reader, which would give us location coordinates, route navigation, messages, and so on. I really didn't use it that much.

Our hiking missions were to last for a duration of four hours and for this particular day, we went out on our mission in the afternoon with six of our guys, plus two marine soldiers. We were told that we were doing a simple reconnaissance mission to get familiar with the area.

We walked down a long hallway on Echo level. The armory was there as well as a small triage hospital. It was a small floor that led into an airlock. One door opened, we went in, then it closed before the outside doors opened into a natural tunnel cave on the side of a hill. As soon as I set foot on the surface, the gravity changed. It was like learning to walk again, but it felt really good. It always feels good to go into lower gravity. It took about fifteen minutes to adjust. And this adjustment phase was built into our mission time.

We exited the tunnel onto the surface of Mars. The sky was blue, similar to Earth but dimly lit by a smaller looking sun. It was just much further away. There was cold air that felt much thinner. It was like walking outside in winter. We fell into line on a trail that was well traversed. You could see that we were positioned between two mountain ranges. We came upon a wide open space with small craters, about six feet deep, round, and about the size of a swimming pool. We were still in our fifteen minute adjustment phase and I went down into one of the craters. I was able to run on the walls of the crater, with my body basically parallel to the surface. I was able to gain speed, which I wasn't able to do on the surface. On the surface, when you ran, you went up. It became hopping. In the crater, I gained centrifugal force. It was so much fun. I tried to get the others to give it a try but they weren't interested and either blew me off or ignored me. A soldier told me to knock it off and quit fucking around. When our adjustment time was up, we got back on the trail.

We must have gone about four or five kilometers from the base. Everything was metric in space. The surface of Mars was a combination of rusty-reddish sandstone, rocks, and sand dunes. At least the parts that I saw were. We eventually arrived at another type of crater, where there were these black jagged rocks piled on top of each other into columns fifteen feet high. They were only about two feet wide and the rocks looked like sharp volcanic rocks. There must have been something holding them together. And there were about twenty or so of them. The black rock material that they were made of wasn't apparent anywhere else around. They had to have been dug up from somewhere or brought in.

"Who did this?" I looked at these monuments, asking one of the soldiers.

"Don't worry about it," one of the soldiers dismissed me quickly.

"It's not our business. We're just passing through, the science guys have already been here, researching these long ago. And don't touch any of them."

"Well, what did the science guys say about them?" one of my guys pressed on.

"The science guys said these columns are extremely old, they've probably been here for millions of years."

We finished that day's mission unscathed. One thing to know about Mars is that the weather changes very quickly, and very often. I remember coming back into base with the light blue sky quickly replaced by hard dusty winds—so bad that I had to turn my face away to avoid eating the dust, and then just as soon as it changed, it would go back to normal again. This could happen in a matter of minutes, even seconds sometimes.

"Get used to it," one of the soldiers said.

"It's always like this here. But catch a good sunset and you won't forget it—they're purple."

When we got back to the base and went inside the doors, there were a half dozen officers cheering for us. When the soldiers came in they were all high fives. Whatever happened, we had no idea. But everyone, including the soldiers, was elated. After a second hiking mission, we got a couple of days off.

"You guys are doing so well with the missions," one of our superiors began, "that we're able to skip a few of the pre-planned steps and are drawing up new plans for the next missions, which are more advanced."

Whatever was happening on this forward base, it was the first time wherein I actually felt like a participant, instead of existing in some type of 'slave-like' capacity. And even though the soldiers would haze us, we all got along in somewhat of a fashion. And the truth of it was that they were probably clones too— just like us. In fact, I believe the cloning technology drove this whole experience. It allowed for my consciousness to be transferred into a "new" body that could be replicated easily.

When I was younger, at Inyokern, they often called me a clone. Seattle people referenced me as a clone. But I had never given it much thought because I was self aware. I knew that I was a person, with consciousness. That wasn't something I thought a clone would have. At some point on the moon, I started hearing comments like "they're gonna put you back" from the other guys. I didn't have the concept that I might be missing from somewhere, because I couldn't remember my family. I was mind fractured and didn't really consider where I came from.

There was one man on the moon, Air Force I think, that I specifically asked if I was a clone. He told me that no, I actually wasn't. But the people who thought I was didn't have clearance to know otherwise. He told me not to worry about it, that I would go back. Back to what, I never questioned. It was like ticking a waiver on a phone app. I just accepted it and went on.

These soldiers knew we were clones and would use that knowledge to their advantage, especially at the cafeteria during breakfast. And not once did we go anywhere without shock collars around our necks. We were given collars the night after the battle with the bug in the arena. It was a thin, braided, metal-fabric band. It had a small box on the back right side of the neck. It fit well and the shock box stayed in the same part on my neck. These collars never came off, including sleeping and showering. If we got shocked, we would immediately stop anything we were doing at once, and no matter how illogical or ridiculous the command was thereafter, we would follow command for three to five minutes in a catatonic state.

At a 7:00am breakfast one morning, one of the soldiers started bragging that he had the device to give us shocks at will. On missions, soldiers have the device in their suits. But never in a recreational capacity. And this frightened the hell out of us clones with our shock collars on.

"Oh yeah, I got the shock device," the soldier taunted.

"We got one of those clone boys like you and shocked him silly...did whatever we wanted to do with him!"

We all sat around, and the feeling was obvious—we were all terrified of knowing that. Breakfast time was always a very crazy time. It was the time when the soldiers would come in, holler and haze, cat call, throw food at us, or do whatever pleased them—they were mostly young guys like us, but the food throwing was a huge one for them. They would do this until someone of rank would show up, and everything ceased at once. It was always humiliating.

One morning, just before our third mission—the most major one yet—the biggest food fight erupted. A soldier threw something at our table and one of us had enough and got up and threw it back angrily. The rest of the soldiers started throwing food at us and several others joined in. I thought that they were all going to get in trouble so I just walked towards the bathroom out of the line of fire. It got so crazy, that even the server behind the breakfast buffet was throwing food. I never once threw food back at the soldiers. I was busy processing a grief that my feeling of being a part of the whole crew was now shattered. We were being isolated and picked on again. We weren't part of their crew at all. What they did was so juvenile, disheartening, and real bully tactics. And we all got in trouble. We were sent back to our sleeping quarters and were told not to move.

"Don't even think about going to the fucking bathroom!" an officer shouted, "Until we work out what we're gonna do with you!"

Man, I'm a blameless victim here, and I'm still getting into trouble! I remember thinking to myself. It was like shades of Seattle all over again.

But nothing much happened in terms of punishment, except that we no longer rotated duties on kitchen clean up like we had before. Post-food fight, everyone had to do chores every day.

Throughout my kidnapped time, which came to be twenty years, I truly believed that there was a world —a culture—that was dignified, that was self-respecting, because I had seen it with certain people that had crossed my path. I believed that maybe one day, I could live and be a part of that, because what I had experienced this far was nothing of the sort. This hope is what kept me going through it all.

Our period of downtime didn't last long. Our superior came and got us while we were in the middle of laundry one day.

"Come on! Let's go! We've got a mission," he ordered. "Suit up!"

The guys and I looked at each other confused. It was already late in the day and it was strange for us to be going out this late in the afternoon. I really had a bad feeling about this. We were getting briefed on our way to the elevator.

"The bugs are more active during this wild type of weather, we seem to think," he said, marching along. "So, we need to deploy this mission, effective immediately."

They had shown us a short video briefing about the bugs on Mars when we first arrived. They didn't show photos or give many details, other than that they were dangerous. That, plus the guys that told me they'd take a limb if they could. I assumed they were something like eagle-sized mosquitoes. I assumed they could be dealt with using the same tactics used on Earth to deal with bugs. Swatted away or something. Plus, we had guns on our suits.

We went up to the armory and quickly got suited up. It was odd to me that the Major in charge who usually took his time to brief us all only popped in for a few minutes or so and then left.

"Just do what these two soldiers order you to do," he advised in a rush.

The Major's evasiveness confirmed my bad feeling. Nothing about this felt right. One of the soldiers held up a data screen.

"Alright, here's the deal," he began, showing us a 3D map of mountain terrain.

"The bugs are all along on top of this range. We will come along the bottom of the foothills, cutting across those dunes," he pointed with his fingers, "and then we wait at an outpost for further orders to come back."

We all got loaded up with the map on our wrist devices. Then the elevator doors opened upward.

"Now listen," the soldier said.

"Just take it easy. And don't shoot anything unless I say so!"

We understood. We were hit with a mass of wind and dust so hard that I immediately regretted what we were doing.

"Holy shit, this *sucks!*" 232 shouted out.

We were all called by our numbers. I don't remember mine. We had mics in our helmets that the Marines controlled and we used them to communicate across the distance.

"Well if the dust clears, you'll be able to see a purple sunset," the soldier called back out to him.

"Isn't that what you guys always wanted to see?"

We made it about a half kilometer out along the base of the foothills. The soldiers broke off from us and went left and up the hill to walk alongside us in an elevated position. We continued on along the side of a big hill that morphed into a mountain with an elevation of about five-thousand feet. We made our way around the lobe of the rocky hillside until the land gave way to a huge, flat, desert-like area.
"Hey, somethings wrong with my map," 344 said, tapping on his wrist device. "This mountain is not showing on my map—I don't have the correct map!"

We all peered down at our wrist devices.

"Oh shit, I don't have the right map either!" 232 called out.

"Well how the hell do we know how to get back?" 344 sputtered.

"I don't know, why wouldn't they check this software before we came out?" 232 said with frustration, "Look at the soldiers on the ridge, we're so far away from them!"

"Come on, let's keep going!" I said, pointing ahead. "Here's the route, let's keep going while visibility is clear, 'cause once that dust kicks up, we won't see anything!"

We pushed on.

"This isn't right!" 344 complained from the back, "We're going the wrong way!"

"Oh come on, would you!" I replied.

"Here's the route, let's keep going! Stick with the mission!"

"No!"

Our tempers were flaring and the weather was getting bad.

"Well this is what it says!"

"But the software's all fucked up anyway!" 556 whined, "We don't know what we're doing!"

"I'm going another way," 344 called out looking at me, "You're gonna get in trouble!"

Three of them broke off from our group and started off in a different direction toward the mountain, and the rest of us just kept going along the route. My group went on for another several kilometers until we noticed huge dark clouds rolling in, very quickly.

"Oh no," 840 said, looking up into the sky. "Look at the huge dust cloud coming at us."

"We gotta keep going!" I said, moving forward. "We gotta follow out the mission."

"Yeah but what happens if the other guys had the right map, and we got the wrong map?" 840 suggested.

"And I'm hearing shit, I've been hearing this rustling in those dunes behind us."

We all looked at each other worried. 840 might be right. We peered around ourselves, searching the huge, six or seven foot high sand dunes surrounding us. Every now and then, one could hear this rustling sound. A sound like someone dragging a lot of sticks over some rocks. And on top of that, every now and then we could also hear a strange type of distant buzzing.

"That's gotta be bugs," I muttered.

"I'm going up the dune to take a look," 840 said, and we watched him run up the side of this enormous sand dune. He looked and immediately came back down. He looked concerned. He didn't say anything to me, but his face confirmed bugs.

"I think we should just run for it," the other guy said.

In the lighter gravity and without the buoyancy of a heavier suit, running turned into hopping, and it was very hard to take bigger hops without having to pause a split second when you landed and hop again. In our panic, we did just that. We all hop-ran along the route. I stumbled a few times and got up.

"Come on, let's just take our shots!" 432 suggested.

"No," I said, turning to him puffing, "They told us the shots were for emergencies only."

"Well you lead us then. Go on," 840 said.

So, we began running again, with me in front now, until I heard 432 behind me shouting out.

"I see them!" he shouted, "I see the bugs!"

Then we heard what sounded like hooves in the distance. We stopped for a second and looked at each other. Petrified. You could hear what sounded like twenty deer or horses running around in the distance behind us. You could see dust being kicked up in that direction.

840 and 432 immediately hit their small thigh devices and I watched them literally fly over me, then flat out past me. I was terrified. I, too, immediately hit my thigh pack and felt the needle push into my back. It hurt at first, and then all the pain subsided, and I really felt like I was superman. I became strong enough to do the hops with one leg at a time and it was more like running. I ran over the tops of these sand dunes—sand dunes that were fifteen to twenty feet apart, and each stride I took was only clipping the tops of them. I felt like I was almost flying. It was an unbelievable feeling.

It was the same situation as on the moon. We were trying to be the one in the front so that they would get the guys in the back first. I started out in the lead and I felt a small measure of safety from that but it wasn't long after that that I fell and rolled on the ground, and that was when 840 and 432 passed me by. Out of all of us, I think I had the hardest time running in the lesser gravity. Most of them were better at it than me.

My newfound confidence soon faded, when I spotted a whole cluster of bugs coming up from behind me. They were doing what I was doing—clipping the tops of the dunes—but they had the advantage of wings propelling them forward. A couple of them were massive, bigger than the rest of the bugs. The larger ones were jumping over several dunes at a time, leaping over my head and to the right of me. I grabbed my gun and shot at one—and missed.

Before I knew it, something grabbed me from behind, and cleanly severed my arm off—my arm with the gun. It happened so fast that I was mid-air when I was dismembered. I didn't even feel the pain at first. I plummeted face first into the backside of a dune. For a split second, my programming was still active and I believed I could kick the bugs' asses. I had seen 840 and 432 fly over me and take cover on the backside of a dune also, but the odds were totally against them. I watched the bugs swarm towards that dune and all I could hear were the terrified screams of those guys, followed by what sounded like total dismemberment.

There were many species of bugs. But they all had a vertical face with pinchers near the mouth. Most of them were the size of a chihuahua, a few the size of larger dogs, and two that were the size of a Harley Davidson, plus another motorcycle size one that had taken my arm.

I lay in the sand in total shock and was bleeding heavily, blood began soaking into the sand around me. I knew I had to get the auto-tourniquet to save my life. I was searching for it in my thigh pocket, but I couldn't move because a huge spider was on top of me. It was the same bug that took my arm off. He was riding me more than sitting on top of me. He pinned me face down on my stomach.

I could hear them all moving around me. There had to be twenty to thirty of them. The one that was holding me down would grab my backpack somehow and shake me around every so often. Then he dragged me up to a flat spot out of the ditch I was in and held me up to my feet. Most of them were ugly to look at.

The spider looking one had huge scissor looking mandibles from its mouth and a tiger stripe pattern like camo. It was much bigger than me and had a flat vertical face that went down into its mouth with six or eight black eyes. Its face was shaped like the front of a ship with eyes down the side. The little ones had antennae and hairs and a big reddish shell with six legs and smaller mandibles at the mouth.

But one, unlike any of the others, was walking towards me on four legs. It looked like a praying mantis. It was dark brown and smooth with two bigger eyes on its face and antennae that were moving. It was turning its head to meet the same angle as mine and it walked up until it was about two feet from my face.

Please don't kill me... Please don't kill me...Please don't kill me...

9

THE BUGS

I HAD NO IDEA WHAT the spider bug was doing. It didn't matter, really, because I was going to die. Either from bleeding out, unable to move my remaining hand with the tourniquet in it, or from the bug ripping me to shreds at any moment. *They prefer to dismember you.*

The mantis-like bug picked me up by my backpack and dragged me up onto the next sand dune. The sand dune was long and flat on top, and to the right of it was another bug—but a different looking bug to the rest of them. He was much darker on the front side and he had a striped, iridescent pattern on his thorax. I was amazed at how much he was *bug-like*, and yet, he moved and behaved more like a human being—walking towards me with human mannerisms. I was freaking out.

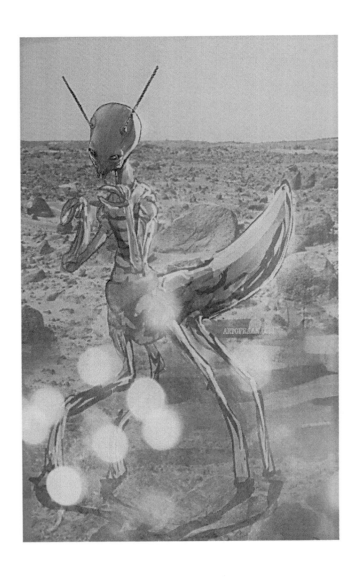

He had two long antennae that looked like a stack of black olives piled on top of each other, about eight inches in height. They moved with precision, though the movement seemed random. He made his way closer to me.

"Please don't kill me!" I begged him desperately. "I don't wanna die!"

In unison, his antennae moved together and pointed right at the center of my forehead. I could feel a telepathic connection being formed and I begged him again. My pain immediately numbed and I went into a sort of dreamlike state.

I was seeing visions of being back in the barracks at the forward base in front of my cot, with the vision of blood pouring out of my arm. Next we were at an empty cafeteria—food still scattered everywhere but my arm had stopped bleeding. We then found ourselves on the spaceship that brought me to Mars— the mantid was traveling with me through these visions. There was no one else in these scenes other than the mantid and me. I could best describe it as him flipping a rolodex of my life, shuffling some years faster until it came across a card of interest and stopped there. The cards where it stopped were the scenes I was seeing.

"Please don't kill me," I asked him telepathically in the dream state.

"Look, I don't want to kill anything," the bug responded, in a very astute manner. "But if I am ordered to do so, then I will have to. We'll see what we can do to allow you to live."

Then we were at the arena where I was looking down at the dead body of the bug that was blown up.

"Hmm, well this doesn't look good," the bug exclaimed, as if he was communicating with somebody other than myself.

Next we were in Seattle, then Peru where I felt the dream shift, then back to Seattle.

"We have to find out who you really are." the bug said.

Then it went to the MK Ultra period at Inyokern, where I was standing in a room, peering through the drapes when I was told not to because the Dr. had told me there was classified activity outside. And then it went back to my old farmhouse—the farmhouse where I grew up—the living room to be exact. The room was so foreign to me.

"Where is *this?*" I wondered.

"This is who you are," the bug assured me. "This is who you are. Your purpose is not to kill, your purpose is love. You don't belong here."

Suddenly I came to, and the pain came back with a tremendous force. I saw more blood on the sand dune. Right then and there, the big mantid bug who had grabbed me, instantly let me go. Stumbling through my pain, I stood up and put the tourniquet on. As I was doing this, an audience began to accumulate around me. Thirty or so bugs were now surrounding me.

Most of them were chihuahua size bugs with a vertical face with several small eyes and scissor-like pinchers about six or seven inches long. I wasn't as scared of them as the larger ones. It felt as if they were communicating together. One came towards me and I could 'sense' from it that it really wanted to experience a combative type experience. The mantis type bug was there, and he gave the nod of approval for this bug to launch at me—and launch he did. He came fast right at me and bit my foot off just above the ankle. His energy was childlike. He seemed excited by the experience. He didn't eat my foot, just sliced it off and left it in the sand. They all moved in unison and started fluttering their wings in place, which created a cloud of dust. Then they all hopped off at full speed away from me into the long crevice of the dunes we were stopped between. They were out of sight in seconds.

I fell to the ground in a slump, and by that time I had lost so much blood that the pain became secondary. I watched them flutter their wings and kick up a flurry of dust and sand and they took off in unison.

Why did he let that bug bite my foot? I thought he wasn't going to kill me.

I was confused. I didn't have a tourniquet for my leg that was bleeding out, but I knew that the guys over the sand dune did. So I crawled over the top of it and saw the guys—well, what was left of them, because it was just a mass of torn flesh, blood, and their suits.

Through the bloody mess, I found the part of the suit that had the tourniquet and put it on my leg. I then flopped down on the ground. I breathed a sigh of relief. I looked down the ditch to the next body that was chopped into pieces and was an unrecognizable pile of bloody parts, and I started crying.

At least now the bleeding stopped...someone can come and save me, I thought, laying there. After only a few minutes I realized that night was starting to set in, and it was getting dark. No one seemed to be near to come rescue me.

"Fuck it, I'm just going to start heading back," I said to myself.

I got on my knees and through my agonizing pain, I crawled onwards, back toward the base. I had tried to walk, but I couldn't find my balance without my arm and I kept falling. It was excruciating. So I crawled over the dune where I got my arm ripped off, and then back over another. What I really wanted to do was to hit that injection shot so I could have those superman powers again—but I couldn't reach it with my remaining arm. I thought that maybe if I could roll on a rock or something hard, I could do it. But my efforts were futile.

I crawled on, for what seemed like an eternity, but in reality, it was probably only a few minutes. Then I noticed movement through the dusty haze coming toward me. Soldiers.

The relief I felt was unspeakable.

They opened their helmets and peered down at me. I knew who they were from lunch at the cafeteria. One was a tall skinny guy, roughly over six feet, and the other was a bodybuilder type guy.

"Where's the rest of your team?" the bodybuilder one said.

"That way," I pointed.

The tall skinny one took one look at me and immediately hit the shot in my pack and an instantaneous feeling of greatness swept over me again.

"Can you walk?" He looked at me.

"No."

"What happened out there?

"They got us!" I said to him, "Those bugs got us."

"Why the hell did they let you go? They killed the rest of them," he wondered, confused. "I don't get it!"

"I don't know."

"Doesn't matter—let's get outta here."

He put me over his right arm and together we hobbled out of there.

"Look, I can't carry you the whole way—you're gonna have to try and walk!"

The other soldier came back with all the shots from the other suits. And he was mad as hell.

"You stupid fuck!" he cursed, and punched me in the face. "What the hell were you guys doing? I couldn't save the others because the bug loving fag-boy here used up two tourniquets."

Then he started cussing at me, saying that they were dead, K.I.A, and it was my fault.

"Calm down!" The skinny soldier said. "We'll get him back and debrief there."

We must've walked forever. It felt like forever. We were a long way out from the base at the foothills of the mountain and the skinny soldier basically had to carry me the entire way back. I kept passing out on him and he would slap me awake.

"Can you give me another shot?" I asked him.

"No way!" he said.

"I need them to carry you back. We're still in a combat zone. You'll get to see your purple sunset if you keep yourself awake. I don't want to lose you because I don't have the equipment to bring you back."

It was a struggle. All I wanted to do was to close my eyes, but I would force them back open and ask the soldier to hit me to keep me awake. This went on and on. And then at last, through the dusty haze, I turned to see the beautiful violet sky lining the mountains in the distance with an incredible purple sunset.

"There you go—there's your purple sunset," the skinny soldier said.

I didn't see the sun due to the haze, but it was beautiful nevertheless. We went on for almost another kilometer or so and out of the corner of my eye, I spotted the door to the base, behind some rocks. *Finally*, I exhaled. I closed my eyes and went to sleep. And the skinny soldier let me.

The door was slightly obscured inside a cave opening, and we disappeared inside.

The next morning, I woke up inside the infirmary, and I felt like a million bucks. I looked down and saw that I had my arm back. A female doctor was leaning over me, with her glass tablet device, entering in data details. There were several other soldiers around me and an older officer that I recognized, plus a few others who were seemingly in administration. I had never seen them before.

"When can he return to service?" I heard the older officer ask the doctor.

"He'll be getting the implants, in addition to some other modifications," she answered him, continuing to fill out her tablet.

The officer soon left. The other soldiers set up a camera in front of me. It looked like a small ball that he set on the folding table and started recording.

"What happened out there?" One of them asked me.

And I went on to tell them exactly what happened out there, almost verbatim. They were fine with all of it—

but they were really curious to know what that Mantid said to me.

He said for me to tell you—"That they are not that stupid."

He had told me this right before I awoke from the dream state. I understood that he was speaking directly to the forward base.

"Well what else did that bug say to you?" One soldier queried.

"Nothing else," I answered.

"Are you sure?" Another asked eagerly.

The soldiers then left the room, and then several minutes later, they came back in.

"Was there anything else that bug said to you?" One of them asked again.

"No there wasn't," I repeated. I had told them about the visions I saw with the bug and everything that transpired with that bug—but the only thing I didn't tell them was that the bug told me my 'purpose was love'. I withheld that information from the soldiers because I felt like it would be used against me.

Satisfied with their interrogation they left me in my room.

I had pretty bad eyesight but when I woke up, I looked around my room and could see the various forms of equipment featured throughout the space very clearly. I concluded to myself that the doctors at the infirmary had somehow re-cloned an exact replica of my body—except corrected.

I recuperated in twenty-four hours and then I found myself back in the old routine on the base—the only difference being that all of our missions were cancelled. The conclusion of those missions was that the bugs adapted too quickly, and everything was scrubbed. I got the sense that the base was there because a resource was nearby. I think the bugs had already claimed the resource and did not want to share. They met any incursion into their area with deadly force.

For a while after, the other clones and I had nothing to do and it became groundhog day all over again. We were so bored that every morning at breakfast we would beg the soldiers to give us something to do.

"Give us some chores! Come on!" One of the clones would ask them as they walked into the cafeteria.

For a while they didn't give us anything to do, but then one morning they came in.

"You want something to do?" One of the soldiers said jokingly, "You can move some boxes after breakfast."

A soldier took us to a room where they had us move these gigantic boxes. They were massive. But being that we were clones, and we were made for a purpose, the prospect of doing nothing day in, day out, was becoming excruciating for us. They were empty boxes and it was a complete waste of time. But we were happy to get out in any regard really. They laughed at us when we showed up for lunch later.

One of us said to them, "Please keep it coming," but that was our last chore.

The groundhog day experience went on for another month or so. Just before we were scheduled to leave, however, something awful happened. During lunch, the hazing really started picking up again with the disgruntled soldiers. There was one in particular, who always threatened to have sex with us.

"I'm gonna fuck all you guys before you go!" he would taunt us, getting his lunch.

One night after dinner, around 10:00pm, that soldier came outside of my door. He knocked on the door.

"Hey—how you doing?"

I felt a sudden jolt to my neck and got zapped by my shock collar. The soldier had managed to get a shock controller and could now shock me at will. There was a keypad on the remote that allowed him to tap into my collar frequency. He kept doing it over and over. With extensive mind control, after one is shocked, one will immediately stop whatever they were doing, and obey any command   given for a few minutes thereafter.

This soldier didn't say anything, he entered my cubicle space, pushed me down on my bed, and began to rape me. The reason why I think he was targeting me on this night is because I had the "newer" clone body after my injury rejuvenation.

"You're the tight one," he said to me.

Because our cubicles were paper thin, I knew the other guys could hear what was happening.

"You're not gonna get away with this," I said to him.

"You're gonna lay there and do exactly what you're told!"

"Well, what the fuck ever, I'm not going to enjoy it you piece of shit."

"Oh no—you're gonna enjoy it," the soldier said, putting himself on top of me, "You're gonna nut all over the place."

The mind control programming is overwhelming. Of all the times I had been raped and abused up to that point, back to the Seattle days, I had never orgasmed.

This time it was different. The soldier reached around and grabbed my penis.

"You're gonna cum!" he said.

"No I will not!" I gritted back. But with any type of mind control, it reigns dominance over any situation, and I did have an orgasm.

Not long after, he did also and then he left.

I felt so bad laying there afterward. I felt so violated, as any rape victim would. But this violation felt different than those in the past, the shame was intensified because my body orgasmed through it. I was disturbed and I felt guilty. I felt a hundred times worse than any other rape I had endured beforehand.

The next morning was a complete walk of shame to breakfast. I had never experienced more embarrassment in my entire life. All of the soldiers were sitting there catcalling, and then I saw him.

"There's my girl!" he called out from the table looking at me. "Right there!"

They all cheered him on like he had won a marathon. I sat down next to one of my clone counterparts 332.

"Did you hear all that last night?"

"Yeah," 332 said quietly, and kept eating his breakfast.

It was an off-topic zone. We knew not to talk about it.

10

ARIES PRIME

Three or four days after that we got our orders. We were to be taken to Aries Prime, tested and trained for new assignments. They told us the soldiers got mad about it, saying that they had never been to Aries Prime and we were dog shit and didn't deserve to visit the capitol. I suspected a lot of the Marines were clones as well, they just didn't know it.

I had never heard of Aries Prime. I couldn't understand what the fuss was all about. I didn't know if I was leaving Mars or staying on the planet. I certainly had no idea that Aries Prime was a major city.

My group of clones was shipped out of the forward base on a smaller aircraft. It had small wings, windows, and we sat in seats that faced each other. I felt torque as we departed on this craft, and it felt the most similar to an airplane. The other transports, up until this point, did not have torque and very little motion was experienced aboard the other crafts.

We flew for about a half an hour before landing on a strip and rolling into a hangar bay in an underground city. I have no idea how the ship entered the surface of the planet to get underground. We de-boarded the plane into a giant hangar room where we could breathe the air. I could see that there were doors large enough for the ship at one end, and through them I could see sunlight. From there we went into a large room that looked like a cafeteria. We passed another set of doors and found ourselves in a location under some kind of geodesic dome that was Aries Prime. I remember seeing the layers of red dirt piled up against the sides of this dome, because it was constructed out of clear material. At the top of the dome, there was a small area that wasn't covered by dirt, and you could see the sky and dust blowing over it. We were in what appeared to be an airport with palm trees and even a water feature. There were civilians and other types of people everywhere.

It turns out that Aries Prime is a plush metropolis city and transportation hub on Mars. It's modern, pleasing to the eye, and very comfortable to be in. Both humans and extraterrestrial races inhabit the city, although the population is predominantly human. There were multiple languages spoken.

"Hello," a man came up to us.

He was wearing a one piece that looked like he belonged in a sterile environment. He actually had a pocket protector with pens.

"I'm going to help you with your reassignment." He pointed to half of us.

"You guys go with that man over there," he said, directing them to another man waiting for them.

This man was in an officer's uniform, much like the man on the airplane who explained the logos to me.

"And you others," he said looking at the rest of us, "Come with me."

He spoke to a woman dressed in formal military-type airport clothing and then came back to us.

"You are to wait here and someone will be coming to collect you."

We must have waited a couple of hours before someone came. When they did, we were chaperoned down to long hallways and ramps to another area of this place, until we were shown our rooms.

I have my own private room! I was given a bag with a change of clothes and left on my own. The room had its own little sink and dresser, a bathroom, and a really nice comfortable bed. Everything was immaculate, as if it were all brand new. The walls were painted a dark, rusty orange color that seemed to absorb sound and noise, which made the room very quiet.

It made me feel like I was part of an organization, rather than owned to some individual as a slave. Like there was some level of respect towards my individualism. All the while sitting in my space, I was worried that another rapist would come and knock at my door. It was hard to push the experience from my mind. I eventually fell asleep in the afternoon and slept all the way through the night. I awoke to someone knocking at my door. I was still wearing a shock collar.

"Get up!" they yelled.

I opened the door and saw two soldiers, in full military camo, both wearing berets.

"You're to go with him every morning and he will take you to where you need to go," one of the soldiers said, looking at the guy with the beret.

I remember how decorated and *shiny* they both looked.

"Make sure you listen to his instructions and do as he says to avoid problems."

Up until this point, everyone I encountered had an American accent. These two men were American as well.

Every day, the soldier with the beret would escort me down long hallways, walking me to the same place— a huge room that resembled a massive computer lab. It was similar to the one on the moon but much larger and had taller ceilings. This room was dark, veneered with a type of black wall, and the only light came from an apparatus fixed above each computer station. There were a lot of stations. It was about a fifteen minute walk and once we entered, there was always someone to advise us—which was a grey alien. It was the same species of grey that was on the moon.

"This is your instructor," the soldier said to me and then left us.

"Oh! Another ape from Earth!" the grey sneered telepathically.

I remember immediately being taken aback by the instructor grey's rudeness. He went to his desk, fiddled with some buttons, and a computer station lit up.

"Follow me," he said.

He sat me in front of a very thin-screen type of computer, which also had an area to sit your chin into —just like the optometrist again.

"Now sit your chin into the apparatus."

I did as told. He fiddled with the adjustments until it fit with my face. He then put droppers in my eyes.

"Now do what the computer asks."

The sound and screen came on and prompted me with a series of audio and screen tests to set me up.

"Okay, you are set up now, you baboon," the grey said to me smugly.

And he meant it. He was not joking about his smugness towards me. I could *feel* it, which is part of the impact of telepathy. There's a lot more data per message than standard verbal communication.

After I was set up, I was taken through a movie showing potential career advances, which was all dependent on a series of aptitude and IQ tests. After each movie, a test would begin. They were multiple choice word questions that would appear on the screen and you had to lock your vision on one that was your answer.

After all my testing was done, I left the disgruntled grey and the computer lab and was taken back to my room where food was waiting for me. It was similar to a microwave meal, on a tray with separated serving spots. The food was warm when I arrived. And even my bed was made. They had a turn down service at this place.

The IQ and aptitude tests were carried out for a few weeks, following the same routine everyday. I would be taken to the computer lab with the soldier carrying the beret, I would do the tests, and then I'd be taken back to my room to eat and sleep.

Then one morning, the soldier knocked at the door and told me something different.

"Tomorrow you're gonna have to get up earlier and take a shower. I'll come and get you."

I did exactly what he said, but nothing changed. I was still taken to the lab, greeted by the disgruntled grey, given my eyedrops, and sat down to do more of the aptitude tests. The drops produced a mild buzz. As soon as the computer booted up, a strange binaural sound would play for about 6 minutes and I finally mustered up the courage to ask the grey.
"What is this sound?"

"It helps you concentrate and become alert," he answered curtly.

"Now do your work."

After that day of tests, the soldier came to pick me up to take me back to my room.

"You remember how to get to this place, right?" he said, nursing that beret.

"Yeah, I think so," I said, peering down the endless hallway, passing a few regular looking people.

"Tomorrow you're going to walk to the lab yourself."

"Really?" I wondered curiously.

"But how will I wake myself up in the morning?"

"There's a box in there that emits special waves that put you to sleep and wake you up," the soldier advised.

"Okay," I said.

No wonder I fell asleep as soon as I put my head down, I thought to myself.

"But don't even think about deviating off course," the soldier warned. "We are tracking your every move. We know exactly where you are at all times—and if you do, you'll be in big trouble."

I didn't even dream of it anyhow. Where was I going to go?

So that became my new routine. I would wake up when the box *made me* wake up. There was no noticeable sound, but I could feel it when it came on. I would say there was less than a minute before I was totally zonked out.

Every morning, I would take a shower and then go to the computer lab. The advisor grey was always waiting for me. You would think being there for such a while that he would warm up to liking me, but no—he really didn't like me.

But this time the aptitude tests changed. There was a series of movie scenarios, and a different set of questions and visualization techniques.

"These different sets of tests are going to get you a job, suitable to your abilities," the grey told me. "You've already failed Command, so let's see what else an ape like you can do."

I kept going with the tests, and the grey would come over periodically to advise me on my progress.

"Well, looks like you've failed in Administration also, so let's try Research."

I started more tests, and the grey was getting more annoyed with me. It was obvious to me that I was failing. I had no clue what was going on, knew nothing about the answers. Every response was pure guesswork.

"You are a miserable baboon aren't you!" he sneered at me. "You've failed Research, so now you're going to go to the next tier down, Engineering. And just so you know, the lower you progressively get with the tier system, the more physically hard the work will get. Hard labor. So let's just get this out of the way because I know you're going to fail this one also."

I completed the engineering tests and the grey was right—I failed.

"But you only barely failed," he quickly pointed out.

"You only failed engineering by two questions."

"Well can I sit for the test again?" I hoped, looking up at him.

"No, that's not the nature of the testing. It doesn't work like that," he answered quickly. "So the next tier down is Skilled Labor. And if you fail this one, it will be Manual Labour. And that's going to be very difficult. No intelligence is needed for that one. And you will suffer because it is very physically challenging and you still have a lot of time left on your tour. So put more effort into it, baboon."

Fortunately for me, I passed. So, it was decided that I would become a skilled laborer. I would daydream to myself what it could've been like if I had passed my way into Command. During the testing, I had no idea that I was being screened for Command roles. Had I known that, I might have tried harder. I really felt like I had dodged a bullet with not being assigned to Manual Labor. I was fearful of what that could entail and I felt extremely relieved to not have to participate in such a program.

One day the soldier came and took me for a round of medical tests and then I returned to my room early. This was the first time that I had a little free time before I went to sleep and I began daydreaming though memories of my time in Peru. I felt a longing to be back there, much like what I'd expect the typical homesickness to feel like. It was the only memory of "home" I had, and I missed it. *If only Manuel and the others could see me now.*

The next morning, back in the computer lab, the grey put my eye drops in and looked at me.

"Okay you big baboon, today we start your training," he advised, with his usual sneering telepathic remark.

A series of movie tutorials covering topics like how to use tools and fire suppression techniques. It didn't take long for me to tire of watching these movies, and at the end of each one, there'd be a test and if I didn't pay attention, or got the test wrong, I'd have to rewatch the tutorial. I passed the tests most of the time.

"You are as unreliable as a broken clock, you fool!" the grey called out to me telepathically. He was a condescending dick and it didn't matter if I passed the tests or not, he still hurled the insults.

"It looks like you passed one. Must have been luck. Let's see how you do next, monkey."

In between some of the tutorials, I was taken to mechanical-type workshops on how to use the buttons, how to open valves for piping infrastructure, and how to read and use gauges. Then I would be taken back to the computer lab, for more of the tutorials. It was relentless.

One morning upon awakening, I saw a different set of clothes on my bedside table. Before, my clothes had been military camo pants with a t-shirt, very much like what I wore on the forward operating base on Mars. This day, there were regular gray pants and t-shirts. The pants were the same color of gray as Ceres —light and dusty.

I opened the door to go to class and there stood a man, waiting for me. No knock at the door or anything. I got the sense that he knew my schedule and knew when I would open the door.

"Hello, you'll be coming with me today," he said.

Without question, I followed him down the hallways. This walk felt like it went on forever. We must have walked more than a mile through the never ending hallways. We eventually reached another section where the hallways opened up and the ceilings were very high. It felt similar to the shopping mall-type area where we first disembarked upon arrival. The ceilings were impressive, contoured in artistic shapes and there were people everywhere—civilian, military, commuters, it was a very busy place. It looked like the transport hub of a city, but there were also doors leading into office and commercial looking buildings.

I was taken into another area that was glassed off with curved ceilings. I soon recognized that it was a train station because there was a gleaming white train with a blue stripe running along the side of it on the track. We stood in line and waited to embark.

"It's my first time!" I heard someone saying excitedly.

"I hope I don't get sick!" I heard another say over my shoulder.

I looked at the man I followed here.

"Where am I going?"

"You're being deployed," he answered matter-of-factly.

"You'll take this shuttle and then move onto your next point of call. You'll find out your assignment from there."

I began to feel nervous. I wondered what that would be.

We finally embarked onto the train and it was great. It was incredibly spacious, and the seats were wide and comfortable, all facing forward. Once seated, a bar came over my body and rested on my lap. There was a long loading process, and I could see that there were other's wearing the same type of uniform as mine being seated. The guy escorting me had a brief conversation with another man who was supervising the others like me.

Finally, the train was fully loaded. You could hear the train switch on, then it bounced in an odd way. I felt immediately airborne, and then we were off. There was no real feeling of speed, but I could see out the window that we were increasing pace towards a tunnel. The windows darkened as we entered the tunnel. The train accelerated to full speed rapidly and then *something* happened and I became highly disorientated. There was a feeling as if my ears were ringing, but without the ring. It was like a poof—then my eyes were out of focus and everything was a little different. And just as quickly as we took off, the train bounced again and then began screeching on its tracks. We had arrived at our destination.

The doors slid open and we found ourselves at another train station.

"Please be orderly as you depart," said the voice over the intercom.

"You will experience an electrolyte imbalance, please proceed to drink water immediately, which is available with the designated officers within this terminal. Thank you."

As soon as we disembarked, we saw officers with water scattered along various water stations at tables. I walked up to a table and watched as others grabbed water bottles around me. I wasn't yet aware of my thirst, but I reached to take one, just trying to do as told.

"No, no!" an officer quickly stopped me.

"You are not permitted to drink bottled water. You must go to that table with all the others and get a *cup* of water. And soon! If you don't drink you will experience serious negative bodily reactions."

I looked at all the people frantically pushing their way through to get a stingy, triangle cup of water. I managed to squeeze my way through the frenzy and got one small cup of water—and then there was no more. It was then that my thirst hit. I *really* wanted another.

My escort took me out of the train terminal and we entered into what appeared to be a huge hangar. It had a metallic, waffle-like ceiling that was massive. To me, it looked like it was over a hundred feet high. I was stunned by my new surroundings, because I knew I wasn't on Mars anymore. Everything was too different. The atmosphere, the architecture, the style —everything.

"Everybody line up!" an order was shouted.

We assembled ourselves into lines and watched a man on a podium speaking in German. I had no idea what the hell was going on—nor did I know where I actually was. I studied my surroundings. There must have been five hundred people, all wearing a navy uniform—mostly young males. I was distracted by my curiosity when an officer came up to us, wearing a grey uniform with a strange hat, gun in tow.

"Line up at *once!*" he shouted with an unfamiliar accent.

It was clear from this shrilling tone that he was some type of drill sergeant.

"You are all slaves, and you will be ordered to take your vows today."

I positioned my feet on the painted lines on the floor. ThenI felt an intense surge of static electricity permeate the air. I saw a chrome-silver disc, zipping past us all. I couldn't believe my eyes. There was a humming noise, and I watched it hover glide over to the other side of the hangar and dip down into another adjacent hangar—equally as big as this one. I was in awe.

"Hey! Concentrate and get in line!" an officer shoved me into position.

I shuffled into line and was handed a green flyer with lines of German words. I had no idea what was going on.

"Just to let you know," the drill sergeant shouted, "We had some slaves last month who didn't want to take the oath, so you know what I did with them? I shot them!" he boasted pointing to an area with what looked like dried blood stains.

"So. Does anybody want to get *shot* today?"

We all quickly shook our heads no.

"Does anyone here have a problem with reading an oath aloud today?"

Again, we all shook our heads.

"Good!" he shouted.

He turned towards his superiors, where one amongst them looked concerned.

"There's no flag here—we can't do this without a flag!" an officer said aggressively. "There's gotta be a flag, and they are not going to salute our flag! So find something else"

Their flag had a fancy eagle with a rounded swastika symbol. It was black, red, and white.

A few minutes later, out came an alternative flag—an eagle with the Earth beneath it, held within chains. This flag was mostly grey and black. The officer put the flag into a holder, and then the officer on the podium began speaking again. This was followed by several other officers saying a few words—all in German— and this ceremony seemed to go on forever.

At some point, all the lines of slaves, were instructed to take their oaths. We were to repeat after the officers. They said each line with such force and punctuation. But when it came our turn, we turned towards the flag we were to be using, hands across our hearts, and just dismally mumbled our way through the oath—it was pitiful in comparison.

"Right, everyone come with me," an officer said to my group of men, chaperoning us to another area.

This time, it was a shop—a barber shop—where we all got buzz cuts, our teeth checked, and a quick, medical-type exam. We were then walked to another train—a stand up train only, so no one would be seated. It couldn't have been more than a fifteen minute ride, underground the entire time. We exited the train onto a small platform, took a few steps down to an intake area, then I was taken to check into where I would be staying for the next ten years of my life.

11

CERES

MY SHOCK COLLAR WAS TAKEN off overnight, only to be replaced by another, and we were given our daily routines. First order was to shower in—we could not come *or* go from the facility without taking a shower first. The showers were literally the entrance and exit of the building. So we would go through one door, line up, hang our clothes up behind the door, take a shower, and then our new, fresh uniform would be waiting on a hook on the exit door, and then we would leave.

My room was extremely basic—a roughly eight foot by ten foot room with a small drawer hanging off the wall, and a cot made with a thin cotton feeling grey blanket small white pillow, and that was it. Then it was lights out. I was to later learn that I was on the planetoid Ceres, and I was one of thousands of slaves living amongst a colony inhabiting the dwarf planet.

Ceres is on an offset elliptical orbit between Mars and the asteroid belt. It's roughly five hundred and eighty-seven miles in diameter. There is no atmosphere, so everything is below ground. The colonies there were set on artificial days at twenty hour days. If they had not installed artificial lights, the dwarf planet would have been dark at all times. The population was two hundred and twenty-five thousand people when I lived there, composed mostly of people brought there from post World War II. The official language was German.

There were two other alien species that lived there. I'm not entirely positive about this memory, but I think one species was called the Altruan. The Altruan had their own language that they spoke between each other. Otherwise, they spoke telepathically. I don't remember what the other species on Ceres was called. They had small beady eyes and wide hips.

The Altruan were human-ish, with skin like ours and long hair. They needed low gravity and it followed them as they walked around. This gravity field was an advanced technology that Ceres had built in everywhere. They had standard "human" anatomy—except they were close to nine feet tall. I would learn this small fact about their anatomy later on as the owner of a brothel I would frequent was one of them and had sex with all the women before he hired them. This species was in charge of all the businesses. They also spoke telepathically.

ALTRUAN

The room had three walls. There was no wall at the foot of my bed, the room opened right into the hallway. There was a bed and a small permanently mounted drawer on a wall. That was it.

Brrrrrzzzzzzzzzzzzzzzz!

An alarm went off, ringing over the entire complex, and then all the lights turned on. I was wide awake— whether I liked it or not.

"To the left!" an officer shouted along the hall.

It was like being back at school on the first day, and I felt excited to know that there were literally thousands of others just like me, in the same boat, and there was maybe even a potential to make some friends—for the first time.

After showering and getting dressed, we were shoved along to the end of the hallway where there were two women, fitting us with our shock collars for the day. They were behind a window where we would wait in line each day. Our collars were taken off each night unless it was a particularly busy day. Then we were left to sleep in them, which was irritable and somewhat painful.

"Where are we supposed to go?" I asked one of them.

"You're in that line over there," she pointed. "Get in the line with those guys for the train."
I was confused as I looked at them.

"I'm sure I'm not going with these guys," I protested, "I'm wearing a different uniform!"

"—No, just get in line there," she replied adamantly.

I did what I was told, and followed the line of men to the train. The platform for the train was about fifty feet from the window. We had walked through a cafeteria to get to the train entry. When I boarded, it was filled with what I would discover were miners. They were filthy as was the train—there was a half inch deep grime on the floor. I looked around myself, knowing I wasn't supposed to be on this train, which inevitably took me to the mines. It was about a twenty minute ride. There were windows on the train but it was pitch black out. There were no seats, standing only. We had hooks to hold onto but there were not enough for every guy. There were no females that I saw and the other guys looked like they were about my age.

"I'm not supposed to be here!" I said to an officer checking in new recruits, as we all piled off the train.

"No, this is you," the officer reassured me. "A lot of workers don't think this is them, but it is. You'll be here for the rest of your time here, so get used to it."

I didn't know what to say.

"So, I'm gonna give you a quick tour," the officer went on, "of safety and regulations."

"Look," I stammered, "I haven't been trained for any of this!"

"Quit talking!" the officer snapped.

"You need to shut up, this is your post, so deal with it. I don't want to hear anything more about it."

We exited onto steel grating, overlaid onto a sort of dirt. There were roughly six hallways that lead into caverns that were actively being mined. I could tell the whole thing was new because a lot of it was still under construction. I think we were deep underground. There were temporary lights on poles set up for us to see.

A group of about twenty of us were led through the first level of the mines. There were little six wheeled vehicles zipping around all over the place, along with much bigger ones—all on the metal flooring.

"Whatever you do, stay on the metal floor," the officer warned.

"If you step off—you'll be exposed to microgravity. Men have been trapped in places."

In some areas, they had erected huge panes of what looked like glass windows, but they must have been much stronger than glass as I knew it.

"So what are these doors for?" I asked, referring to the huge doors in certain areas of the mine.

"We're digging for water," the officer said, "and sometimes when we hit it, it floods the mine. You need to shut these doors in order to stop the flood of the water from reaching other areas."

My mind raced. "But what if you don't make it to the doors in time?"

"Don't worry about that," the officer said flatly as we walked past them.

We walked deeper into the mines. We came across a few workers standing on a huge tripod with a massive gun that shot out red laser beams. I was curious.

"What are they doing?" I wondered, watching them point the laser into the rock, pulverizing it.

"They're building the walls for a new cavern, from the floor up," the officer replied.

A thick cloud of dust developed and I watched the red laser beams illuminate through the opacity. It looked so cool.

Man — that's the job for me.

"It's not the laser that is blowing up the walls, it's sound. It's uber-sonic."

The dust was so light that it almost *wouldn't* settle. Another work crew would come in, encapsulate the area with a type of plastic film, and then vacuum all the dust, finishing the job by watering the area down. Then a different crew would come in and start with assembling the gravity plate flooring. This process went on and on.

I later found out that once the flooring was in place, I was to be part of the crew that would go and pick up all the remnants of pulverized rock that had been blown to smithereens. We would load up these pieces of rock and dust on a small cart, which would then be transferred to a bigger cart to be taken out by the six wheeled vehicles. They looked something like souped-up golf carts.

"So, this is your area," the officer advised me, along with three other of my co-workers. "You're working on the edge of the gravity field."

A terrible feeling of dread rushed over my body. It was going to be your standard, pick and shovel job. Back breaking labour.

And if I were to be exposed to the micro-gravity, I could be left floating in the middle of a room and forgotten about if I were alone. It had happened in the past and someone had been stuck and forgotten about. I don't know if they died but it was a bad situation and people referenced it often.

The makeup of the walls was like chalk, but light grey in color. It was a fluffy and lightweight material, more like dust than dirt or traditionally mined coal. We were given rags to put over our faces because it was impossible not to breathe it in. Most of us just pulled our shirts up over our faces when it got bad. It was messy to pick the material up because it would often break and we would have to shovel it up in pieces.

Something's gotta be messed up with my work. I thought to myself, *How could I be working these damn mines with a pick and shovel? All my training was inside the ships.*

The officer left us, and it was straight into it. Manual labor.

After a while of shoveling with my co-workers, I wondered why we were mining for water and what was the importance of it.

"Why are they mining water?" I asked one of my co-workers. "Like, why do they care so much about it?"

"Well, don't you get thirsty?" he joked. "Actually, in all seriousness, there are rumors that when they find water, they believe there are buildings hidden within it. They think there'll be tech they can use to trade with. That's what pays everything. They're all about the tech, these Deutsche. So finding giant pockets of water is the main objective."

"Well what happens if we break through to water and we get flooded out?" I asked.

"Well if you outrun the water, then you'll be fine—if not, well."

"Well what?"

The co-worker looked at me, "They're not gonna care about whether or not you got stuck in a flood. You are dispensable. Like all of us."

I stood there looking at him feeling very unsettled, then went back to my shoveling.

"I can get promoted, and get onto that drilling crew."

"Keep dreaming!" Another worker called out. "The system is all rigged. And besides, the line for promotion is endless. You'll never get on there!"

At the end of the day, we left the mines and got back on our train, to the check-in point where the two ladies at the window took off my shock collar. Beside them, there were two officers waiting for me. I was absolutely filthy, covered in dust and soot all over.

The officer's face looked hard.

"Why didn't you report to duty?" One asked, pissed. "You know we're here to kill you."

I stared at them blankly. I had no idea what was going on.

"I went over there!" I pointed to the desk, "There was a girl there that told me I had to line up—I told her I wasn't supposed to and she just told me to shut up and get in the line!"

The officers left me and went to the girls at the window.

"Who was assigned at that table this morning?" one of them ordered. "You can go!"

I was confused. And tired. I felt disgusting covered in the grey, chalky dust. I left to shower and go through the whole re-entry routine again before laying in bed, totally exhausted and sore—like my ass had really been kicked.

The entry and exit routine of the barracks was this: remove your clothes and drape them on a hook, enter the shower through a long line of naked men (probably five hundred), take a twenty second shower, exit to a room where your new clothes would be hanging on a hook—identifiable by a number, go through a hygiene routine, go to work, return, eat at the cafeteria, shower in the same way, go to bed.

We had just enough time in the shower to lather up the main spots—crotch and armpits, rinse, then exit. Imagine a hand soap dispenser, but for soap, shampoo, and conditioner. The water came out by pulling a chain and it was warmish. There was an intentional effort to avoid creating steam so that we could stay under video surveillance. I chose to only wash my hair every few days because of the time constraints.

Every once in a while, the shower line would pass two men having sex or giving hand jobs and blow jobs. A pair would step aside before the shower and some men would clap, cheer, or even smack them as they passed by. The guards encouraged this time for sex and would often remind us that this was our chance.

Bisexuality was a part of our conditioning. It was a mostly unspoken reality that the majority of us had been raped by a man at some point in our journey. I believe they did this to first establish dominance, and secondly to normalize bisexuality or homosexuality. In the current military environment, it's a don't ask don't tell thing. But here, there was no shame or need to hide our sexual endeavors. The Ceres Colony and the operating fleet were aware that people who were sexually active were more productive in their day to day job than people who were not. These were facts straight from data and they encouraged sexual activity.

The cafeteria we ate in served a buffet, but there were no chefs. The bulk of the food was made in a replicator each morning by one of the resident slaves. The food we were served was garbage. Imagine oats and mystery meat. The Deutsche had a tradition of eating bread with meals and we were always served rolls. If the buffet ran out, you would just go to the replicator. It looked like a 1960's microwave. You would put your empty bowl inside, covered by a lid, then push one of a few buttons. After three to five minutes, your food would be ready in the bowl under the lid. It was piping hot. We were aware that they had the ability to replicate anything and we often complained that it wasn't necessary to serve us such shitty food. But the newer, nicer replicators were reserved for the free class. We were slaves.

The next morning, I woke up, went through the morning routine, and found another officer waiting for me when I checked in with the girls to get my shock collar back on.

"You're coming with me," he said, escorting me through the crowds of people.

"Okay."

We walked in a different direction and the officer vented his frustration, heading towards several doors with armed guards surrounded by thick grey walls of concrete. Two women were also sitting at a desk with a scanning machine.

"I knew they would mess it up!" he spat, "You were meant to come to the hangar *yesterday*. You'll be here from now on."

We came up to the door marked A11. "This is your gate." He peered at the women. "Please scan him in, he missed his start yesterday."

One of the women looked amused as she took my picture. "Someone's going to get hell for that," she mumbled.

"They sure will," the officer answered her. He turned to me. "Okay—let's go inside."

We entered a long hallway that stretched into an umbilical, similar to those at airports on Earth. It was air tight, flexible, and at the end of it, was a watertight-style door, akin to those on naval ships. We went through this door. Inside, it was very cramped. It was filled with pipes and metal—top to bottom. The ceiling was not more than seven feet high, and in some areas it was closer to six feet.

"Hello, and welcome," one officer, donning military gear, poked his head through the narrow walkway.

"Come with me."

His uniform was sleek, formal, and well-fitted. It was grey and black, with a captain-looking hat. But he was not a captain. He was a dark blonde Deutsche with blue eyes. He spoke what sounded like German to me but I heard it in english because we had all been given translators. The translator was advanced, and it sounded like his voice as it translated into my ear. There was no hardware, so I've always suspected it was implanted during my time on the moon.

There were six of us slaves there. We followed the officer until we reached a bigger room, where we found ourselves standing in front of more officers, also wearing military uniforms.

"Welcome everyone," the one in charge stepped forward. "Today we will be actually leaving the dock, undertaking an exercise." He pointed to a TV screen. "By now, you should all be familiar with this, the LDS 12 System."

The TV screen looked just like the flat screen TV's we have on Earth, only that this one had a touchscreen keyboard filled with German words, and a keypad with numbers beneath.

"Every morning, you are going to come in and report to duty, signing in at this screen. It will then proceed to give you your tasks for the day and is also your instruction manual."

At that point, I was quaking in my boots—I had no idea about this system. I don't ever remember receiving training for this LDS operating system back on Mars—not once. I could feel my eyes glazing over.

"That will be all for today," the officer closed.

We all immediately stood at attention and gave the required salute—hand on the chest and then jarred outwards. The officers then left, taking with them two of the guys that I had some with to other areas of the ship. I was left with four co-workers.

I felt a small, hopeful excitement sweep over me.

I can finally make some friends with these guys.

I longed to make new friendships on par with what I had eventually developed with Manuel, and in the beginning, the guys that tended to be assigned to this work, like myself, were so mentally damaged from the programs they were a part of, they were very disconnected to everyone and everything. They weren't capable of making connections with others, and certainly not of creating friendship.

We were in a compartmentalized section of the ship and couldn't see anything outside. There were no windows. We couldn't feel any movement, aside from one initial vibration when they started the craft. Apart from being told that we were traveling, we didn't know where we were going or what we were doing. I still don't know where we went most of the time. I had no concept that we were star-travelers, which we actually were.

Life on that ship was like groundhog day. Day in and day out, it was the same exact thing. We completed different tasks, but the routine was the same *every. single. day.*

We would report to the big black screen, it would identify us, clock us into our shift, and finally give each of us our tasks for the day. My initial fear of the screen was unwarranted as it was the most simple, intuitive instruction one could possibly imagine.

"Number 23849, you will be assigned Number 3 today. Your duties for this shift will include the following…"

The instructions were always very detailed and explicit. "Go to the tool kit. Look inside the compartment for Tool D. Close it. Now go to compartment C. Open it…"

I depended on the screen for everything.

At the end of the day, the officers would chime in over the intercoms.

"Everybody report to the instruction room," a voice would bellow.

Everyone went to the instruction room where we were made to stand in front of a camera. There was a very specific way we were supposed to stand for the camera in order for the officers to see us. One of my coworkers didn't do it right, and they shocked all of us. Not a huge shock, but like a jab to get our attention.

Each day we were scored on our performance. My first day I was terrible, but so was everybody else. Using a scoring system out of one hundred, we all scored in the low thirties.

"We are now docking. Stand in line toward the EXIT door."

The voice over the intercom always sounded as if it was being bothered to talk to us. Sometimes it would come over in German, and we would stand there wondering what was said and then it would come on in English immediately after and tell us what to do.

So, we would leave the craft, get on our train, go through the shower routine, then return to our pod. It was weird, but sometimes only a few minutes had passed from when we left for work earlier that morning.

"You know you've only been gone about 20 minutes today?" One of the girls would remark, removing my shock collar at the end of the shift.

What?

At first, I thought I was being lied to and I didn't like it. I knew I had worked a solid, full day's work, but I came to learn we were time traveling on our job. Temporal missions are what they were called. And time travel would become a regular thing. At the time, I had no clue how this worked. Later in my term, I learned more about how time travel worked and more about the places we would visit.

So this is how it was—everyday. But it could've been worse—I could've been down in the mines like so many others were, doing back breaking work, but I wasn't. And when we completed our daily tasks we would return clean. Or at least most of the time I'd be clean. Sometimes I was filthy, but it wasn't often. There was always the odd oil spill, or some type of liquid to mop up. There were spills and leaks all the time. Turns out, our ship, which I came to later learn was called the *Blitzbus,* was an old ship, a converted post World War II submarine that had been made into a nuclear powered spaceship. The leaks and spills were never ending.

This was the start to a very long, predictable time at my post on Ceres. In the early years, the workload really wasn't that bad other than some days there would be tasks that would be very annoying. For example, crawling in a pipe to clean an oil leak, or laying down on your back to wrench out something inside the pipes, but it wasn't that bad—nothing could compare to the mines, but there were also a lot of days that were super easy to complete.

We would get our work list, and I could tell straight away what kind of a day it would be. I learned quickly how to navigate myself around the valves and the pipes, as well as the tools necessary to implement the outstanding tasks. Sometimes the valves were so big that I would need the use of a machine operated tool that was a type of "assisted wrench." The tool would help me with my work of cleaning the filters inside the valves. And that's all we would do some days. Just clean filters of these valves, sometimes up to twenty per day.

We got really efficient at cleaning the filters, and so if we finished that task, then we would do easier tasks like clean.

"Get to work, and if you can't finish your duties, then just *clean*," was the instruction we got most of the time.

When the cleaning was done, we would take the liberty of '"lounging" around and cruising through the rest of our day. When we did "cruise" through the rest of our days though, we had to be wary of the cameras situated around our work areas. If we weren't careful to watch for the cameras, we would be caught, and our officers would correct us at the end of the shift.

"What were you doing slacking off today in Section C? Your score is deducted for today's shift!"

Our scores were cumulative as a team, and we did eventually get our scores up to meet our quota.

We would also warn any new guys on the job of where the camera's were hidden. "Don't hang out here too much," we would say, "there's a camera there."

Our crew aboard the ship worked out amongst ourselves which areas of the ship were heavily surveilled. In the early stages of this job, we were strictly disciplined—mostly in the form of getting shocks to the collar. Over time, though, our score rating for our crew's productivity increased, and the discipline eased off.

One time, there were four of us workers on the job— two of them I got along really well with. The other, Shaun, well not so much. One day I found out the two that I liked were being transferred to another area of the ship.

"You have been working very effectively as a crew," an officer informed us. "And due to this efficiency, no longer will these two workers be transferred over to this ship to undertake tasks. From now on, this is your permanent crew onboard."

So I was now stuck with guys that had chosen their own non-number names, Shaun who I didn't like, and one other new member, Jeremy. I tried to give myself a name and they refused to call me by it. They kept me as a number. The next few years with this crew would become a blur.

Shortly after this new team was formed, our fourth crew member was removed and transferred elsewhere. We were good enough at our jobs that we didn't need him anymore and so it carried on just the three of us. Myself, Jeremy, and Shaun.

It was *same* jobs day in, day out. And they were forming a friendship with each other, sharing a bond for not liking me. They had become seemingly best of friends. As a result, every time there was a shitty task to be taken care of, it was put to a vote as suggested by the voice over the intercom. I got the shitty task. Every time.

I never really had the thought of killing myself. I was programmed not to. But I knew that this felt like it was going to go on forever and ever, which leads to some dark feelings. Time was so malleable, and their ability to adjust the time-space continuum was thorough. Going to work in the morning for a full day's time, then returning only a few minutes later was a mind fuck. It was like a double-long, terrible day. One time I asked the girls at the counter on my way out of the train about it.

"How long am I going to be here doing this job? When can I go do something else or be done with my tour?"

The girl looked at me with solemn eyes.

"You're going to be here for a very long time. You have a lot to go."

My heart sank. I remember feeling that I just wanted to die, I was utterly depressed. The hopelessness I felt of never having anything else happening to my life was an unthinkable reality for me, and I couldn't shake it.
One day on the ship, we had all completed our duties, and were finished with our jobs for the day.

"Come with me," Jeremy said, the taller, greasier one of the two said.

Jeremy was the type of guy that would take a shower, and still come out looking greasy. He had a criminal type mind, always sneaking around and very convincing.

He led me to an area which was off camera, and totally secluded. It was there that I found out that Jeremy and Shaun had not only bonded—they were lovers. And they would come to this area to have sex and make out. I was totally dumbfounded.

"We want you to join us," Jeremy said, taking me to their love spot. "I want you to go down on me."

"What?" I protested. "No way! I'm not into that. If anything, you can go down on *me*!"

"No, come on—" Jeremy replied.

"You go down on me."

"No fucking way!"

I was already so damaged from what had happened in my past, there was no way I was going to participate in this.

"Fine then, fuck off!" Jeremy dismissed me.

Another dickhead Jeremy. At least he didn't force me.

I later found out that the reason why their daily scores were so high was because they were helping each other finish their tasks. My score was always lagging because I had no help with what I was doing. Thinking back, I really noticed a change in their behavior six months prior, so that's when I believe it began. And it killed me, because I knew there was nothing I could do to be in their 'club'. I was a total outcast.

One day, not long after, two officers came in at the end of our work shift.

"You guys have been here long enough, and after a certain amount of time, you get offered a different type of service," one of them informed us. "And if you like, you can volunteer to undertake new jobs— but these jobs may be at times, very dangerous, and could put you in harm's way. However it you complete a few of these jobs, you *will* get rewarded. You may even get a promotion."

I didn't even hesitate.

"I'll do it," I said quickly.

Here's my chance, I thought. *I'll get on one of these missions, and I'll fucking die. Anything's gotta be better than this.*

We had been told that there was an end to our service. We knew that we were going to be returned to earth. But my state of mind at the time made even a month, let alone years, seem like forever. The thought was unbearable. I tried to look forward to my earth return, but I couldn't emotionally connect to any form of excitement about it. The only longing I had was to return to Peru.

I didn't hear back from them and as time passed, I lost the dream of getting any kind of promotion. It wasn't as if I had someone, such as a supervisor or even an officer, to ask whether or not they were going to take me, or if I was even considered to go on one of these riskier missions that I volunteered for. I reported to a black screen and followed a voice over an intercom. So, it was on the back burner for months upon months.

During this stretch of time, I also didn't have any friends back at our quarters where we all lived, because in their minds, I was a part of the flight crew, and they were all miners. That caused an instant discrimination and divide amongst us.

Even when I began to potentially make friends with a miner, someone else would come up to him and warn, "Hey—don't even try to make friends with someone like him. He's a flight suit."

Most of the guys that were in my section of the barracks worked in the mines. They were jealous of other workers because they believed we were spoiled and had it easy. They came back from work each day filthy and exhausted. I came back pretty much the same as I left each day—or at least never as dirty as they were.

We had weekends off for the most part. There was a random pool to do barrack duties on the weekend, like laundry and cafeteria work. I didn't get called in that often. One weekend evening, an officer came to the ladies at the window, who then buzzed into my room and told me to report to the front. There was a blonde man in a Ceres Colony military uniform.

"Come with me," he said.

We took a short train to another connecting train and ended up at an administrative type office. I was excited. I thought something good was about to happen to me. He was explaining to me that they had met a new group of advanced, grey ETs, and that a lucrative trade for technology had been struck. They needed labor and I was in the pool to go help. They were going to test me for the role and decide if I would be sent off.

I was apprehensive but excited, thinking it would be a better position than what I currently had. We went through the administrative building, down a hallway, where there were about fifty guys like me lined up. I could hear someone screaming towards the end of the hallway, blocked off by two doors. Two men approached me and the officer and took some information down.

"He's going to be tested, right?" asked the officer.

"No, they don't need testing. He's going."

And then my escorting officer left. I was instructed to just wait in line and do as I was told. The screaming guy was brought out of the room and escorted another way, further from us. I was in line for another fifteen minutes. Three or four more guys went in, then another came out screaming.

He was skinny, extremely disturbed, and screaming at the rest of us in line.

"Don't go. Don't go. It's more than ten years. Kill yourselves," he shouted as they hauled him off.

At that point, two armed guards came out and told us that we were to remain in silence. Otherwise, we'd be shot. They moved the line back some so that when new guys came out from the room, they could be shoved off without passing and interacting with us.

When it was my turn to enter the room, I walked onto an inclined table. There were two greys that I'd never seen before, with wider heads than I'd ever seen and much darker grey. I was strapped into the table, where I was told that I was going to be serving another ten year term.

"You can't do this. It's illegal. I've been told it would make me go crazy."

"That's not true," a German officer in medical gear responded. "This is completely different technology and you'll be fine. You'll be right back."

They stuck a needle in the back of my neck, and another into the tear duct of my right eye. I did go for ten years, but that's another story.

The only thing I knew of the trade was that the deal was cancelled because of multiple suicides on the other end. But Ceres Colony considered it a success because they had enough personnel to honor their agreement and get paid out something like 70% of the agreement.

I returned to my body a few minutes later, right in the same room. They pulled the needles out and walked me right back to the barracks. I was told I had the rest of the weekend off and to rest. I remembered nothing of it at the time. It was back to work as usual for me after that. But the devil steals.

Over time, our ship began to degrade. We were constantly fixing the same parts, in the same areas, and the piping was wearing out and breaking down. Even our tools began to break down. All of our tools were battery operated, and at the end of each shift, we would plug in our tools to recharge, so that they would be ready for our next shift. And even though we reported the defunct tools, it could take ages for them to get replaced.

Each tool had a case that opened up, where inside you would click the tool back into its specific place. This is where they were charged. On the ship, there were a few outlets for electricity. They were similar to the outlets in the US, but two much larger prongs. Again, our tools were battery operated, and the only thing I ever saw plugged in was a motor or pump assist machine that was brought in for special repairs.

There were zero point energy generators for the entire planet that were leased by the Ceres Colony Corporation from an ET species. They were made of exotic materials that were found towards the center of the galaxy. This area of the galaxy has been claimed by an ET race who's sole industry is free energy generator leasing. Our ship got its energy from a smaller generator that was also leased from the same species. Some of the older ships had nuclear power.

We had one tool, an auto-welder, that would cut the pipes we worked with. And then there was another that would fuse the joints of the pipe together. So, we would attach the auto-welder on with a collar to fasten it to the pipe, and then the welder, which was the size of a shoebox, would move around the perimeter of the pipe, cutting through it as it did so. The other type of auto-welder required a specialized gas cylinder; a canister the size of a coffee cup in diameter, and it also had a sort of brazing rod attached to it. That one always required a bit of smarts on how you attached it, as it needed plenty of clearance space.

In the beginning it was rare for our crew to use these types of tools, at least for the first few years. But after time, we began changing valves more and more often, from corrosion in the pipes and the general poor condition of the ship.

The pipes in the ship carried various fluids like coolants, water, radioactive water, hydraulic fluid, and oil. These fluids ran the systems on the ship to keep it going. I worked on this ship, the Blitzbus, for eight years and can honestly say that I do not know how it traveled through space. I never once saw out a window. When I walked off each day, the doors closed and that was it.

One morning, I got up for work, business as usual. The buzzer went off, we lined up for a twenty-second shower, brushed our teeth with a horrid disposable toothbrush made out of wood with toothpaste from a dispenser, and then threw away our brushes.

Same as always, I went into the dressing room to get my work uniform where I found it hooked up with my number on it. But this time, there was a different suit hanging on my hook.

I looked at the suit. It was a type of tight fitting, spandex suit along with a very comfortable pair of work shoes—much better than the boots I was used to wearing.

What's this all about? I thought.

I made it to my ship and reported for duty and instruction. A military officer was there.

"Today is a special day," he said looking at me. "Today is the day you will be embarking on your mission. You are ordered not to clean, not to touch any chemicals, you just sit here and wait for your instruction."

My other two crew members were in regular work clothes and were not coming on the mission with me. They went about their regular duties.

"Don't think you're anything special!" They barked at me. "That suit you got on couldn't be any tighter—it's sexy."

We flew for a couple of hours and then the door of the Blitzbus opened. There was a short catwalk with railings on the side which I walked over into a sort of receiving area—small, but gymnasium like.

I received an instruction manual and was ordered to wait by the EXIT. Not long after, two younger military officers came to collect me, both in very fancy military uniforms—both blonde, and much more "together" than the other military officers. *Gleaming* almost. Like something from *The Empire Strikes Back* in Star Wars with short tailored shirt arms and gloves—the whole wham.

"Come with us," they said.

12

THE REPTILIAN

I FOLLOWED THE TWO OFFICERS through the umbilical until one turned to me.

"Do you know where we are? We are on the moon," he advised me.

"You're lucky to even be here, most people that come here, never even get to be at this level. We are on a deeper level—a top secret area of the moon. And just because you're not wearing our uniform, that doesn't mean you're gonna take any shit from anyone because you're from Ceres Colony. We are the best there is. Best of the best. Take shit from nobody. Don't forget that."

It was actually called Ceres Kolonie Gesellshafte, not Ceres Colony Corporation, the way I'm referencing in english. I think Gesellshafte translates loosely more as "organized society" than corporation, but most everything was "Corporation" out there.

The two of them were pumped and drilled me with this rhetoric.

"You're no slave today," the other said over his shoulder.

"You're Ceres Colony Corporation Personnel, and all these people here need to show you respect. You need to *walk* like it."

The other one seemed like he was selling me something. Trying to pump me up.

"Zero Hour is here! We are Mittenachtwoffe!—The first to travel space other than these American fuckers!"

I felt that they were both a little too exuberant. I tried to get in the spirit though, thinking that maybe this frame of mind is what it takes to get promoted.

One gave me a pen-like device. "Here," he said, thrusting it in my hand. "You'll need this. It's your translation device. With this, you can understand any language being spoken on the Moon."

We eventually made it through the hallways to a checkpoint supervised by grey aliens. The same species I'd encountered on the moon before. Condescending and cold.

The officers were handed some paperwork they needed to fill out at a nearby window.

"Wait here," they said, lowly.

Upon their return, we went through a door and began our journey along several more very tight hallways with different colored lines on the walls. As we turned a few corners, we came across several other ET species that were walking the hallways. There were humanoid ones that looked like us but with elongated heads and longer faces, a little taller. That and more greys. There were also humans in one piece uniforms, akin to a jumpsuit.

My surprise was obvious to the officers.

"Don't look so impressed—even if they are an advanced race of species—you're from Ceres Colony. You are representing the finest colony of this Solar System."

To be clear, I was receiving their commands through the translator. They were speaking the same dialect of German that everyone spoke on Ceres.

These guys must've had years of confidence boosting morale, and I'm not going to lie, it felt really good to be amongst them. I had such low self esteem, it really did make me feel valued and important for a change. Upon learning of this mission, I had mentally prepared myself for death. So any type of life threatening situation that would come across my path on this mission, I would not avoid, as it was my ticket out of this damned life. I had been so miserable for so long, this was exactly what I needed to hear from these young shiny Ceres Officers. It definitely stroked my ego, and it was the first time to even remotely hear this kind of talk.

As we turned another corner, the Ceres officers got sidetracked by a person and stopped to talk. In my distraction however, I kept walking a little farther ahead. Around the hallway corner, I noticed a young black boy being escorted by two greys. And these weren't the typical greys. They were much skinnier darker in skin tone than any I had seen up until that moment. This young boy, no more than eight years old, was in a medical gown and had tubes sticking out of his body. There were bandages, predominantly on his head. It was as if he had just come out of surgery and he was not being cooperative with the greys.

The boy saw me and made eye contact with me. Within an instant, he came screaming at me "Ahhhhh!!!" with his arms stretched out as if to hug me. In a knee-jerk reaction, I put my foot up to stop him and he bounced off my foot onto the ground. I'd caught him square in the chest and he had the wind knocked out of him. It was like a kick that he ran into. It wasn't until I saw him start to cry on the ground that I realized from the disappointment in his eyes that he had only wanted to hug me. I felt crushed. The two greys came up quickly and motioned for me to stand back.

"What happened?" One of the Ceres officers said, running up to me.

They then looked at the greys who were busily sticking something into the boy to sedate him. "What happened? Is there a problem?"

"No—no problem," the greys shook their heads quickly.

"Please do not raise this as an issue. He is unruly. We are sorry for any problems caused," we all heard them say to us telepathically.

I watched the greys stand him up and stare at him for a moment. He stopped crying and looked hypnotized. Then they guided him with a hand on his shoulder back to where he had started running from. The three of them disappeared inside a door just off the hallway. This would be an important event and memory for me years later on earth, post recall, because this young boy and I found each other in 2017 on Earth.

So here I was, with these slick young, blonde German officers with egos bigger than the sun itself, walking along a deep, underground level on a base at the moon, getting through with only a extremely high security clearance. We eventually made our way to a large, multi-level room. I spotted two men behind a desk, eyeing the curved screens in front of them.

"Excuse me!" One of my cocky chaperone's called out to the men. "We need some assistance!"

"Yeah," one of the admin guys behind the desk answered, still preoccupied with the computer screen in front of him. "Just wait a minute."

"Hey—we're here with a guy on the *mission!*" The other blonde officer next to me piped up.

The guy behind the screen glared at the two officers beside me. "I *get it.* Please, just wait a few moments. Or your mission won't get done."

I felt the ego's of the blonde officers deflate quicker than they liked. Finally, another behind the desk got up.

"Okay," he wandered over to my chaperones.

"Whatta you got for me?"

"This is one of the recruits for the mission."

"Okay, have him wait over there," the admin guy pointed, next to three other guys who were dressed exactly like me.

Beside the guys were suits with climbing gear, hoists, and backpacks. The suits had suction cups looking devices on their knees and feet. I peered around that corner, and noticed a set of stairs to the right, leading to a doorway—except that it wasn't a door, it was three steps and then a grey wall. *Weird.*

"So what's the process?" One of my blonde chaperones asked the admin guys.

"Is there going to be a long wait?"

"We're calibrating right now," an admin guy responded from behind the desk, busy on the computer.

"It's gonna be a few minutes. Besides, they still need their briefing."

Soon thereafter, another admin guy showed up and together, all the admin guys and my German chaperones started having a conversation. I listened to the tone of their words, what they were whispering, and I was immediately disappointed. My chaperones were quick to dispose of me.

"Our guy is just a slave—we don't care about him anyway…"

I couldn't believe what I was hearing! After all that pep talk they groomed me with, revving up my confidence on the way over here, in an instant, they had snatched it away from me. I was appalled at how quickly they kissed the asses of the admin guys.
I watched another admin officer walk in, from the direction of one of my apparent counterparts. Others that were like me were starting to trickle into the room. This counterpart was wearing the exact same clothing as me, most likely a slave like me also, but donned a huge criss-cross harness around his torso. Not only that, he was wearing the suit with the suction cups on his knees and feet, and also a pair hanging from a wrist.

An admin officer turned to me. "You're going to be fitted into this gear just like he is."

He then began a briefing, explaining the power system, the roles each of us needed to carry out.

"This here is the quicksilver" he said, "you'll be needing to use these," pointing at a basket with silver looking bottles the size of a two liter soda.

Just then, another officer walked in.

"Stand at attention!" He ordered.

"Now, you select few are volunteers for a risky mission. I commend you on your courage. There is an EBE5 currently stationed on Earth, and he needs anti-gravity, as his unit is broken down. There was already an Alpha team that has serviced the unit and are on their way back to the base. You are the Charlie team. And your mission is to go down to Earth and refill the quicksilver. However—" he peered at us sternly, "This EBE5 is classified as something potentially very dangerous, and if anything is to happen to you, you *must* remain still. Under every circumstance, do exactly as it says. If you lose your life on this mission of this kind, you wouldn't be the first. But if you make it back here alive, you wouldn't be the first either. If you complete this mission, there is also a window for promotion, so keep your thoughts on that."

EBE5 wasn't the exact abbreviation that they used to describe what I would soon learn was a Draco Reptilian. But they did use some code for reference and at that moment, I didn't know what we were doing or what he was talking about. I learned that "Charlie" team meant that we were the "C" team, or the third to go in. Nothing else he said meant anything to me.

He then whipped out a screen in front of us. "Now look. This is the building," he said pointing to the computerized image.

"You're going to be portaled into a stairwell inside this building, then you will suit up, and climb up and outside of the building."

He motioned to our harnesses.

"This is a new climbing apparatus and we're field testing it. We've used others in the past but this is an upgrade. Don't be fooled, these packs weigh almost thirty kilos. However, when you activate them, they reduce your total weight by sixty percent. "

He flipped to another image. "Now this is the refill unit. There's a nipple type device where you attach your canisters of quicksilver. The unit will automatically accept the liquid and refill as quickly as possible. After, you are to line up and face the unit intake and wait for a signal on your wristbands to advance. You will face the moon. You will all walk single file into target and be portaled back here."

We knew that quicksilver meant Mercury and that it was a poisonous liquid.

He stood back. "Do you all understand?"

One of the others spoke up, "How will you know when to open the portal?"

He responded "We will be watching you the entire time."

We all stood in silence.

"Very well. Now wait here."

We waited for sometime after that. At this point in my life, I welcomed death. I wasn't frightened because I knew what kind of life was waiting for me back on Ceres, and I knew that it was a long, endless day of unhappiness. I never thought about what would happen to me if I died, meaning the afterlife, but I was sure that it was better than this. I had done the exact same depressing job for about four years now and it wore on me.

There had never been a more suicidal time in my life than this time, my life working aboard the Blitzbus. The prospect of a promotion *did* give me a glimmer of hope of something new, of something different. I'd also been heavily programmed not to kill myself, both at Inyokern and on the moon.

"Okay, the time is now," an admin officer walked up to us, cutting my thoughts quickly. "Line up, please."

We did as we were told.

"Now, that doorway up there is a portal. It takes an astronomical amount of energy to power this—It is quite unimaginable. And fortunately for us, we have access to one of the power nodes of this facility that can power this device. It is crucial that you do exactly as you're told once you are standing within the device next to the bright light. Do not touch anything as time and space will be distorted and you can get hurt if you do not follow our instructions. We will call you, one at a time, so stand by for departure and walk at a constant rate straight into the light."

We lined up toward the stairs. Up close, I could see the stairs and the entire floor area was made with stone. A sleek black slate-type stone that looked like polished Shungite. As we got closer, the wall to the left became transparent. This was so the entire admin team and operators could watch the process taking place.

An operator, kitted out in protective gear, glanced at me.

"Okay stand right here," he ordered.

Right in front of an enormously thick, square piece of the black slab stone. It was shaped Into a square, and another one hung right above it, about ten feet in the air.

The remainder of the room was made out of another lighter colored stone. All of it was amazingly smooth. It was surreal. We lined up, single file, and moved one at a time. Suddenly, a blinding ball of bright, light green light appeared in the center of the room. It was hovering about three feet above the ground and was the size of a beach ball. The operator turned to me.

"Okay. This is it."

We walked one-by-one along the stone catwalk towards the blinding ball of light. The first guy in our line up got to the bright ball of light and for a split second, the ball of light grew bigger and then he disappeared. Then the second guy followed, it flashed again, and he was gone.

Now it was my turn. I was scared shitless.

"Go now!" The operator said, "Whatever you do, keep your walking speed constant. Don't hesitate as you grow closer to the light. The guy before you did this and it's dangerous."

I took a deep breath and walked along the catwalk closer to the ball of bright, pale green blinding light. As I grew closer, I knew I was within its field because I could feel the static electricity engulf my body, and oddly enough, as I moved toward the ball of light, I could see it was actually more of a *chrome* ball. Through the chrome ball, I could see a dark room on the other side. I even saw a door knob. I kept pace and walked straight into the light and instantaneously I was in a stairwell, looking now directly at that same door knob—a door knob for an EXIT door, right outside the building.

"Whooah..."

I glanced at one of the guys who got there before me and was feeling immediate disorientation. The first guy had already exited.

"Here, drink this water," the guy handed me a liter bottle of water. I guzzled it and felt better. There were bottles of water on the floor already. So were the backpacks and harnesses that we were to use. Team Alpha or Bravo must have left them.   Suddenly another guy appeared behind us, and we handed him a bottle of water also.

We went through the door to find ourselves outside on a roof where we were slammed by a hot summer night. Hot and humid somewhere in a city, more than fifteen stories up the side of this building where an apparent EBE5 was living. We were back on Earth. I could see the moon. I could hear the traffic of the night humming down below us. We were positioned on a roof, but as I looked above, I saw the building had another tower above it way up into the dark of the night sky. We had been told in the briefing that we were going to Chicago. All I knew was that it was a city on Earth, but this didn't feel like a big deal to me. My goal in joining this mission was to die, after all. I was hoping this was the end of my life.

We rigged our suits up, got our harnesses on, had *no* practice whatsoever, and proceeded to try to turn them on. I weighed about one hundred and sixty pounds, the gear was about seventy pounds, and for my weight to now decrease to about ninety pounds, made the climb significantly easier. We had to leg over a parapet wall and attach the suction cups to the glass panels of the building. The suction cups were advanced. They could be turned on with some kind of electrical field, and self-adhere to the glass. They looked like velcro. We knew that it was after hours and the building was shut down for the night, so we could complete our climb in the relative obscurity of the night.

I had trouble getting on at first. I hit the switch and it came on but I didn't feel anything. Another guy came over and said no you have to turn this dial as well. "Keep it on the eighth one, just under full power, you don't want to have the battery die almost at the top and fall."

When he said that I started to contemplate falling to my death and it didn't exactly excite me. Even though I was of the mind that dying on this mission would be some kind of life improvement, the thought of smacking the ground really scared me.

We came to learn we were climbing up an office building. Thankfully no one was still at their offices, despite a few lights being left on. We could climb up the endless glass panels and all the rooms were empty, all the way up to this EBE5. Truthfully, the suction cups weren't all that great. If the wind picked up, I could feel them sliding along the pane of glass, which was very unsettling. I did manage to get the hang of it. The timing of letting the button go and re-hitting it when applying it to the glass was the entire trick. The times I had a close call I had just lost focus of hitting the activate button on time.

The climbing went on forever, and by the time we made it to the top, all four of us were utterly exhausted. It felt like we climbed for an hour. We must have scaled up at least twenty stories. It was a massive effort, and we carried the unnerving thought in the back of our minds that our packs could run out of battery life, and we'd plummet to our deaths. By this time, I couldn't make out things on the street that I was able to see when we started the climb. We were very high above the street.

Since my return to Earth, I've searched the Chicago skyline to see if I could identify the building. There are a few that are candidates, the closest being the Sears Tower. But I can't verify it without going into the building to see if the same stairwell is there, leading onto the roof.

We approached another parapet wall that was finished in smooth metal and rolled over the top, helping each other over. It felt nice to be working with a team of guys like that.

We stripped from our harnesses and handed them to one counterpart who had instructions of where to stack them. After, another counterpart had instructions on how to handle the canisters of quicksilver.

"I had to take a class on this, on how to inject it into the unit."

We glanced around the rooftop and found the big, square air-conditioning unit in the corner. We made our way over to it. It didn't look like anyone had just serviced it—it looked like nothing was wrong. Coming out from under the air-conditioning unit were two braided chrome lines and some type of a nozzle. The nipple of the canisters fit right into the lines. It only took a few minutes to empty the canister and move onto the next one. We'd each carried one in our backpacks.

Once we were done, our instruction was to stand in a straight line, at attention. As we stood there within the hot winds of that summer night, we shared small talk with each other while we emptied the canisters.

"Why did we even portal all the way down there, if they could've easily portaled us up here already? Doesn't make sense," I said.

"Seems dumb."

"You know, testing the new equipment," one guy replied, "And also, they wanted us scared."

Once done, we all talked about the best place to line up and then we did as we were told, facing the moon. It was all a little vague and confusing. We stood there for only a minute or two.

Without any warning whatsoever, we were all paralyzed. No one could even talk. I was instantly nauseated, wanting to both throw up and shit all at once. It felt very violating what was unfolding. I didn't get any of it. And even more disturbingly, it was all mental.

I heard a voice inside of my head. A very loud, deep voice. Fucking frightening as hell. Up until that point, all of my telepathic encounters were of a normal exchange. Felt much like the volume and intensity of my own thoughts. This was anything but.

"What do you think's going to happen nooooooow?" The deep voice seethed. "You probably think you've done a verrrrry good joooob."

This must be EBE5, I thought to myself. It was a voice that reached farther into my mind than it should have.

Every last word he spoke was dragged out and there was a feeling that he was intentionally messing with us. It was like we were being bullied, but mentally.
I was compelled to look up at the unit we had just serviced, and about thirty feet up in the air were these two eyes, floating. Looking down at us. As he came close to me, I only saw one, giant yellow eye.

"Do not think you are the first to do this type of thiiiiiiing." The shrilling, dark voice went on. "But it just may well be your laaaaaaaast."

It was trying to scare us and, not lie, it *was* scaring the hell out of all of us.

"Which one of you is the most afraiiiiiid? Well, you don't deserve to leave todaaaaaaay."

This EBE5 could hear our thoughts, but none of us could hear each other's thoughts. He was responding to each of our thoughts.

And even though it was scary, I realized that I wasn't actually afraid. In fact, I a part of me was looking forward to being killed quickly. It was a liberating moment for me because I knew that this was how I could escape going back to Ceres.

"Which one of it is todaaaaaaay?" EBE5 kept jabbing. "Is it yoooooou? Is it yoooooou! Oh? What about yooooooou! That's right, you cannot see meeeeee! I can do you the honor of looking you in the eeeeeeeye!"

Then the EBE5, appearing as only a single, yellow eye, floated down to us so that he was less than ten feet in front of us—all of us still paralyzed, unable to do anything but listen to his sneering. Then the huge yellow eye came right up against my face. It was yellow with a slit, very similar to snake eyes. It must have been over two inches tall. I could tell then that EBE5 was wearing some type of invisible suit to obscure his body, because there was a gas coming off around his face. The gas somehow bent the light around it.

He glared at me, into me, with his erratic yellow eye.

"Not you!" He grunted. He quickly moved to the guy standing beside me. "You?" Then to the next one "What about you?" And then onto the last. "It must be you! You're the last one in line!" And then he went on to abuse the poor guy at the end for who knows how long.

"Who do you think you are? You insignificant idiots. So it's none of you, then. What? You don't like the way I smell? Well I do not like the way you smell either!"

I didn't smell anything from him, not that I remember.

And then, in an instant, he made us all piss our pants. Literally. He had the mental ability to do these kinds of things. And there was not a damn thing we could do about it.

Then the yellow snake eye shot back up to the top of the air-conditioning unit, and he turned around and walked away. And that was it. As if on cue, our wristbands started blinking. This was our signal that the portal was being opened up for us.

"Line up!" One of my counterparts said. "Face the moon!"

We all turned, faced the moon, and when the blinking on our wrists transitioned to a solid line, we knew that the portal was opened and we walked forward. And within an instant, we were back in that same large room, with the portal deck up the steps again. This time, there were a bunch of officials and personnel in the room.

"Wow, you guys made it back." One of the operators said happily. "Congrats."

"Can we change our clothes?" I asked, feeling my dampened groin.

"No."

Within minutes, the group of us men were separated and whisked away.

I was taken away to an office where I was debriefed, asked a few questions about EBE5, then within five minutes, I was chaperoned by my two blonde German officers back to the ship. The officers wanted to know what he said to us, what he asked, and what he did.

When I got back, I went straight back to work. They promised me new pants but I had to wear the soiled ones for the rest of the day. In the back of my mind, I now had the hopes of getting some type of promotion. It was a new wind in my sails and I felt excited at the prospect of having one. Not as good as dying on the mission, but better than I'd felt prior to leaving.

I wasn't allowed to talk about this mission to anyone. It was classified and my orders were to keep my mouth shut. So that was basically that.
Weeks turned into months, and anytime I would see a superior officer coming in to check our working progress, I would take the opportunity to ask him about it.

"Look those types of missions you are a part of, are sporadic and do not always automatically guarantee a promotion—do you want to be taken off the list?"

"No—no!" I answered quickly. "I was just wondering."

"Sometimes you have to do perhaps two or three missions before you receive a promotion."

I was disappointed and it was depressing, but it was also the one thing that kept me going—a glimmer of hope of a potential promotion. Other than that, it was the same old miserable routine over and over and over again.

As the months wore on, we did get new tools for our jobs, small upgrades here and there, or a new training. And my two lover colleagues eventually tired of picking on me and came to just ignore me altogether.

Finally, another mission came up. I was elated! They took me right out of my work to a smaller ship. I was heavily drugged this time. It was eye drops and I was totally stoned when they explained that we were going into an active combat zone. If ordered, we were to sacrifice ourselves to prevent harm from any soldiers or officers. We were considered fodder, a buffer for the people that mattered.

We did not have a long commute. It was less than an hour of flying. I was hallucinating, tripping balls actually, and the only thing I remember about the ship was that it was smaller. We landed on another planet, with an environment very similar to perhaps Northern Europe—densely forested with a huge burning house in the middle of it.

It could have been Earth for all I know, but they said it was another world.

There were armed Deutsche troops surrounding the home and it was engulfed in flames, burning to a cinder. I still have no idea as to why I was even there, with six other men just like me, but the Captain of my first original ship was in charge of this mission, and put the other guys to work before me.

They were made to clean up a mess and there was something of great importance the soldiers were looking for—what it was, none of us knew. There could have been about fifty people total. We were only there for a short time, perhaps thirty to forty minutes. We went inside the house as it burned and they were searching for something. There were five or six dead bodies, humans, that had been shot dead on the floor.

They talked like we were not accomplishing what we were there for. It was a failed mission. Either fear or just passed time was causing whatever drug they gave me to wear off. I was thankful that they decided to not have me start searching the house for anything. The commander called it, and then we were out of there.

That same day, I went back to work as usual. I was at my post on the ship. I was able to sit down and sober up. I didn't have to work that day, I just sat there. I was not debriefed, nothing was spoken of this mission ever again.

The Blitzbus that I had been working on for years, was basically breaking down daily. When I got off the train for work in the morning, and we were waiting in line to board, I would hear other men talking about how parts were constantly breaking, the continual power failures, and parts of the ship losing gravity.

"That sounds like fun, being weightless" I perked up to one of the workers, remembering being in a zero-gravity situation on my descent to Mars orbit that one time.

He turned to me. "No way is it! These guys were stuck up in a completely dark room, weightless, unable to get out for like six hours."

It would be like being trapped in a closet, with the lights off, but also floating.

My co-workers and I were also starting to hear other strange noises coming from one of the huge pipes that we hadn't heard before. It was hitting what seemed to be the hull of the ship.

"I hope something bad doesn't happen to us," I said to one of them, on one particular day.

"Don't worry, it won't because if it did, they would anti-telephone it," he assured me.

"We won't even remember it!"

"Yeah—yeah, you're right," I said in agreement.

We always talked about anti-telephoning. We had been briefed that the ship would leave base and when returning to base, it would come back five minutes before our departing time, flying a distance of slightly more than five minutes away from base. This way, if it didn't come back at all or was in the wrong place, they could scrub the mission and never launch the ship. This was known as anti-telephoning.

They could schedule very dangerous and aggressive missions with this technique. There was a loophole in time that was policed by other beings, somewhere else. If needed, we could negotiate with these time-police beings to basically reprogram the past and not let the ship leave that day.

The times that there was a mission scrub, we would still work all day in the hangar bay cleaning or organizing. They would usually come and debrief everyone on the ship after an anti-telephone incident. Then for weeks after, they'd ask us if we had any unusual dreams. I never did. There were times when some guys did dream about it and had to report their dreams.

13

THE BURN

There was a large pipe on the Blitzbus that must have been twenty-eight inches in diameter. It ran through a junction room and it had a huge valve at the top of it, just before the pipe ran out through the wall. The valve kept failing and it was an essential component to purge one of the engines allowing the ship to switch modes to return home. It left us stranded on two occasions. Other ships came out and got us. I have no idea how they got us back home, but they did.

Some officers had been down to tell us to try to figure out how to access the valve. We tried beating on the side of it with a hammer and it didn't work. The auto-welders we used to cut into pipes and replace valves were not big enough to fit this pipe and if they were, there would be no way to cut up where the valve was because of the wall.

One morning when I arrived at my post, there were a bunch of people in our work area. Jeremy had figured out how to break three of the biggest auto-welders and hook them together as one, big enough to reach around the pipe and then cut it down near the floor. There was room for the welder to travel around the whole pipe near the floor.

This allowed one of us to crawl up inside the pipe and pry or tap on the valve and release it closed. We didn't have to do it all the time, but when we did, we made sure to have someone else there to pull us out of the pipe by our ankles. We then had to leave the room and seal the door because even with the valve closed, radioactive boiling water and vapor would still seep down the pipe.

I never went inside the pipe because I wasn't the skinniest. The skinniest co-worker usually went up there to tap the valve.

It became pretty standard over time, that we needed to enter the pipe and release the valve. It became a routine. It would usually take my coworker and I about an hour, just before we finished work for the day, to do the pipe routine, and then we would go back home.

On one particular day, however, we had a huge maintenance schedule for that day, and one of our co-workers wasn't with us. He had called in sick, and so we had to pick up his duties for the day. The extra work meant our work schedule was ramped up for the entire day.

As the end of the day drew near, we heard an officer come over on the intercom.

"Stand by the purge valve."

We both knew that we would have to make our way up the room where the big pipe was in order to fix the valve. But because my work colleague had to complete the other mandatory jobs before we finished, there was only one of us to deal with the purge valve this time. I went up to the room.

"Can you send someone else to help with this valve? There's only one of us here," I said back over the intercom.

"Negative—you need to purge immediately!" the officer came back.

"There is a protocol in place," I argued, "We are not allowed to do it on our own! You know this!"

Silence.

What the hell is going on? I thought to myself. There was nothing for maybe more than fifteen minutes. The lights were flickering on and off. I couldn't hear a thing. Suddenly a voice boomed over the intercom.

"Purge the valve immediately! PURGE THE VALVE! PURGE! PURGE!"

Well, if this doesn't work out for me, they'll just anti-telephone it in, I reassured myself. I didn't buy into his fear mongering tone, because I really didn't think it was as bad as he was exaggerating it to be. After all, they could anti-telephone anything in.

A few minutes later, something hit the side of the ship, and there was a huge bang that reverberated throughout the compartments. Seconds later, the same officer came over the intercom. This time I knew something serious had gone down and he was terrified. I could hear people screaming in the background.

"Purge the valve immediately! Do whatever it takes! Purge the valve! ALL HANDS, ALL HANDS, PURGE THE VALVE!"

They'll just anti-telephone me in, they will, I kept telling myself looking at the pipe. But I knew in my heart that this wasn't going to be a good ending. Some voice within me just told me, 'Go, you will be safe'. So I did.

I grabbed the pipe wrench in my right hand, and crawled up inside the huge pipe. I had to keep my left arm above my head as well because the width of me barely fit inside the pipe. I could barely move. I had to shimmy my way up into the pipe—a filthy pipe covered in disgusting rotten slime.

I finally got to the valve and hit it hard. Nothing happened. I did it again and it shifted a little, but not enough. I beat on it some more. I knew that the valve had closed over, but not all the way. The officers also knew this upstairs because they had a light notifying them when it had closed over. If it had fully closed, they would have notified us.

There was no way I could've bent my knees to try and maneuver my way out. Knowing what was coming next for me, real fear took over my body. I took another crack.

Within seconds, a hot steam started bellowing out of the pipe. It first burnt my arms, and I dropped the wrench, which hit me as it slid down and out by my feet. Then it immediately burnt my face. I was shocked and inhaled a chest full of steam. I couldn't breathe.

This is it, I thought to myself. *I'm dying.*

Within moments, I blacked out, lost consciousness entirely.

When I woke up, I was laying shivering on the floor, looking up at five or six people inside the pipe room. They were superior officers, in sharp uniforms, from the top decks—the bridge of the ship.

I remember looking up at them while shivering, absolutely freezing to death.

I was in agonizing pain. My body was totally cooked. My right arm, my head, and my face were burnt so badly that the skin was peeling off. I saw my co-worker, and assumed that he was the one that came to pull me out and saved my life. The officers were talking quickly amongst themselves in German looking down at me.

Then the Captain walked in. All the other officers immediately straightened their backs. The Captain began talking in a brisk tone to them.

"What?" my co-worker said to the Captain.

The Captain turned away from him and then talked to one of his officers in German and suddenly, I could understand what they were saying.

"When I walk into the room, turn on the *fucking* translator! What the fuck happened here?" He asked his officers.

And they began an in-depth technical conversation as to what happened. Another officer burst through the door and ran to me, examining me in detail, surveying the damage.

"Am I gonna be okay?" I asked through my wheezing.

"You poor bastard! You're gonna serve the rest of your days disfigured," the officer quickly answered.

"No ones gonna spend the money on fixing you up! You can look forward to being this ugly for the rest of your life! The medics are on the way, but they won't do much."

A few minutes later, the Captain walked over and looked down at me. We shared a deep eye contact.

"No, he's getting the full treatment," The Captain ordered, still looking down at me.

"We're gonna fix him. Full repair. He's earned it. You're going to get some rest."

The Captain was mad. *Really* mad. Mad at everybody else in that room—but me. But that was the last thing I cared about. I was in so much pain I just wanted to be put out of my misery.

Eventually, the medics arrived and hoisted me up on a stretcher. The doorways were so tight that I remember the searing pain shooting through my body as they bumped me into the doors and walls moving off the ship. I was freezing cold. They put me onto the back of a golf cart vehicle, then injected me with something. Within seconds, I blacked out.

Sometime later, I woke up in a hospital bed, fully healed. I am sure to this day that they put me into a new body. I vaguely remember the procedure of a needle into my eye—a sensation of feeling like being punched in the eye, to instigate this process.

I was absolutely thrilled that I had no pain in me whatsoever. This was a pinnacle moment of my life, because nothing was ever the same after that. I didn't yet know, but after what I estimate was over seven years, the dismal routine was over.

I later learned that the Blitzbus was in combat when I purged the valve. Me putting myself at risk and entering the pipe when I did actually allowed the ship to escape just in time. It's considered an honor to sacrifice oneself while in combat, which is ultimately why my burned body was repaired. It was an award worthy action, but I would never earn a medal or a badge of honor because I was a slave.

Not long after the incident, the Blitzbus ship was decommissioned. That was the last mission on the ship and we received orders that we were going to be retrained.

In the days that followed, I sat around my room at the barracks, cleaned, or did domestic duties until they were ready for us again.

14

THE PROMOTION

A week or so later, officers came and got me. I was being sent back to school again. Everyday, there were training classes. A lot of time seemed to pass me by, but once a week or so, our superiors would schedule a meeting for us to attend at a facility that resembled a gymnasium. We would all convene, perhaps fifty of us, and listen to our officers.

"Look, you are never going to know all the details," the officer said.

"These missions are classified. Everything is compartmentalized, and because of this, you will never entirely know who you are working with, how many workers are onboard, how many staff are involved," he went on.

"So listen, we need a name for our new ship. What are your thoughts? We're going to conduct a poll, to see what name fits best."

We all looked at each other, but because of my rank of being a slave, I didn't get a say—nor did any of my peers, but we listened and had high hopes for a good name. I loved the name of our old ship, the Blitzbus, which translated to something like the lightning horse.

There were a couple weeks of time in the name consideration process. We had high hopes that it would be fierce. We heard of a couple front-runners that would work well. When the naming day came, there was an assembly of the cargo department in the gym area.

We listened, anxiously. The new name for our ship became *Max Von Laue.*

The official name would produce a long acronym that would be on the side of the ship, as signs where we would board. My memory recall of names from the entire twenty years is very, very bad. But it went something like this:

Mitten Nacht Woffe
Ceres Kolonie Geiselschaft
Raumschiff
Max Von Laue

M.N.W.
C.K.G.R.
M.V.L

By the time my peers and I returned to our slave barracks, the opinion of the name of the ship was out —everybody hated it! It was weird.

Middle of the night fleet, Ceres Colony Corporation, Starship, German physicist.

But that was it. The ship was named.

Training continued on for what seemed like an eternity. But then again, everything there felt like eternity. I received orientation training on a small pad that had the same software as what would be at my new workstation.

One day I was ordered to report to a different area of the hangar on an upper floor. When I arrived, I was impressed. The room was a big waiting area but far more plush than anything else I'd seen in the hangar. The floor and the chairs were polished to a shine. It was a large room with a glass office in the center.

There were windows with a line and women in uniform sitting there. I walked up and reported to them that I had been sent there from the barracks that morning. The woman told me that the officer was running late to meet me and give me my briefing. I didn't even know I was getting briefed. I felt relieved that it didn't seem like I was going to be put to hard work. She told me to just take a seat and wait, and that I could look out the observation window.

I looked to the area behind the office cube and there was one long wall that was all glass with chrome and blue chairs that were lined up in small waiting areas. When I walked close enough to the window, I discovered that it looked out over one of the parking stalls for spacecraft in the hangar. About seven hundred feet below, on a hanger, sat the Max Von Laue. It was love at first sight. I could only see the front half from above as the rear end stretched outside the bay from my vantage. The front was smooth and came to a point. There was scaffolding towards the center that looked like it was part of construction for a tower being built on top of the ship. It was a blueish black and had lines along the leading edges. Like a B2 bomber. I stared at it in awe.

Just a few minutes later, a man in a uniform similar to office clothes walked up to me, seemingly agitated.

"Have you contacted the floor master?"

I thought to myself, *oh here we go, I'll be in trouble for nothing.*

"No, sir, I was told to report here only."

He was clearly in a hurry.

"You don't need me to go with you, take the lift and go meet the floor master, I will tell him you're coming."

He pointed at doors to the right of the glass windows. When I went out the doors, I found myself in a giant hanger bay. There was a platform with a gate, behind which seemed to be only open air. Then an elevator-type lift came up with someone riding it. It only had a railing around it and it was made of steel.

As he exited through the gate, I asked, "What do I do?

He hit the button for me and closed the gate behind me saying it wouldn't move without the gate closed. I took it down. It was a sketchy experience. The elevator rode its track loosely and it was a very long drop.

When I got off at the bottom, no one was there. I stood and waited. A few minutes later, a six-wheeled golf cart vehicle approached, driven by a man in overalls.

"Floor Master?"

He nodded and told me to get on. When I asked him about my briefing he said that because I would be in charge of a cargo bay and the loading process, I needed to have an idea of the logistics from underneath the ship. We rode all the way to the rear of the ship, then turned around and rode back. As he drove, he pointed out all of the cargo bay doors and where each loader was located. The ship went from a triangle shape in the front to a rounded edge along the sides to a tapered square shape in the back. The back was where the main C cargo bay was. My bays were the two on the port side of the ship. We could barely see the doors where mine were located. The C bay in the rear was open and there was scaffolding and men working. He dropped me off at an exit, which led to a hallway, which led to a train stop, where I got off and went back to school. I was relieved to not have to take the elevator back up.

A few days later, we were shown the inside of the ship, which I marveled at. There were pocket doors that were pressurized to close. I loved them because they didn't have the huge thresholds that I would always trip over on the Blitzbus. The thresholds of these doors were only a couple inches to step over. It was such a relief.

I learned the details of my new job and became accustomed to the new ship. The area where I worked was on the second floor, above the Cargo bay in the center of the ship. Everything was painted in a white, epoxy finish, featuring fast ladders and staircases for quick maneuvering around the ship's areas. The middle decking was carpeted. The C deck was a vast, wide hallway area which was also within the center of the ship. There was a ring-style hallway, where our hub was with a food replicator and a bathroom.

The ship was made on a sort of assembly line, far from Ceres. When we received the shell of the ship, men went to work making it suitable for humans and the tasks we would undertake—hauling cargo.

I began wondering if we were ever going to get back out into space. There were days where I would stand at my post and do nothing, the entire day. Ceres has a twenty hour day. I would get to work, eat lunch, and then stand at my post and do nothing. We were not allowed to sit. At 3:00pm, a progress officer would come by to log us into the system. I was baffled.

"How are you gonna know my progress if I am doing nothing all day?" I asked him as he punched my ID number into the system.

He looked at me.

"Every position on this ship there are at least 2 people doing the same thing on this ship, and we compare your productivity scores in a numbering system. So we can make comparative observations. So we know who's slacking. It's a science. There are rewards if you do your job. Do what you're told and be productive, or there will be corrections if you are consistently bad."

Wonder what the corrections are.

We found ourselves competing against our other workers to get a better score. We would race to eat lunch, race to use the bathroom. We were always looking for small jobs or things to appear more productive, to up our personal progress scores. Even just fifteen minutes of extra work would increase our score. I knew there was a worker, just like me, on the opposite side of the ship, doing my exact job, and that my score was being compared to his. We were always trying to outdo the other.

"So when are we going out?"

"Things are still being built, areas are under construction. In due time," the progress officer replied.

One morning, the loud buzzer rang and all the lights came on. I got up, lined up naked for my twenty second shower, pulled the chain, washed, and then went into the side room. My uniform and shoes were waiting on my numbered clothes hook. I went into the sink area and used my disposable toothbrush, then through a short line to get my collar put on. I walked out past the cafeteria, where I would catch my train, and I was stopped by an officer.

"This morning you're going on a different train, the Dash-1."

Well that sparked my interest.

"Okay," I answered.

I got on the Dash-1 train and was taken to a new area. Guards were waiting for me and escorted myself and several others to the front of the ship. I had never been in the front of the ship. I went through double doors, climbed a stairway, where I found myself in the bridge area of the ship. It was split level with a huge white room upstairs, navy flooring, a darkened atmosphere with a huge screen, and officers working at individual panels. There was also a railing wrapped around an overlook where you could see the bridge. Behind the overlook, was a briefing room. We were called to an official meeting with the Command Crew.

I had met the Command Crew several times already, but I had never really interacted with them on this scale. I discreetly inspected my surroundings, and noticed a pantry behind the railing, full of food, baked goods, coffee, and a food replicator. It looked like luxury to me. Then there was a huge white table, with twenty chairs around it. There had been meetings before, but in the back of the ship. This was my first time being called to the front for a meeting with my superiors.

"You sit here," a superior guided me to my seat.

I was definitely feeling apprehensive, fear creeping over my body. The Command Crew began the meeting, speaking in German. Suddenly something switched on and I heard the translation of what was transpiring.

"Okay, we're talking to you, we're introducing ourselves, we'll go around the table. I'm Captain Zoeggler, this is the first officer, this is the transport officer, the training officer."

And they went on like this down their ranks. They then read out our ID numbers. They went around the table. 1247055, Do you know why you're here?

He spoke up, "Sir, I'm here to access cargo data and make sure nothing poisonous or hazardous exposes the crew to danger."

"No," the Captain said.

"You are here because in your last post you performed steadily above what was asked of you. I have all your scores here. He read the history of his last posts. You are here because that's what I expect of you here, and what I'm trying to do is assemble a crew capable of performing higher than anticipated. The High Command advises that it is not possible and that genetics are the limit of performance. That the scoring system is accurate and you can do only that good. I believe otherwise."

He continued around the table and it was a theme. He asked each man what their job was, and then he would read off their entire history, landing on something they had done in the past that stood out.

My ship counterpart sat across the table from me and he had a unique number for his ID. I didn't know what it meant at the time, but the last three numbers were 007. One of the flight crew was absolutely excited about it. Enough so to pause the reading of his record and insist that he get the nickname Bond. There was some back and forth between the officers before they shot him down. They settled on calling him Keven or Seven from time to time.

Seven had an air of arrogance about him. He had an outstanding performance record and was gifted at time management and data entry. When he found out I was his counterpart, he would glare at me. He was confident that he would outperform me at every turn, and he made it known.

The Captain got on to reading the others. It was like pulling teeth. Some were actually misfits that had a spark of talent or just blind luck, like me.

And then I heard my number.

"99252270—do you know why you are here?" Captain Zoeggler looked at me.

"I'm your Cargo Engineer, Sir," I replied. "I manage cargo."

"That's not why you're here," the Captain responded. He picked up the papers in front of him.

"This is your entire report. I will say that your scores do not merit this position. You are from maintenance and do not qualify for an Engineer position, however..."

Then he proceeded to read out my report. It wasn't just my time from the years on Ceres, or getting burned in the pipe, fixing the valve. It was my time as an empath in Peru, as a sex slave in Seattle, and then my position of combat on Mars and even on the Blitzbus.

"I picked you because you were distinguished in that you volunteered for high risk missions and on your last mission into space you were distinguished. I think you will perform well where we have assigned you now."

"Is there anybody else sitting at this table that qualifies for a Badge of Honor?" Captain Zoeggler spoke up, peering at all the faces. He was met with silence.

"Is there anybody else sitting at this table that won a Badge of Honor? The *Bundeswehr*?"

"You, Sir?" one officer spoke up.

"I'm not talking about me," Captain Zoeggler answered tersely.

"Well, I had a citation credit," another officer perked up.

"Me too," another said.

"—Okay, those are great," the Captain nodded. "But they are not the Badge of Honor. The *Bundeswehr* ."

The Captain turned his attention to me. "If this man were not of a slave rank," he spoke to everybody, "He would outrank every single one of you sitting at this table. And *that* is why you are here. I chose you because you are distinguished. I chose you because you got a promotion to do what you're doing—above what you are qualified for, because you earned it—

and I'm going to keep my eye on you," he focused on me.

"We expect great things from you."

"Yes, sir," I answered.

And Captain Zoeggler continued on with the meeting.

At some point, later on in the meeting, my nickname came into question. They mulled it over but never came to an agreement that day.

The next morning, however, I went in for the daily meeting and they were already talking about it.

"You're Gerostet," an officer said, chuckling with the others.

"That's your new nickname."

I hated it. *It's better than Shelly though.*

It means toasted, or dry roasted, because I'd been cooked by the radioactive steam in the pipe. *Fuckers.* It stuck though. The Americans shortened it to Jerry, which most everyone would adopt unless trying to insult me. Then it was Gerostet.

I actually felt ashamed of my newly acquired status. I thought it would be another reason for me to get picked on, or singled out now, undertaking my new job. After a few weeks of docked daily meetings and very little work, we were ready for our first mission.

The Max Von Laue ship was one thousand feet long, about six hundred feet wide, and about five hundred feet tall, roughly. Everything there, again, was in meters. It hovered ten meters, or thirty feet roughly, above any surface. It never touched the surface, even if the power went down, there was a backup system to keep the ship hovering.

There was an elevator with cables mid-ship on the bottom. There were four big cables and four small cables. It was meant to hold four people but we never loaded more than two or three because it was really wobbly at full capacity. We called it the spider web because of the cables.

"Meet me at the spider," we'd say when it was time to disembark for trade.

This elevator was how we got down when the ship was in a hover.

Our missions were to trade goods for technology. We also carried cargo for other races or organizations into places they weren't allowed to go. We also had a service on ship that allowed people to move cargo anonymously.

We carried everything under the sun—pharmaceuticals, missiles, clothing, other people, soldiers, you name it. The crates we carried were varied as well. From cardboard boxes to chrome containers, I saw every kind of packaging imaginable. I rarely knew what was in my cargo bay.

For a while, all of my cargo bays were empty, the main five bays, and even the under-bay. The technology with our bays was impressive. All bays could transform into one big bay; the ceilings and floors could drop and move, the walls could fold down, accommodating whatever cargo was to be transported using a huge hydraulics apparatus. We referred to the bays according to the Greek alphabet. In the under-bay, we kept our 'sample packages', which were used to conduct trade with other worlds and civilizations.

The first month of missions, my cargo bay saw absolutely no action—I was simply positioned at my post. All the action was happening on the main bay, the C Bay. It was filled up, and then unloaded. And I was just positioned at my post. Sometimes I was given other people's data to enter in the system, but perhaps ten missions went by before I was assigned tasks at my post.

After a while, a routine began forming in my work schedule. I would go to meetings, then afterward, I would walk along a long wide hallway with elevators. I'd walk towards the back of the ship from the command deck, where the hallway would taper down to a small crammed hall, with stairwells, all the way back down the end of the ship.

I couldn't go back to work via the C Deck, as it was too busy most of the time. And anytime I would pass this one soldier, and officer in uniform, I would have to immediately stand to the side, no matter how crammed the hallways were or weren't.

"Moooove!" The soldier would bellow, rudely, shoving his way past me.

It wore on me. And any time I had to go to meetings, I would always time myself, hoping I would miss this imminent encounter with him. Sometimes I could, if the meeting ran overtime, or ended earlier than usual. But more often than not, we could 'clash'.

Down at the end of the B Deck, there were five stairwell ladders. I learned to take one of them, and this allowed me to avoid him most times thereafter.

This stairwell had a gravity distortion, and we called it the "fast ladder." It would reduce your body weight by about fifty to sixty percent. I would sometimes take the ladder up and down multiple times in one passing just to play in the gravity distortion. Avoiding this soldier had led me to a fun discovery.

As we continued on with our missions, the cargo bays began filling up, and we became very productive. In one meeting, our superiors were talking about how much profit they were beginning to make, and that they were going to start implementing profit sharing with the crew.

All the officers were happy about it. Everybody received a base salary, but they were now going to get supplemental bonuses.

"Well what about them?" An officer pointed out, looking at us slave engineers.

Everyone turned.

"Well what about them?" The trading officer answered.

"They are slaves, and the other cargo crew shouldn't be getting anything!"

The trading officer was an absolute psychopath if you asked me. He was made for the position of trade relations, because he was ruthless, cold, and sadistic.

"Well shouldn't they and the cargo crew be getting

some kind of profit, too?" Captain Zoeggler questioned.

"Well, let's vote on it."

So it was voted on. And approved. And as a result, I started getting a bonus. It was the equivalent to about $20 per week spending power. I was elated. My mind raced with what this newfound freedom could bring to me. I was also scared, because I wondered how this would change things. To now be finally getting a salary every week. It was unfathomable to me.

"Okay, well it will be a couple of weeks until this comes into being," I was told by another superior.

"We will have to create a new trading window account for you—you'll receive an account and get paid regularly. You can go out and travel into the Colony of Ceres."

The trading window was their idea of a bank, and it was at the very end of the entire hangar area. It was a huge department. It's where all the trading went down. They handled all the currency, and acted as a sort of customs office as well. All ships docked at this part of the Colony would be assessed and their cargo issued a monetary value by this point. When ET's would visit that didn't have currency, they could barter at the window to gain purchasing power. They would barter knowledge, usually. But some of them had a status that allowed them to spend without limit.

The excitement within our crew lasted for weeks surrounding this decision.

"So what are you going to do with your salary? Go to a restaurant?" A crew member asked me.

Wonder how much that would cost me?

It was a totally new concept to any of us, and we all dreamed of the endless possibilities this money would give us. That's all we talked about. Little did we know at the time just how expensive everything was in the Ceres Colony.

A few weeks later, an officer pulled me aside after a meeting. He was older, and seemed like the trustworthy sort.

"Hey, do you know what the red light district is?" He wondered with intrigue.

"No—no I don't know what the red light district is."

I must've looked blank, because I sure felt it.
"Well look, you gotta go there, even if it's just once, you may not ever get to go there again, especially if they take your salary away. So try to get there. If there is anywhere you should go first, it should be there."

"Where is it?" I asked him.

"It's on the train line, you'll see it on the map. The train will get you there."

15

KRUMS

I was so excited to experience the freedom of *my own* time, out in the colony, that the thought of being afraid about anything I might come across never entered my mind. There had been such a build up for this moment—not just all the hype with the guys on the ship, but all the years from the date of my capture to now. I'd never had money to do anything, let alone the opportunity to claim my time as my own.

When the time came, a few guys at the umbilical exit on the ship asked me what I was going to do, and if I wanted to walk with them to the trade window to get paid. I asked how far it was and they said almost two kilometers. I turned them down.

"I don't have time. I have a lot of exploring to do," I assured them. "And hey, do you think the red light district is a good place to visit?"

Two of the guys looked at me like they had no idea what I was talking about. The other laughed with a giant grin.

"I will find you tomorrow and you can tell me."

With that, I was off. I decided to take the train to the trading window instead of walking. It was a short ride to the trade station stop at the end of the hangar —it was the first stop, ending at an ornate, tiled, 1930's looking station that was bustling with people. The atmosphere was mostly stressed, as if everyone was late for something very important.

A personnel officer back at the barracks had given me detailed instructions for my trip. I followed the signs to get in line at the trade window. I had a printed paper with my personal information and instructions on it. The line moved pretty slow and looking back, it was basically the same as waiting in line at a bank. When it was my turn, I walked up to a woman in uniform. The window was tall and I had to look up at it.

I offered up the paper I had. She was curt and somewhat rude, saying, "I don't need that."

"I'm here to collect my money for working on the Max Von Laue."

"Yes I know. Your file comes up when you're at the window. The computer recognizes your face and probably that beautiful necklace you're wearing too," she said expressionless, never meeting my eyes.

"You have F20 Francs plus an initial bonus of F10 Francs from opening an account. Would you like to start a blockchain account? You could collect another opening bonus. Also you can sign up for hands free facial recognition that would require a monthly maintenance fee of F4 Francs."

I was stunned. Chains? This window was supposed to be the key to my freedom and the verbiage she was throwing at me was scaring the shit out of me. Monthly fees?

What the fuck do I do.

"Please no chains or anything. I just want my money and I'll go, please."

Looking back, it was her demeanor that was the largest source of my anxiety. She gave the impression of someone who really hated her job. But I was out in a social setting enough to not take it personally. It felt *at me.* She was so short with me about everything, it was unnerving thinking I was an idiot, annoying her. But she probably spoke to every customer that way.

"You stand to make a profit off of your money with a blockchain account. But suit yourself. You'll need to create an account to deposit into and maintain at least F5 Francs balance."

I nodded and agreed. She pointed at a big poster on the wall next to the window.

"Read that while I set it up".

It was a digital screen and the words turned to English when I looked at it. It was basically my bank account agreement. I tried to do as told and read it all, but it was fine print and after the first few lines, it became Greek to me. I had no idea what it was talking about. So I pretended to read it and when she seemed to be finished with what she was doing, I turned and said okay.

She asked for my signature on a glass pad, explained a few more details about my account, then handed me F25 Francs. I walked away feeling like the wind had been taken out of my sails.

The money was made out of plastic feeling paper. It had some toughness to it. It had multiple colors and displayed scenes from battles in the 1600's.   There were German looking men on the bills as well, and battle scenes with men on horses and cannons.

The people on Ceres were extremely proud of the thirty year war they fought in the 1600's. I heard the story over and over again from people that were born on Ceres—how the Deutsche had defeated an ET influence in Europe and they had done so by "using horses".

In the thirty year war, there was an ET presence trying to control Europe. The ETs had advanced technologies, and therefore a true battle advantage. But the Deutsche revolted and fought them off using "horses"—meaning they used archaic, inferior technology and still won. The result was religious freedom.

After receiving my money, a magical moment happened for me. For the first time ever, I walked to the public train. Not the slave one. But the nice, clean, toll train. I stood there looking at the map of the routes. I stared at it, realizing that I could go wherever I wanted. In that moment, for this short time, I had complete freedom. I was overwhelmed. I teared up.

The lines to board were full and the whole area was very busy, so I knew I had to pick somewhere and go. The red light district wasn't even on the map. I looked at the graphic of the map, chose a town with a pleasant name, then purchased a one way ticket for F4 Francs.

So I boarded and went on my way. These trains were so clean, with seats and proper lighting. I was allowed to sit, but the trains from the hangar were always full. No one paid me much attention from the hangar, but after a few stops when civilians entered, I did get funny looks. There was no way to conceal my slave collar and we were not allowed to disguise our status. That was made clear by our superiors.

I exited the train into a busy shopping strip that was brightly lit with shops and restaurants along the side. There was a huge ceiling in the cavern with lights shining up on it, illuminating a fake sky complete with fake clouds and all. The shops all had flat, digital signs above their storefront with graphics and videos playing to entice your entry. Sometimes the screens were ten to twenty feet long and wavy or had just a slight curve so you could see them from an angle as well. It was impressive.

I walked for a bit then began to feel hungry. I went into a small corner diner and ordered something that was basically chicken teriyaki on a stick, on a small paper plate. It wasn't bad, but it was pretty small for F12 Francs. I finished it in what felt like two bites. Then it dawned on me that I had just spent F16 Francs out of my F25 total—and I still had to purchase a ride back to base. And I still wanted to see this red light district that everyone had a weird look on their face when I asked about it.

The city areas were much easier to navigate than the hangar at the barracks. The train stops were presented in a friendlier way than I had been used to. There were signs that lead you to the nearest train station, and the train stops had a much more complete map of the planet's train network posted at the ticket kiosk. I found the connection to the red light district easily this time and took the connecting ride.

When I got off the train there I was immediately disappointed. It was messy and dark. The ornate construction of the buildings in the city was replaced with concrete and brick buildings. The street was simple. There were street lights everywhere but above them, the cavern ceiling was darkened and there was no view of the cavern ceiling. There was an obvious difference in presentation for this area compared to the bright, shiny city cavern I had just come from.

Still I knew there must be some spectacle there, or it wouldn't have come with such a strong recommendation. I walked for quite awhile. There were tunnel-like areas that you could walk into with better looking buildings built into the sides. It was basically rows of pubs that you would expect in a modern college town.

I realized that everyone was in plain clothes and I was the only one in a uniform walking around. I started to feel a little worried about the way people looked at me. By people, I mean men. It was almost all men on the streets there. There were women, but very few. I wondered why there were no women given that it wasn't a military area.

I tried to enter a few places to see what it was like inside, but they all had a cover charge of more money than I had on me. So that idea was ruled out fast. I decided to just make the most of it then and walk around and explore as much as I could. I had plenty of time. I had to be back in time to report to my shift in the morning. It had been made clear that I could be severely punished or even put to death if I didn't report for duty. At bare minimum, I would lose my position on the Max Von Laue and be reassigned to a terrible position, something way worse than I had on the Blitzbus.

Eventually, I came across a club with display windows, as well as digital screens showing what they really had to offer in the area. Nude women. All the conversations I'd been hearing of other men walking by started to make sense. The funny look on the faces of guys that told me to go here, or when I asked people about it. It all dawned on me. I got the joke. It wasn't funny to me.

I did appreciate their sentiment, but I had a disdain for the sex industry. All I saw were women that were living the loveless, lonely life I had experienced in Seattle. I wasn't intrigued and I wasn't aroused or even curious. I felt pity for them when I realized that the last mile I had walked was full of these clubs—and that meant hundreds of women being treated like I had once been treated.

I understood the system in place. I could rationalize that at least they get to be with someone of the opposite sex, and it had to have a more natural experience than what I had gone through. But I still knew that this place was an absolute factory of despair for the workers—and I wanted to leave.

I started to look for signs back to the nearest train stop. But there were none. I realized I was in fact quite lost. The fear of not making it back to base on time was now manifesting into a real possibility. I started to panic. I increased my pace, moving up and down streets in a search pattern, which I think just made me more lost. I had no sense of direction. There were no maps to look at like in the city. In fact, there was an absolute absence of posted information. The streets were intentionally vague. I started asking for help from passersby, but because they were all civilians, and I was in a uniform, they avoided me. They would say something in another language or simply dismiss my attempts with a discarded, "Don't talk to me," and walk away.

Finally one man said to me, "We aren't supposed to talk to military personnel, we can get in trouble".

I *knew* I was going to get in trouble in the morning and I remember replaying in my mind what they had told me would happen if I didn't make it back.

They didn't say kill me right? They said demotion and discipline? Not kill? Kill?

I summoned up some courage and a small amount of determination. I knew I had time. I just had to find a train stop. How hard can that be? So I just decided to walk slowly and be methodical and quit doing circles, which I realized that I had been doing.

I walked to an area that had an upper and a lower tunnel ramp, choosing to go down. I didn't recognize it, so I figured new surroundings were a sign that I was making progress. When I got below, the streets were more like large hallways. It was much busier and even more crowded. And then I saw it—a train stop! I went to the kiosk to buy a ticket, where I found a map with military stops marked by numbers and I suddenly realized that I had no idea what my stop was called. I had no idea where I was supposed to return to.

I noticed there were non-human people a little more often than had been in the upper level. Finally, I came across someone in uniform. It was two ET's in baby blue uniforms with hats and ID badges. One was heavy set and had orange hair. His nose was just like a cat's and he had whiskers like a cat would—but he was otherwise human looking, with strange hands. He was taller than me and overweight in an out of shape way. He wasn't very pleasant looking at all.

The other was a dark grey, fish looking man. His eyes were very wide and far apart. He had a mouth like a fish, with big lips and no real nose at all. His skin was smooth. He was shorter than me and very skinny. He probably weighed less than one hundred and twenty pounds. He had two large fingers and a large thumb for hands. Nevertheless, these guys were in uniform and wouldn't get in trouble for helping me. I was desperate to talk to them, even though I had been instructed on several occasions not to interact with non-humans. My desperation took over and I walked up and gave the salute, chest bump then hand out, and asked if they could understand me.

Immediately the larger one telepathically said, "Go Away! Before you get hurt!"

I looked down away from their faces and said that I needed help, "Please I'm lost."

Before the big one could finish saying anything, "What do I...." the smaller one started.

"Hear him out, are we not lost as well?" he responded, very formally.

The big one was clearly angry from something that had transpired before I had approached them and said, "He's a slave. What are you even doing out here? Who are you with? You don't have money to get here. Is this some kind of scam?"

Inside my head, he was being loud.

I was desperate to defuse him. reassuring, "No I'm by myself. I have a position that pays me, I just need to find the train stop for my barracks. See I have money for a ticket right here."

I reached in my pocket and pulled out the money I had left and showed him.

They looked at each other and the small one sort of nodded, then the big one clocked me square in the face. I went down. He got on top of me and hit me again, then grabbed the money. The smaller one started to kick me as I curled up in a ball. Then they just walked away.

I crawled over to the wall nearby and sat up against it and started panicking. *I'm never getting back, and this is it. They are going to kill me.*

I looked down and saw blood dripping on my pants from my nose. I completely broke down, full on crying. Minutes passed as I kept trying to come up with a plan. People were avoiding me. They would just walk right by.

All of a sudden a girl dressed in a lace blouse said to me, "Sugar, are you ok?"

I shook my head no and said, "I'm lost."

"Oh sugar, come on, come with me."

She escorted me across the street through a large wooden door, across a sort of breezeway, then ushered me over to a table. I glanced around and noticed a very empty "Cheers" looking bar—a bar in a sunken area in the middle of the space, featuring a stage with curvy neon lights. There was a stairway flanked by another two stages, so three in total, and they were all surrounded by booths all along the walls. Further towards the front of the stages were much more comfortable lounges with large couches in a C-shape formation.

"Hold on," the woman said. "I'm gonna go talk to the boss."

I watched the woman briskly make her way to the corner at the right of the stage. There was a booth with a very tall looking ET. I would guess about nine feet tall. His wide hips and his elongated skull, covered in a mass of curls, stood out the most to me. But he had human-like features as well. His eyes, black and dark, were disconcerting. He looked scary. A few moments later, she came back with a glass of water and a handful of napkins.

"Here," she soothed, sitting beside me blotting the napkins with the water and then began wiping my face.

"This should make you feel better. I'm still not sure what we're gonna do next, but we're gonna take care of you, honey."

The woman caught me still examining the boss.

"Sugar, just a couple things I need to tell you. The boss never ever wants you to talk to him—ever. So anything you need to say, you gotta say through me. Otherwise he'll throw you right out. You're a slave and he doesn't like interacting with any slave, so any talk has to be through me or one of the other girls. Do you know where you're going to, or were at least trying to get to?"

"I'm so confused," I replied, "I don't know the train network well enough to figure out where I was going back to. I have no idea what my stop is on the train route."

I honestly thought there was only one hangar area so it would be easy to find on the map. But out in the colony, the train maps at the ticket kiosk changed slightly from place to place and there were apparently multiple hangars around the planet.

"Hang on," the woman said, "We'll see what we can do."

Luckily for me, the bar was empty. Another girl came over—she was gorgeous. She had long red hair, was a little thinner than the first woman, and the look on her face was hard to forget.

"Holy Moly! What happened to you? You look like you got into a fight!"

"Yeah, I got into a fight outside the bar."

She came and put her arm around me.

"You don't need to be a fighter, you could be a lover."

Just then, the first woman, Monica, came back and listened in.

"Look," she began quickly, "Don't even bother—see?"

She pointed out, "Look at what's around his neck. He's a slave. That's a collar. He's got no money."

"Oh," the redhead said quickly.

Her entire demeanor changed immediately. It was obvious she was doing a job here.

"Oh okay, well, nice to meet you!"

After some discussion, the women finally decided to call the police. About thirty minutes later, two blonde, German looking officers in military uniforms with side arms walked up to the bar. One noticed the insignia on my shoulder.

"Oh, he's on the Gamma Block. He goes on the K Route. Don't worry about him, we'll get him sorted."

They were entertained to have been called to a titty-bar and joked that they didn't get calls like this often.

Actually, they decided to order a couple of drinks and stayed a while talking to the women. They were the typical arrogant Germain officers that were so common around the Ceres Colony. Soon after, they left, and I felt a rising anxiety.

"Where did they say I needed to go?" I asked Monica.

"Don't worry honey, we'll write it down for you," she assured me.

"—But I don't have any money! Can I borrow some money? I promise I will pay you back next week."

"Hang on, I'll go ask Krum."

Krum?

It turns out, Krum was the nickname of the boss, and the bar itself was called "Krums."
Monica came back with money in her hand.

"Here—here's F4. Krum is 100% convinced you will never come back and repay him. This will be enough for a pass back on the train to your designation. Prove him wrong, honey!"

"Next time you get some money, come back up here and see us." She placed her hands on my cheeks.

"I would really love to see you again."

"Thank you."

We got up and she chaperoned me outside the entrance of the bar on the street.

"Okay, so go left behind that corner and then take a quick right and you will see the train stop. You can't miss it, honey."

And that was that. I got on the train and felt the

embarrassment of the onlookers. They must have known that I had been in a fight by the look of my face. I heard the snickers from the Colony teenagers, saw the stares of the civilians. I felt it. Finally, I made it back to the barracks.

The ladies behind the desk were quick to advise me.

"Oh, you must file a report immediately. You've had an altercation."

I spent a time explaining to them exactly what happened.

The next morning, I learned that a report was filed and given to my flight crew. The meeting with my superiors was an interesting one. I tried to walk in and act like nothing unusual happened. If I played it off well, then perhaps they wouldn't notice my gigantic black eye and fat lip. With an awkward good morning, they immediately went into discussing protocol of ship personnel and violent confrontations. Then a debate ensued as to what would be the consequence of this incident.

"He shouldn't even be let outside again, because the next time he will probably get killed!" One of the superiors said.

"He was lucky this time, next time for sure he won't be so lucky!"

"—No," another argued. "We'll give him another shot. It was just bad luck. Let's see what happens the next time around."

Another superior turned to me. "Well, what do you think? What are your thoughts about all this?"

I thought about it. "Well, I actually promised the people of Krums I would go back and repay them the money they loaned me. So I'd like to at least do that, and to make arrangements for that to happen."

"Right, that's good enough for me," the Captain said. "But if something else happens, or if there is one more incident like this one, you are going to lose your leave privileges."

The following week was a tough one to endure. Not only did I have to walk around with a black eye, noticeable by everyone that I passed, but my scores for my work performance were terrible. It wasn't just this week, my scores were always low. I had never in my life been made to work with data or a computer, and it was all completely new to me.

"Where are you at with your progress?" the routine officer checking my daily performance would ask.

"Well…"

"—Well let me tell you, Gerostet," I watched the officer thumbing through his clear circular iPad looking device rimmed with rubber, "007 is beating you again."

He looked up at me.

"You know they're going to hammer you at tomorrow morning's meeting."

"I know, I know."

007 was always doing much much better than me. It was embarrassing to go into the regular morning meeting and listen to my superiors constantly remind me of my inferiority. It was unfair because 007 had been doing data entry for years.

"007 is at 110, and you are barely making 90. You can at least close the gap a little."

Eventually, not wanting to be demeaned more gave me enough spark to get into gear. I started doing the very best that I could. Undertaking whatever effort I could to increase my score. I quit chatting so much and asked my fellow officers what I could do.They laughed and really didn't care about my wanting to do better.

I was on the Port side of the ship, D & E. 007 was on the starboard side, A & B, respectively. I came to learn very quickly that he was a machine. Despite the stiff competition I got from 007, I kind of liked him. But he had not endured anything remotely close to what I had. He had basically been a laborer ever since he started in his program. I learned he was younger than me, and had nine years of service remaining. He had zero concern about making friends. He didn't care whether you liked him or not, all he wanted to do was to get the job done. He wasn't rude to me, but he also came across as arrogant, aloof sometimes. He knew he was there to do a job and that he was very good at what he did.

That following week, when I got paid, I kept my word and returned to Krums. My face was mostly healed. I sat down at the same table and another girl approached me. It wasn't Monica. Monica was nowhere to be seen.

"Hey, I'm here to pay Krum back his money," I began.

I even offered to pay more.

"Sure!"

"And if I am able to, I would like to purchase a drink and spend time here, so that I don't have to return to the barracks and do chores."

The girl left to take my money to Krum. She came

back with a look of bewilderment.

"Krum is absolutely shocked that you have come back with the money," She said with a smile.

"He is pleased that you would do this. And actually, not long ago, another woman working here—a coworker of mine, was assaulted in one of the back tables over there," she pointed out, visibly upset having to speak about it.

"I don't want to get into details, but Krum is unable to see the table from his booth, and you know, he can't leave the booth because of his low-gravity situation, but he said that you could sit there, free of charge, as a placeholder so that the other patrons of the bar would have to sit elsewhere."

I was dumbfounded.

"Really?"

"Yeah," she went on. "You don't even have to buy a drink. Krum will let you sit there for as long as you want, and just keep an eye on things in this area."

"Well, how often can I come back and do this? Like sit at this table?" I wondered, taking Krum up on the offer.

The woman smiled, "Come back every single day sweetheart."

I was elated and felt my chest swell. So I budgeted my pay every week, and instead of buying a two-way pass for the train each day, I could purchase a cheaper day pass, which allowed me to go to Krums every single day after work.

I was terrified of being in public every single day, wondering what may potentially happen, but it wasn't enough to stop me from going. I had an eyeful of beautiful women surrounding me everyday, and I got out of barrack chores, which were always tedious. What more could a guy ask for?

Eventually, I got to know most of the girls that worked at Krums—and they were good to me. One day, towards the end of the afternoon when the next shift was starting, a new girl came over to my table and introduced herself as Lynne. Lynne and I were talking, but I was completely taken by another girl. She had blonde hair with black highlights, and a petite, athletic frame.

"Marie, can you go serve that other patron," Lynne said quickly.

Marie looked at with a scornful eye.

"I am not going back over there, you go there and do it! I just finished two rounds back to back, so it's not my up, sister!"

She then turned her attention to me. "Who's this guy?" Marie smiled coyly.

She reached up and grabbed my collar, giving it a little jiggle.

"It's a shame he has to wear this thing because he's kinda cute."

I watched Marie get up and go back to working the room. I was totally taken by her. Nobody had ever grabbed me by my collar like that, and it made a huge first impression on me. Her confidence in touching a stranger was something completely on another level. Plus she was stunning to me.

This period of my life was the most exciting I had ever experienced. Earning a profit, feeling a small sense of freedom, being able to go and watch the girls at Krums— it was all something that I could look forward to every day. In all honesty, it did take awhile for me to acclimate to this newfound freedom, given the strict parameters that had conditioned my life up to that point.

During this time, my counterpart 007, was continually exceeding my performance score. Nothing I did daily could ever outdo his score. I really was applying myself, breaking my back to catch up with him and do better. I did increase my score somewhat, but I never could beat him, and nothing seemed to work.

One morning, after our regular daily mission briefing, everybody was dismissed by the Captain, except me.

"Look, you are a good worker, and I like you," The Captain began.

"There is…something about you, that is admirable, and if we existed under different circumstances, we probably would be friends."

"I agree with you," I replied.

The Captain and I had a bond, despite the circumstances I found myself in, so I felt glad to hear him say this.

"With regard to your counterpart 007, don't try to beat him, just expect to," he advised.

"You know, as if you've already done it. Trust me. Don't listen to what everybody else is saying."

I absorbed everything he told me. Then we shot the breeze for a little while.

"So, what do you do with yourself in your spare time?" The Captain wondered.

"How are you liking the colony?"

"Well, it's nice to be able to get out after work. I have an arrangement at Krums. I sit in one of the back corners, and watch the girls. Make sure nothing happens to them."

"That's good."

"To be honest, I'm still a little apprehensive to venture out, after that attack where I got robbed. So I still always have that in the back of my mind. You know, just keep cautious and stay out of harm's way."

"I understand," The Captain nodded.

"And you know, it's better for me to go out and be somewhere else, so that I am not drafted into after work chores. It's only costing me a day pass on the train, so it's affordable, and of course, I'm not complaining about being around a bunch of half naked, beautiful women."

The Captain sat back and laughed. "Yeah, I can't argue with that," he smiled, "but don't overindulge yourself. Don't let it distract you too much from your duties."

I wished that the Captain would have asked me to stay behind every morning. We had a real rapport. To confide and have someone of great authority to sit and listen to me was a wonderful thing, and honor, and I would call him a good friend. And truth be told, it was nice to have someone treat me with respect.

Over the next few weeks, I kept my daily routine of daily visits to Krums. One night, I was folding napkins with Lynne and Nat for an upcoming party. Meanwhile, Marie sashayed over, and the sensual dress she was wearing was ripped down the front, exposing her breasts. I felt my cheeks immediately burn with embarrassment. Their quarters were being cleaned, and she was unable to go upstairs and change.

"I'll just sit and wait here with you guys until they finish," she said, sitting next to me.

"What happened?" Lynne wondered.

"Jeff tripped and ripped my dress, that's what happens when you're old."

As Marie sat next to me, it was difficult for me to contain my blushing face—Marie on the other hand, carried on folding napkins with us, oblivious to the impact she was having on me. I caught a quick glimpse of her chest, then looked away quickly, just in case she saw me and maybe slapped me across the face. She intimidated the hell out of me. Not enough to stop staring at her when she walked away, however, and a few of the other girls picked up on this—especially Lynne.

"You stare at her more than you stare at anyone else," she remarked one night with a smirk.

"I can't help it!" I retorted.

Several days later when I went back to Krums, Lynne came up to me in her bikini top and denim shorts.

"Oh! We've been waiting for you," she said, her long, red, curly hair bouncing around her shoulders.

"Come with me—you get a free one!"

"What?" I stammered, "What do you mean? With you?"

"Oh no. You don't want me!" Lynne snickered, grabbing me by the arm. "You want Marie."

"—Oh no, not necessarily!"

"—Honey, we all *know* it's true!" She laughed.

"Someone came in from your ship—an officer, and told Krum you would've got a medal for what you did. The officer said that we needed to take care of you!"

I was dumbfounded.

"All the workers or officers that get a medal of some sort, get a *'free one'*"

So I learned that an officer had come in and talked Krum into letting me experience a woman for the first time.

I was shocked! I was expecting to go to Krums that day and relax, having no idea that something else was planned for me. We walked by Krum, this time sitting in his square office, and went down a hallway. To the right of him was a doorway, and it opened up to a long line of doors. It was the brothel part of Krums.

"Go up there to room number five," Lynne pointed to the door.

"Just wait there."

I did what I was told and just waited. The room was no bigger than ten feet by ten feet and had a standard countertop with a sink, displaying a line of jars—all full of condoms.The bed that was shaped like a 'C', with a red mattress extending up the wall and folded over above you. It even had tassels on it to grip onto. A few minutes later, Marie walked in.

"Don't worry, I'm gonna take care of you," she assured me, "Trust me."

As we got on the bed, I noticed a dial with five settings on it. It was used to turn the artificial gravity down, and each turn of the dial reduced the gravity by twenty percent.

"Oh cool," I remarked, "I'm gonna turn it to five."

"—No, don't do that!" Marie insisted. "You will have to pay for it otherwise. Just put it on one. Trust me, being weightless is absolutely terrible! It's a horrible experience—I won't do it."

So, Marie and I had sex, and it was the first time that I had experienced real sex with a woman. And whatever went down between the two of us during the encounter, despite my awkwardness, it was as if both of us were struck by a bolt of lightning. Literally, there was a bolt of energy between us.

After we finished, she helped clean me up, shoving the tissue into a small, five inch hatch that was automated by a vacuum to suck up the contents. Throughout the entire experience, we only had a few minutes.

"Come on, we gotta get going, we can't stay in here," she said to me, chaperoning me out of the room.

We walked back down the hallway, passed Krum, and then we went to a table where she ordered me an iced tea. She sat beside me and gave me a kiss on the cheek. I was flattered, and wondered how my performance was.

"So, uh, was that okay?" I wondered.

"You did fine, babe," she assured me. "Now listen, I gotta go make my rounds."

It wasn't very crowded that day, and she was back in about ten or fifteen minutes. By the time she came back, I was absolutely mad for her. We were both mad for each other—head over heels in love.

It was *far* beyond the point of, for example, finishing each other's sentences. It was as if we joined together, unlike anything else or anyone else I had known. And it only took that long, moments, to set in.

Marie became the focus of my days. I would try not to think about her during my ship duties. When I would see her, we would sit together and talk without end— me asking her about her day, her life, anything I could think of. My curiosity was insatiable. Then she would take her turn asking me about my missions, places I went, and the things that happened to me.

Marie was in the seventh year of her twenty-year "career return program." She was taken in 1993, and by the time we met, I had already served seventeen to eighteen years, and was almost ready to go back home. She had told me, in the beginning of her program, that she had spent a short time on Earth.

Almost everyone I met out there was serving twenty years. When I was first taken, the stocky reptile guy with an affinity for Bruce Lee told me that twenty years was more or less the standard term. They had the technology to do it for longer, but the probability of someone going insane increased dramatically if their term was longer. There were exceptions however, as some people had the genetics to serve multiple terms. The terms were still twenty years, however. There was a law set by advanced, intergalactic ET's that governed the twenty-year increments—so that's what we all got.

"I miss the sun so much," she said to me.

"One day on Earth, I woke up with amnesia, and had no idea who I was, or what had happened to me," she pondered.

"The people told me where I was. Something about an animal hospital. I had an apartment, and every now and then, like once a week, men would stop in. It was easy back then. I would stay locked in my apartment and just watch TV. Then I was sold off, by some illegal faction, and was sent to Mars. It was brutal—illegal, even by Mars' standards. One after the other, a never ending stream of men. Sometimes up to eighteen hours a day—*everyday*. And if there was a mean or nasty man, I couldn't deny him. I *had* to do it. At least here at Krums, I have protection over that, and we are allowed to deny a man if he is rude or bad to us. It makes all the difference to me. So, I was on Mars for about a year, and then our place got raided due to all the illegal activity. The soldiers took us girls, and we were sold off to Krum. At least we are treated much better here—but I *hate* not being able to feel the sun on my face. I miss the sun. They told us that Earth had been destroyed."

I had been sworn to secrecy about revealing any details about Earth. I knew I could get in a lot of trouble for disclosing any information about *anything*, especially Earth, but it wasn't enough to stop me from telling Marie.

"Listen, the Earth is not destroyed," I told her. "I was only there just a few days ago. It's there. There's a base where we land our cargo, called Diego Garcia. It's warm and nice there."

Marie gave me a scornful face.

"I don't believe you."

"No—really! Earth is not destroyed. I'll prove it to you sometime. I am being completely honest with you."

Krum, the ET, required that I pay to be with her. He was running a business, after all. Otherwise, she would have never charged me. Because of this, and my financial situation, we weren't able to be together physically very often. I would have to save basically until the end of the year to be with her. In my mind, if I budgeted properly, I could be with her twice more before being sent back—and still be able to take my day passes to see her regularly. I could have slept with her more if I didn't take the day passes, but I couldn't go without seeing her for that long. So it was a trade off.

We had a system worked out, though. She would sneak condoms from the room and sometimes the other girls would do the same for her. I'd put the condom on and she'd give me a hand job at the booth almost every time I visited. It was clean that way, I'd just go to the bathroom and flush the mess down the toilet. It was great. Not as satisfying as being with her —I loved her, *craved* her—but it was enough. One time we had sex in the booth. Krum could see it and we got in deep shit.

In the beginning, I was okay with her doing her job— providing sex for other men. But after some time, it wore on me, and I hated being at Krums not being able to see her. I had to sit there knowing that she was in the back somewhere, with someone else. When I would return to the barracks at night, I had literally five minutes before the light of my room would go out. And as soon as that light went out, I would cry myself to sleep—I loved her that much.

Marie's love had a lifelong, lasting impression on me. So much so, I believe my relationship with her is the reason why I have retained as much memory as I have to this date. She was the motivation for me remembering. Before I left, I committed myself to not forgetting her and her love. Intense emotional connections seem to be a trigger for the memory recall process.

16

MISSIONS

So I began settling into a nice routine with life and work. Mornings of course, began with our debriefing meetings. There were even some days, at work, that I actually started outperforming Kevin 007—my work counterpart.

I'd like to say it was the Captain's pep talk about visualization that did the trick, but I don't think it was. I learned to eat quicker. Everyone else would be standing around, talking and eating, and I'd inhale my food and get back to work.

The Captain was a deep man, however. And his beliefs did influence me. He was a part of a type of secret religion where they believed that only a certain echelon or class of people were called to. They believed they had a more important destiny than the average person. It was illegal in Ceres to practice religion, so he kept it low key. But his group worshiped the creator of the universe. They all tended to be leaders or in leadership positions. Their religion kept detailed records about people. They said that people like me, who sacrificed themselves the way I did, went on to do great things. They made an impact on society.

"Well, I can't believe that for myself as a slave."

"People who come in with karma to even find themselves in a situation where they can sacrifice themselves *in combat* are here to do great things," he assured me.

"This is an uncommon fate. So we'll see about you. There's still time for you."

One morning after leaving the regular kickoff meeting, as I was wandering back down towards my starboard deck, I decided to play on the fast ladder. The gravity disturbance allowed my weight to decrease by about sixty percent and I enjoyed dropping myself down and catching myself mid way through.

Well, this one morning, I had a coffee, along with my clipboard, and accidentally dropped my coffee all the way down to the bottom of the ladder—A deck. There were always men standing around that area, because it was a cargo bay.

"Hey, you asshole!" One shouted back at me.

"We're gonna report you! We're sick of cleaning up after you!"

They often reported me, after which I would stay away for a few weeks, only to return at a later date and do it again. The gravity-distorted fast ladder was addictive.

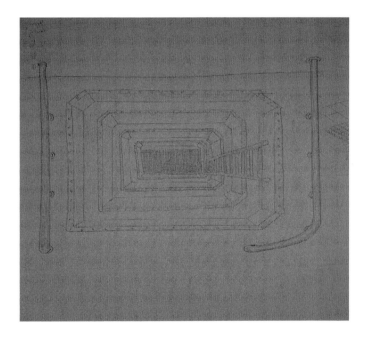

The back of the ship was entirely industrial looking. Everything was off-white, epoxy coated, and had grated flooring—which eventually led to foot problems for me. Our days aboard the ship were long at times, and the leading officers would prep us in the mission briefings how many stops we would have for that day, who was unloading what, what was going to which cargo bay. One particular time, we were assigned to somewhere near Jupiter.

Around Jupiter, there are several areas that are called temporal bubbles. One of these bubbles actually had a base within it—outside of the actual time dimension. When inside one of these bubbles, you could not see stars—it was completely black within them.

This base was well lit, rounded, and white. Imagine a public trading organization that was inter-galactic. It was here that we had to request permission to visit other worlds and points in space to begin trade negotiations. Other worlds would list items to trade and we used this space station to communicate with them. When we'd get a hit back on our goods, we'd then plan the trade route and agreements. We'd only visit for an hour or so before our travels and trades would be set in place. There were all kinds of races there, and innumerable different craft coming and going at all times.

Certain temporal bubbles were only used for housing space stations like this one, while others were entries to natural portals that enabled extra-galactic travel.

Entering the temporal bubbles and portals came with many conditions and many complications. First, our ship had to have permission. Second, we had to use an ET computer to give us the coordinates, the correct speed, and the correct angle at which to enter it. This had to be done before entry, as well prior to exiting this bubble, in order to end up back into the same time signature from whence we originally entered.

On this particular day, the Captain came over the speaker of the ship.

"Thanks to Dimitri, our flight navigation crew member, we have re-entered into current time-space *sixteen hours in the past!*" he spat. "By law, we cannot re-enter Ceres Colony until sixteen hours have passed. So, use your time wisely. Extra points for those who manage to keep working for this time!"

So, on top of an already eight hour working day, we then had to wait an additional sixteen hours. Re-entering earlier than this would break some type of temporal law, which was strictly forbidden. And so began our slow, long crawl back to the Ceres Colony —a sixteen hour journey that would enable us to enter the colony at the correct time. I had already made up my mind that I was going to keep working the entire way back to the Colony, so that I could accumulate points. They would go towards spending more time with Marie at Krums. It was hard. One time I almost fell asleep at my station, standing, and through my exhaustion, my knee tapped the floor. I was deducted points. I was so disappointed in myself! *I fought to stand for so long.*

I was even planning on going back to Krums that night, but I didn't—exhaustion got the better of me, and I went to bed instead.

The time-space timeline that we lived within could never, under any circumstance, be altered. Slipping in and out of the timeline, we came to learn, was heavily policed and under constant surveillance by superior energetic entities. For example, regarding the high risk temporal missions, our ship would leave Ceres Colony at 8:00am. We would work a full shift, traverse huge galactic distances, and then return to nearby the Ceres Colony at 7:55am. We would enter about five minutes away from Ceres at full speed, and the superior entities could physically see the ship to know if the mission was a "success" and still not technically be back yet. If it was a success, we would use the remaining five minutes to travel back to Ceres, arriving just moments after the linear time we had left.

We had to return at this time so that Mission Control could see if the ship had re-entered upon the coordinates agreed on initially only known by the Captain for each mission. If re-entry went according to plan, we knew that the mission was a success. However, if the ship did not show up, or re-entered near Ceres Colony at incorrect coordinates, an accident happened, or that a hostile takeover was imminent, Mission Control would cancel the mission. It would then be anti-telephoned in, before we had even left. As a result, we would spend the entire day cleaning or doing other work that needed to be done. I was informed by an Officer that the 'anti-telephone' technology was a loophole in this heavily surveilled time-space continuum that we existed within, and that the energetic entities that governed our time-space exist beyond the timeline.

One time, according to the Officer, someone had tried to aggressively go back and change the timeline. Within a matter of seconds, the superior entities contacted the person and served him a punishment of one thousand years living an unpleasant life of hardship.

Once he had completed the thousand years, this person was inserted back into the timeline just before he had tried to go back and aggressively change time, but he was never the same person. He was debilitated and scarred for what he had endured. He could remember it. I knew this feeling from my additional ten year service while on the Blitzbus. I couldn't remember it then, but it messed me up. As a result, everyone was terrified of the possibility of such a punishment. But many pushed the anti-telephone technology as far as they could possibly take it.

We usually flew outside the solar system in the mornings. Then for the remainder of the working day, we would do our cargo runs within the solar system. The Ceres Colony Corp had an enormous warehouse out on an asteroid within the Kuiper Belt to take all their cargo. It was a white looking asteroid, similar to the geological nature of limestone. This warehouse, despite its size, was always full. Physical space was a real premium for the Ceres Colony and running out of it was always an issue. Every time a new cavern was mined, it was filled with "city", meaning people and buildings. The Colony would always promise storage space, but they didn't honor their word. Having stored reserves for trading was important and there was never enough storage space to match our ambitions.

A couple of months in, I came to learn that Ceres Colony had made an alliance with an extraterrestrial species extremely far away. They were from another galaxy. And one day, we went there.

As mentioned, there are temporal anomalies (or bubbles) around Jupiter. In addition, however, there is also a natural wormhole. Upon entering this wormhole, one is able to be transported to dozens of other galaxies. And once at the other end of the Jupiter portal, there are other natural wormholes that will take you to yet another several dozen galaxies, and so on, and so on. And it is through this process that intergalactic travel is possible.

The Max Von Laue had the ability to jump to any point in our galaxy on its own, and very quickly— instantaneously actually. But in order to travel to other galaxies, we needed the portals. There may have been other ways to reach other galaxies, but we didn't know of them. It took way too much power too.

When the intergalactic missions began utilizing these wormholes, we were warned that traveling through them would come with consequences.

"Listen," a superior officer began, "when we go through these portals, you're gonna get sick. Everyone is going to experience different symptoms, but most likely all of you are going to get sick for up to approximately ten minutes."

This was a given.

"However," he went on, "in order to preserve your performance scores, we will waive these ten minutes so that you may all recuperate. When the red light above your station comes on, the ten minutes will commence. During this time, you are not to touch your work stations. When the red light goes out, you can commence work."

When we finally did travel through the natural portal near Jupiter, everyone did get sick to varying degrees —I certainly did. I was nauseated, disorientated, and eventually vomited. Some workers adjusted better than others, and gradually, I became used to this incongruent slip in time-space. Instead of needing the entire ten minutes, I would feel better in three to four minutes. There were others that never got used to this.

On one particular mission, the Captain came over the loudspeaker.

"Congratulations crew," he remarked jovially. "Our ship, along with the crew, is now the first ship from our solar system to become record holders in the farthest distance travelled from our home world. Nobody from Ceres, nor from this Solar System as far as we know, has ever travelled this far from our star— meaning the sun for us."

We all erupted into cheers and it was a memorable, exciting moment. But our title only lasted for about six weeks before we were out traveled by another ship.

"Can't we just traverse back over the cosmos and break another record?" I asked my superior officer.

"No, it doesn't work like that," he replied quickly. "Those guys were on a mission, and you need permission to gain entry into certain sectors of the Universe. We must prove legitimate reasons for our trips."

My days on the Max Von Laue always started with the same: hot coffee. I would always wait to use the bathroom until lunchtime because it saved me having to walk all the way back up to the C Deck to go. If I waited until lunchtime, I would already be up there getting lunch and could use the bathroom at the same time. I would however, always get in trouble for doing this, because I liked to take my time on the stool. At lunch time, there were always others waiting.

"Five minutes only!" Someone would call out from behind the door, waiting on me.

I hated it. I literally got written up for it and had to have a discussion with an officer where I was told again that I could only be in the bathroom for five minutes. I don't know how many people were on the ship because the total number of people was classified information. But I knew about eighty, composed of a mix of men and women. Different sections of the ship were assigned to different bathrooms. And they were much like airplane toilets.

We had a food replicator to produce lunch that looked similar to a microwave. There were several buttons on the side that represented different food options. You would make your choice, press one, and then the replicator would *print* the food. If you picked macaroni and cheese, the food replicator would give you a sloppier version of that. Sauerkraut, mashed potatoes and gravy with mystery meat was one of the other options. Pot roast was my favorite of the mediocre choices. The quality of all of the options was the equivalent of a microwave meal, sometimes worse. It was always slimy, like a milky version of whatever dish you chose. Worse than the quality though, was how boring it became to have three or four selections and being stuck with the same thing for lunch.

My 007 counterpart Kevin, was a very slow, deliberate eater. He was like this from birth, another coworker had told me. And I took advantage of it. As I mentioned, I learned to inhale my lunch, sometimes still finishing it and burning my mouth at the same time, all while walking myself back to my station along the galley.

And you know what? When Kevin learned about my method, he refused to even try to keep up with me. So the extra minutes he took to eat his lunch, in conjunction with the trick I learned about my bathroom time at lunch only, it all started to add up. I became the dominant, highest performing worker out of all of the cargo engineers.

It gave me newfound confidence, and I was a little cocky about it. But it felt good because for so long, Kevin overshadowed my performance. I still to this day inhale my food. Learning to eat fast for me at that time was literally life changing. I went from crew meeting whipping boy, to hero in a short time.

All the guys that worked in our two cargo bays were proud of me—and that felt great too. And to my delight, some of my fellow workers even started asking me to walk with them, and sort of hang out and sightsee. So, instead of taking the train from work back to my quarters on paydays every Friday, I began joining three or four others for the walk from our dock, across the huge hangar, and then all the way to the trade center.

The hangar was indeed an impressive sight. At the right end of the hangar was a huge airlock that could easily fit a ship at least two thousand feet in size.

There was a marble stairway that led to massive revolving doors. This kept the air from escaping as much when patrons entered and exited—standard swing doors would have created a suction draft. The revolving doors separated the hangar air from the air in the trade room.

Sometimes the entry and exit doors to the airlocks on the hangar would get stuck, and if one was close enough to the area when it happened, you would feel symptoms of hypoxia. Mostly you would feel light headed, dizzy, and weak.

There were huge windows and tiled floors similar to what you'd expect in a 1950's bus station. The first moment through the great revolving doors from the hangar to the trade area gave a good hit of clean, crisp, fresh oxygen—and it was a total rush, a buzz actually. It was awesome. I remember those walks with my colleagues fondly and I'm glad that I decided to take them.

We would often pass ships under repair. There was an area with ET's that always worked on smaller ship engines and they would yell at us to not walk by the area.

One of us would yell back, "There's no sign!" and then we would do it again the next week. Until there was a confrontation. When we returned a few weeks later, they approached us, armed, and aggressively displayed their level of seriousness.

"Don't fucking come back here again. You're going to get your ass beat. Each of you," they promised, telepathically.

After that, we walked down the upper level hallway that was a lot more boring than the hangar, but still not a bad walk. I always loved the edge of the hangar area just before we got to a long, huge corridor with natural stone pillars. Not because of the grandness of it all, but because there was a fire and rescue and security post there. Fire and Rescue had Unimog vehicles that were the most badass trucks I'd ever seen. They had been converted to electric motors and usually had cables plugged into them.

Just before my twenty-year time was up, the stone pillars that we had walked by for months came under construction. I was told that they had abducted a few of Europe's finest stone sculptors into a twenty-year program just to have them sculpt a few monuments throughout several colonies in the solar system. These sculptors would be working on Ceres for years to come.

They started their work carving giant horses out of two of the natural pillars and over time, it really came together. I went home before it was completed and remember always feeling disappointed towards the end that I wouldn't get to see the final product. They were truly grand.

I was still sometimes required to undertake work-specific training. I would return to classes in order to receive needed certifications, especially on days that had been anti-telephoned. School was usually two to three hours in the morning. Myself and a few crew members became certified as a V- Loader—it was a very quick certification, but a good one to have. It was fun, and we often fought over who got to V-Load when the time came.

The sole responsibility of the V-Loader operator was to man the vortex room situated above the doors of the ship at the cargo bay. We'd look through a window above the bay, focus the cargo under a sort of target, then press a button to activate the vortex. From there, the computer would take over and levitate the cargo into its appropriate bay. The target was operated by a joystick, and the target was a crosshair. You'd lock it in with the button on the top of the joystick. It was like playing a video game. It was the easiest task and we all loved being the V-loader.

This vortex was invisible to the naked eye, except for in snow or a sandstorm.There was a white laser which indicated the perimeter of the vortex. If we didn't have an indicator to outline the perimeter of the vortex, we could very easily enter the vortex and become severely injured. We heard tales of arms being snapped and were warned to stand back.

One time, I did actually witness a vortex in motion when we landed on a planet amidst a snowstorm. Visually, it looked like two lines forming a spiraling funnel right above the cargo load. The only thing that revealed the shape of the vortex was the snowflakes. It was otherwise invisible.

My position in my cargo bay allowed me to use a manual crane apparatus too. This was important in the event that we couldn't generate a vortex. Under certain atmospheric or energetic conditions, sometimes the vortex just wouldn't work. Under those circumstances, I would operate the crane arms to pick up the designated cargo. Rarely was the manual crane apparatus used, but it was handy to have the certification nonetheless. I was consistent in my work performance, and it became noticed.

One time, I was handed a piece of paper from an officer with a list of directions. I was called to the Bridge, which was the command center of the ship. This is where the captain sat—I'd never been allowed anywhere near that area and it was even the first time I'd been given permission to use the elevator inside the ship. As I was about to enter the elevator, I caught two German officers conversing with each other. Until the translator kicked in, I had no idea what they were talking about. But as soon as it did, I learned that they were talking about destroying an asteroid.

"Oh, you should've seen it!" One officer remarked excitedly.

"We did it at point four of a wavelength! We expected it to simply fragment but it completely blew apart haha."

The other German officer was much more aware of my presence.

"Silence," he gasped at the other officer, looking at me. "He can understand what we are talking about— that's classified information. Stop talking at once."

These two men were in shiny black uniforms that I'd never seen before. I became aware that there was much more going on within the ship than I ever knew about. I had an epiphany in that moment, a realization even. We were not just moving cargo.

In the Bridge, everything was surprisingly modern. There were vast glass doors leading into the space, and inside there were about twenty people, all stationed along curved desks with VR headsets on. Their screens were curved and appeared black to the outside observer, but it was a technology used to obscure the display. The VR headsets allowed for each officer to see his or her computer screen exclusively.

All of the screens were connected to a main screen, which the Captain sat in front of. Behind him were two officers, assigned to their own screens. Their screens were full of color and display as they were not using headsets. It was all very Star Trek-ish.

The Captain turned to me.

"Please take a seat. Your work this week has been outstanding, and this is your reward," he smiled. "I knew you had it in you."

He turned toward the screen. "Have a look at the screen. Show him where he works."

The officers directed the screen to the light stationed above my workstation.

"You wanna see what your competition is up to?" The Captain offered. "Here—let's take a look. There's 007 Kevin. And here, here's another worker from your bay. We can basically see anything, anywhere," he assured.

As they were taking me through the ship surveillance technology, one of the pilots had been doing figure eights and tricks with the ship.

"Okay, that's enough messing around, Pilot. Take us back to Pyramid Base."

Immediately, the ship re-orientated itself and through the screens we saw Al Hannah Mons Kryo volcano (NASA has called it this). We flew directly down inside a massive crater.

"Captain," air traffic control came in over the speaker, "We are having trouble with the door. Standby."

Our ship was hovering waiting to enter a set of hangar doors at Al Hannah Mons.

"Hold here," the Captain ordered.

So, we just sat there and waited until further notice.

"What's the ETA on the doors," The Captain sent back to the radio officer for air traffic control.

"We are still waiting on the doors, Sir," the voice over the speaker responded.

"Well. This is damn inconvenient," the Captain muttered.

We sat there for a good long while, awaiting information to proceed. It was kind of awkward. Five minutes passed, then ten, and the Captain was growing increasingly agitated.

"They can fix the door," he grumbled. "It's never taken *this* long before!"

The officers were talking amongst themselves.

"If we were a triangle ship they'd let us in straight away," an officer said, referring to the fact that if the ship were a warship, they would let it in immediately.

Triangle ships are built for combat. The Max Von Laue was no warship.

"Right, I'm done with this!" The Captain spat. "Pilot, tell them we're coming in."

The pilot immediately opened up the airway.

"Coming around at 0.025 field. Clear to patrol to the tower."

We could all see on the monitor how fast the ship was moving towards the crater.

"No! No!" The tower came back hurriedly. "Hold your position! You will cause problems."

The pilot ignored the tower's orders.

"Coming around at 0.035 field."

He started flying and zigzagging around the crater very erratically. Luckily, the comms at the tower came over the speaker.

"Okay, you are clear to enter. Cue to enter."

The pilot brought us to an abrupt halt right in front of two stone-like doors, which were slowly sliding open. Then enormous flood lights shone over the ship. Were it not for the lights, we would have never seen the entrance. It was hidden inside a smaller crater, tucked in the side of the large crater. In addition to that, when the hangar doors were closed, they beamed a hologram over the entrance causing it to appear as dirt.

"Whoever built this entrance knew what they were doing," an officer spoke.

"Because the sun never shines in this area and the blackness obscures any hint of industry here."

The Captain turned to me.

"Well, you should probably make your way back to your station and conclude your report for the day. Keep up the good work. You are dismissed."

This was a sort of field trip for me. It was a reward to actually get to see what was going on outside and around the ship for once.

I honestly didn't want to leave the Bridge. Everybody had a strong working morale with the other, there was great coherency, and it was almost a fun environment. It was also the first time that I could actually see imagery of where we were, what the base entrance looked like, where we were docking—all things I'd never seen before. It was an eyeopener, for sure.

I headed back to my station to finish the day. As I walked back through the ship, I got to look out the windows during a docking for the first time. On a standard day, I wasn't allowed to access the parts of the ship with windows because I was busy with cargo. *I could freaking see out.*

Inside the hangar we'd entered, I could for the first time see all the action taking place around us. I saw huge ships with holes in them being repaired. I could see a metal worker welding the side. There were sparks flying out and dropping to the floor. I saw other ships, mounted on vast scaffolding, and parking bays thousands of feet wide. There really was an incredible industry going on.

I left immediately from work that day to head to Krums, where I told Marie everything that happened. I was so excited to share with her all of it. It's a funny reward, looking back, to get to see what you've been a part of for the first time. But it was an appropriate reward, and it had an impact on me.

17

THE PSYCHIC

My best estimate of my service aboard the Max Von Laue is that I was there from late 1997 to 1998.

It was within this time that I learned of a combat engagement between the Orion Group and some other unknown species. Being that our ship was a cargo and trade ship, we were considered lower tier than battleships. Most officers aspire to work their way up the ranks to become an officer on one of these kinds of battleships— everyone wants combat missions.

In this specific combat situation, we ran supplies for the combat fleet engagement, near the location of the Trapezium. The Trapezium is a star cluster in the Orion Nebula, which meant that we were covering vast distances of space for our shipments. To give one an idea of the magnitude of this point in space, you could hide a fleet within this area, and it would not be found for the next hundred years.

Our wages were increased, as was typical for combat cargo missions. We collected a lot of military cargo that was produced on Earth from Diego Garcia, the US Military base off the coast of Sri Lanka. We would then head back out into the Orion Nebula, drop the cargo into 'dead space' wherein it would simply float. Once we were gone, other ships would come by and take it.

In the beginning, I never actually saw the Trapezium itself, because we were amongst thousands of ships that had amassed there. But after a few days, only a handful of other ships remained in the area. When the ships cleared, the crew began talking about how much they could see. Before we left this designated area, we started requiring a confirmation from the Fleet that the cargo had been collected. This resulted in layover time. They didn't seem to rush to get back to us with this confirmation, and so this 'extra time' allowed us to wander up to the observation deck to sit at the windows and observe our vast surroundings.

There was an odd phenomenon that occurred. When officers took turns looking out the window to observe the Nebula, each one reported seeing different colors. One officer may see only blue or red, another may only see yellow and orange, and there were even other humanoid species on the ship that could see more than six or seven colors at one time. More often than not, however, most officers only saw grey. And some didn't see any color at all. I saw the majority of the nebula to be grey, with some hints of the color red — sometimes with shades of purple. In the distance, I observed a cluster of stars that were extremely far away. But to me, they seemed quite close by. It was beyond beautiful, and it's one of the experiences that has stayed with me. Those moments looking at the stars within the Trapezium.

At the time, I assumed that the war going on was a big deal. But I came to learn that it was just 'business as usual', and that wars like these are more common than one may think. Sometimes battleships would even be repaired and serviced on Ceres Colony, because of the space in the hangar.

Things eventually settled down with this war. Over the duration of it, I hadn't spent much time with Marie. Eventually, I got to Krums early one day, and by chance, hardly anyone was there.

I want to cover a few key conversations I had with Marie within this book because of the impact they've proved to have on my current life. We would talk about anything and everything. Marie and the girls who worked at Krums would mainly want to ask me about the Earth and the weather. They were *all* led to believe that the Earth had been destroyed. And all of them, not just Marie, talked about how much they missed the feel of the sun on their skins.

I, on the other hand, wanted to ask them about their lives working as sex slaves, being that I had my own experiences working on the fringes of the sex trafficking world. I was so curious about what they did, *who* they were with, the course of their days and how many partners they would be required to be with.

"We used to have to have a lot of sex when we were trafficked on Mars," Marie told me.

"But here, it was maybe once every two weeks, where someone would actually *pay* to want to have sex. Most people just want to watch us dance and have a few drinks."

My curiosity got the better of me and the questions were swarming in my brain.

"—Well what about ET's?" I wondered, "Do you have ET's coming in here for sex?"

Marie and Lynne looked at each other across the table.

"Yeah, we do," she answered.

"Well, what's that like?" I pressed on.

They looked at each other again. I could tell they were trying to slide their way out of answering this one, but I wasn't going to let up easily.

"So—what's it like? I mean, like, how many different ET's have you been with?"

"Well, it doesn't happen very often," Marie finally answered. "But it does happen."

"So, how are they?"

"Some are very good to be with," she said, still looking at Lynne, "and some are very bad. With specific species of ET, it tends to be more of a mental connection, rather than a physical."

I immediately thought of one specific grey race that didn't have any kind of genitalia.

"So what about that group of grey's that have been here?" I asked, "The ones without genitalia?"

Marie smiled. "Oh, we manage. To them, they are more after the mental experience. It can actually be really beautiful with them."

Well that piqued my curiosity.

"But there is a group of ET's that have come through Ceres Colony that have mentally damaged some of the girls that they've had sex with," Marie pointed out.

I glanced at her. "How so?"

"First of all, they have to pay *a lot* more money to be with the girls, because they can make them go mad. I have been with one of them. So what happens, due to a part of their mating process, is that they imprint on the female they are having sex with that they will come back for her," Marie told me.

"So the girls, as a result, would become fixated on this ET, obsessively thinking they will *come back for them,* and they are utterly consumed by this salient fact, to the point that it literally makes them insane. It happened to me with one of them. I started thinking about him all the time, that he was gonna come back for me. I wasn't that bad though."

"—No, you were *really* bad," Lynne interjected, her eyes wide at Marie.

"Okay, so maybe I was," Marie replied, "But he did come back for me, and released me from this imprinted thought. Then I was free of him. But I've also had a bad experience with a Reptilian," she continued on.

"He wasn't supposed to touch, but he did and he forced himself onto me. It was awful."

She was actually injured badly by this experience. His penis was barbed and he beat her during their time together. She was taken to the hospital. This kind of treatment was not allowed, but this guy got away with it and left the planet for good.

"But other times, other ET's would come, and would want to simply have us as an escort," Lynne said, "And they'd basically sit and ask us a bunch of questions, our only job being to look pretty."

"Oh, I love when those types of ET's come," Marie said. "We all love these kinds of jobs. Sometimes they would take us shopping to buy new clothes. It's nice."

For the most part, I was totally fine with her doing her job and being with customers, but it was when she wouldn't tell me about certain encounters she had experienced, or something I knew she was keeping from me, that I would become jealous. Mostly though, she was good about sharing things. We both lived vicariously through each other—her's being a very sexualized experience, and mine, more like a voyager's experience. This was one of the main reasons why I loved Marie so much, we had such transparent communication with one another—more than any other human I'd encountered before, or since. I looked forward to nothing more than spending hours upon hours talking with her.

There was one specific event when the Ceres Colony was in talks of negotiating a trade deal with an important ET species, and hundreds of them came to visit. It was such an important deal, that the top echelons had ordered every business to accommodate them. This included offering them specific food, replicating their styles, and even playing their music.

During this trade negotiation, I went into Krums to hear them playing the music that was from this other species. It was certainly not the style of music that we were used to. It was horrendous to say the least—it was squelchy, screeching, barely organized music— more like painful noise than anything else.

I look over at the girls dumbfounded. "How can you even *dance* to this?" I asked them incredulously.

Every few songs or so, they were required to get up and dance—even to this *music*.

"We hate it!" Lynne voiced. "But what can we do?"

When Marie got up and danced, it was funny because she just did her same dance she always did, and it somehow worked. We all smiled because she still, in an absurd moment, found a way to look amazingly cool.

Marie and Lynne had just returned from the shopping mall. They were in a good mood and not that bothered by the disruptive "music." A huge mall had just been completed across from the red light district, and it had everything a woman could possibly want.

"It's the only time we get to dress up without having to look slutty," Marie said. "But we still have to go with our chaperone who keeps an eye on us."

She smiled at me. "Why don't you go and check it out sometime?"

I thought about it. *Why not?*

So, I went. I wanted to see a part of her life that was not based at Krums. To get there, I had to walk through a dank, dark tunnel—a couple of kilometers in length, and it was full of trash, dripping water, and water drains that were seemingly not in use. It was a scary place. At the end of the tunnel, there was a water reservoir with its own gravity. As I passed it, I came to an enormous cavern—hundreds of feet tall with a blue sky painted on top. Pillars littered this cavern, and there were shops carved out of stone in between the pillars. I took a look around, bought a soda-pop, and then returned back through the tunnel.

There was always plenty of construction going on around Ceres, and rumor had it that another area similar to this shopping center was being built, but with a moving sky.

Marie and Lynne were the focal point of my more memorable times of the twenty year program. We spent countless hours talking together, sharing the spiritual aspects of our journeys, and discussing how special it was that we surreptitiously all came together. We talked about how much time we had already done with the program, and wondered if we would remember any of it once we had completed it.

"Well, for what it's worth," Marie began, "I wanna double shot, of whatever it is they give us to forget all this because I don't want to remember any of it. I know being this—this woman of this kind of sex life, is not in my character on the outside. I feel it. This is not me."

I thought about it.

"Well, don't you wanna remember me?" I said to Marie, looking at her. "I want us to be together!"

"I want to remember you," she said, "But I don't want to remember all of *this*."

"Well I want to remember," Lynne chimed in. "I feel open to remembering this experience."

One day, I took a different route through the hangar to avoid an overcrowded train stop. I was used to being pushed and kicked to the end of the line, and today I wanted to try a different stop. As I was walking through the hangar, I noticed a shopfront with a video playing—it was a woman attached to an IV bag, doing psychic readings.

"Peer into your future. Get your reading today," it displayed.

I was totally curious as I walked by.

At the next morning's mission briefing, I asked some of the guys about the psychics.

"Ah, don't bother yourself with that crap—it's all fake," one of them said, dismissing it completely.

But I knew better, I knew it was real, because that is what happened to me when I was in Peru. I was put on an IV, and went into the subconscious, and revealed expanded information to others about their destinies.

As fate would have it, about a week later, we had a huge trade deal go through. Every paid officer got a bonus in their salary—including me. It was something like F80 in bonus pay, and so for the week, I got F100 Francs. I took F40 of that, and excitedly, made my way to the shop with the psychic readings. I had to find out what it was like to be on the other side of the readings, and what information would be given.

When I went inside, it was one of the shadiest shop setups I had ever seen. One of the taller ET's was in charge—I think he was the same race as Krums. It was basically a room with tables covered in sheets. The girls weren't human—they were like hybrids, with straggling hair, balding heads, it was awful. They were more like greys in appearance than humans, and must have only been nine or ten years old.

"You get three questions," the gray towered over me.

"You want more, you gotta pay."

So I went to one of the girls and started my reading.

"Why am I here?" I asked her.

She gave me a weird response that I can't remember.

"Well, am I gonna end up with the one I love?" I asked again.

She opened her mouth. "You are the witness...and there are three loves...and you'll see one, but it won't stay. You'll find her back in the world, but you are to be the witness. You will remember your life."

It was very cryptic, but I took it as a sign. I knew I only had one more question to ask. I asked if I would get promoted, and how? Her answer was complete nonsense and looking back now, it was just a polite way of saying no without creating in me a placebo effect that would sabotage any effort I might put into receiving a promotion.

After the psychic reading with the hybrid girl, I was super excited and went earlier than expected to Krums. I couldn't wait to tell Marie! I waited there for hours until her shift started that evening. When I eventually did see her, I could tell straight away that she wasn't in a good mood.

"Hey," she said flatly, giving me a kiss.

"You gotta listen to this!" I spluttered excitedly, "I had a psychic reading! I bought one, near a shop that I found walking to a new station. Listen, the psychic told me that I've got three loves, and that I'll remember one, and that I will be a witness and remember all this, and that I've got some kind of destiny—"

"—Wait a minute," Marie interrupted my haste, "you *bought* one? Those are fake—totally fake!"

"No!" I disagreed.

"Well, how much did it cost?"

"Uh, like F40."

I could see her face changing immediately.

"You're supposed to be saving that money so we can be together! Are you crazy? That was for us to be with each other one last time!"

She went on, totally livid.

"But you know, I had to hear this!" I protested. "I wanted to know my destiny!"

"—Don't you love me?" she questioned. "I thought you wanted us to be together! I can't believe this!"

Nothing I said could calm her down.

"Look, I gotta go do my rounds."

She walked off and left me there at the tables for at least a couple of hours, playing sour grapes. When she came back, I could sense how she felt and how disappointed she was, but I didn't regret getting the reading. It was profound to me, and meant more than she could know. I empathized with those psychic girls hooked up on IV bags, because that was me—I knew how that felt. I knew how that was.

A few days later, the psychic shop had packed up. The lease had run out and everything was packed up. Just like that, the psychic readings were over.

During one of the morning briefings with my crew, the Captain pulled me aside and started in on one of our sometimes sporadic conversations.

"So, how are you?" he would ask. "How's things going down there? I haven't been keeping my eye on you lately, but often wonder how you are. You know, I always remember your bravery and what you've been through, and had it been other circumstances, for what you did, you would be accepted into my religion."

I had learned over the course of my service on the Max Von Laue that nearly every ship captain was a member of his secret fraternity. But, like our Captain, they all kept it a secret because of the ban on religion.

We kept talking.

"Well, you know, I've gotta ask you something," I began, "I went and had one of those psychic readings, and the psychic told me that I was going to remember everything from here."

"You're not *allowed* to remember your time up here," the Captain responded.

"You are not of the kind that is going to remember what you have experienced. And if you do, the consequences of what you remember will be severe.

They may even kill you first and not even slip you back into your earth body."

I was curious. "Well—how will they know?"

"Don't worry about that. It's more complicated than you think."

"Well, I'm gonna remember it!" I said to him, "I'm in love. I want to remember it."

The Captain looked concerned.

"Well, are you planning on going back to have another reading? I would not recommend it."

"No, no—they've packed up. Gone."

"Good. Better for you then," the Captain nodded.

"And don't be telling anyone else about the psychic's prediction that you'll remember your time up here. It's dangerous information. It could draw unwanted repercussions. Keep it quiet."

"Yes sir."

18

THE RAT WORLD

One day at the morning briefing, there was an officer mix-up. I watched an officer, unknown to me, sit down two seats to my right.

"So," the Captain began, "we have some changes today."

It was odd, because usually the majority of the meeting was first done in German, and then the translator would turn on and facilitate multi-languages. This particular morning, however, it was different. The translator was turned on immediately.

"Kronig here is now the Korvetten Captain. He has volunteered for reconditioning duties, to become a negotiations officer."

We looked at this Kronig person, sitting there to my right, smiling.

"I've already done some training, and I'm going to be really good at this," he assured.

The Captain then went on to read his report from his file, and right from the get-go, we could assume quite comfortably, that this guy had baseline sociopathic tendencies, so he was perfect for this role. Negotiations officers were nuts.

Kronig had gone as far as to receive trauma-based mind control training to enhance his 'negotiating abilities.' Which to me was pretty much enhancing these sociopathic traits, and I would even go as far as to say psychopathic tendencies.

This way, when he encountered certain other ET races, he would have no empathy, nor harbor any kind of remorse. Some of the ET races we encountered were, in fact, very aggressive to deal with. Kronig would go in without a tinge of fear. It seemed to me that some bad deals had gone down in the past, and they didn't want the same mistakes to happen again. So it was decided that Kronig was the perfect fit. I will never forget that bastard, either. He absolutely hated my guts.

Not even three days had passed, and I'd already had my first encounter with Kronig. There was a morning mission briefing, and the team needed to know the available space within the cargo bay.

"We have a huge load booked, and I need to know exactly how much space is available," Kronig advised me.

"We have six hundred and thirty-eight cubic meters," I answered him.

"Come on—you gotta do better than that." Kronig retorted.

"I can't. That is all we have. That's it."

"I know how this goes," Kronig mocked.

"You guys always exaggerate your numbers so that if something happens, you have just enough extra space. A margin of error—in case there is a mistake! I know you guys do this—but I need you to fit more in there!"

"There are six hundred and thirty-eight cubic meters, and I haven't changed the number at all." I was adamant.

I could see Kronig getting pissed with me, and quickly.

"I guarantee he's got more space," he spat.

"I guarantee he's got more than what he is letting on."

The Captain turned to me.

"So how many cubic meters are in the cargo bay?"

"I guarantee there's more!" Kronig went on, speaking above everyone else at the table.

"—Okay," an officer interrupted.

"Gerostet, this is your job today—you need to go and re-tally your numbers and as of *this* moment, give us the exact correct numbers on the space available in the cargo bay. Report to us tomorrow morning."

The following day, the exact same number of six hundred and thirty-eight cubic meters came back in my report. And, as a result, the officers erupted into laughter at Kronig. Because of this, because of all the laughing and taunting that he was wrong, he absolutely despised me. It made it even worse because I was a slave. He took every opportunity to make my life miserable. It was another bully situation unfolding, and it was only going to get worse over time.

One particular morning briefing, I learned that we were undertaking a special mission, of what would be called a "first contact" meeting, with a new ET species. Again in this meeting, my translating implant was turned on from the very beginning, and the Captain focused his attention on me.

"You're going to be going on this mission. You have been chosen, as you've been doing an excellent job with your duties. We're now advising you on the specifics, and will continue to do so, over the course of a week or so."

So what I came to learn was this: they were planning to sneak into a far away planet, somewhere in our galaxy—a planet that was very much like Earth, predominantly a watery planet, and the inhabitants had evolved from what we would typically know as a *rat*. They stood approximately 3-4 feet in height, had the physical traits to that of a rat, but had a humanoid looking face.

These inhabitants were still unaware of other ET existence, let alone our presence, as most had been kept in the dark. The species was yet to discover life elsewhere in the cosmos. They had very similar governmental structures as the earth, wherein they were withholding information about life beyond their planet, as well as being behind in technology. They were like an entire world still in the 1960's on Earth.

So since this was a stealth mission, we had to go to lengths to keep our presence discreet. The ship would come in from space to their ocean that was uninhabited because it was full of poisonous chemicals. We would fly to a place in the ocean near a base and take a hovercraft in to meet with them.

The hovercraft we would need for the trip to their base would need to be cut in half, reduced by ten feet, then welded back together in order to fit within the C Cargo Bay. Two US Navy personnel from Earth had volunteered for the hovercraft reconfiguration mission and then agreed to have their memories erased upon completion of the mission. One was a mechanic, and the other was a pilot who knew how to operate the craft. In return, these personnel would receive some type of compensation—like a promotion or something along the lines.

Over the days leading up to the mission, the back cargo bay was totally emptied—floors lowered, walls dropped, sample packs all cleared out. The packs were either moved into my cargo bay or stored at a facility composed of ice, located in the Kuiper Belt. We had created one huge cargo bay, large enough to fit the hovercraft.

Two days before the mission, I was given a wrist watch.

"Time is of the essence," the Korvetten Captain advised me.

"If you don't make it back in time, the mission will be scrubbed."

Because we had to get that hovercraft off the ship in the sea of this planet, and then ride it for some great distance to land, there were the issues of time-space distortions. Weather that could slow us down, along with a few other variables. Many considerations had to be made, and a lot needed to go as planned, in order to bring us back into our correct time-space. The Captain was gravely concerned about everyone onboard this mission keeping precise time, so everyone was given a watch—I was given a basic Casio G-Shock.

"So what kind of watch do you have?" I asked the Korvetten Captain.

He smiled at me. "I have an OMEGA. You wouldn't believe how much this watch is worth."

I later learned that the Captain had a passion for fine watches, but at that time, I knew nothing about designer watches.

"But that's not important," the Korvetten Captain said.

"We must, at all costs, keep our timing impeccable."

That G-Shock was special to me. Later that night, I put it neatly in the only drawer of my room—and felt proud. I had never owned a single possession, never even had anything in that drawer except for paperwork on one occasion. Even though I had to return the watch after the mission was complete, for a few nights I got to at least feel what it was like to own something. It was a great feeling. I remember waking up the next morning before the buzzer and grabbing the watch. I started to look through it to see if it had any games or online access, but it was pretty disappointing. I was happy to have it. But I knew from things that I'd seen that there were other devices that I would enjoy more than this simple thing.

When the time came, we went to Diego Garcia to pick up the LCAC—that was the official name of the hovercraft. It looked like an airboat, or something you'd see a Louisiana swamp person cruise around on. It was lifted with enormous cranes into the rear main Cargo Bay C. The logistics of actually getting it on board our ship seemed to be a nightmare to us. We had been speculating how the loading would happen. We couldn't vortex it onto the ship because of its size.

When the loading began, there was a thirty minute delay, and we started to worry that something had gone terribly wrong. The cargo crew laughed about a bunch of different possible scenarios. We had to stay at our post and couldn't watch. When I got a chance later, I asked one of the guys from C Bay, and he said it was nothing to see. It was a little tricky and some box fell off that wasn't secured the way it was supposed to be. That was the reason for the delay. But it was otherwise routine.

Once done, we left Earth, and began our mission. I was excited by this mission.It felt like a luxury to be on a mission that did not require drugs beforehand, nor be classified as high risk. I was going to be a participating member of a command crew mission. This was a first in many ways.

Once we arrived on the planet far away from our Solar System, we went to work straightaway. It was the middle of the night, and the hovercraft, along with nine of us, were lifted off the ship by cranes and lowered into the water. They other guys and I actually rode the spider down onto the craft.

I was hoping I would see the stars of this new planet, or perhaps something amazing, like five moons or star constellations unknown to us, but unfortunately, it was a misty, cloudy night. The smell of the ocean water stood out. It was like a combination of our Earth ocean smell and a large swamp smell. It wasn't pleasant. Not unbearable, but you couldn't ignore it. I felt immediate freedom thrashing through the open seas aboard the hovercraft. We were told not to go too close to the front of the hovercraft, to stay behind the gate, and so I did. I struck up a conversation with the US Navy officer.

"What's it like?" I asked, "You know, to elect to do this? And then have your memory erased?"

"I had to do it," he said.

"I had to know what it was like. It was totally worth the choice. I needed to have this experience—even at the expense of not remembering it after. I hate those Germans hazing us though. Not much we can do about it now."

I knew all about the hazing.

I'm speculating, but I would say the time-period of this event was around 1997. The soldier mentioned that they couldn't get enough of these hovercrafts. He wished he could start a business because he knew the US Army was being overcharged for them.

"Well, they are kinda neat, almost as if we're flying," I replied.

"They're just way too loud."

We stopped half way as the environment went from ocean to swamp. It became very marshy, kind of like the Everglades. There were lots of dead trees sticking up through the water.   And it was getting very shallow.

"Don't fall into the water!" An officer called out.

"Fall in and it's certain death."

The ocean was full of poisonous, noxious chemicals, so we had to be extra vigilant. We weren't given suits or any kind of protective gear. The trees resembled Earth-like trees, except they were dead. They had webbing all over them, like a type of gossamer. Every now and then, we would come across a tree that was alive with amber-green, spiraling leaves—but those were few and far between. Nothing looked healthy.

The ride inland took us about forty-five minutes—I made sure I timed it. The crew took a lot more time than expected to unload the hovercraft, and we were all worried that it would take even longer to load it all back onboard. We remained concerned that the mission would be scrubbed—and we all knew how important this mission was.

There was a political or military motivation associated with this mission, and we all knew it was a big deal, despite not being briefed on the full details. It had something to do with the Orions and Dracos surrounding Jupiter, and this mission was somehow tied in with it all.

When we finally landed, we disembarked on a beach covered in leaves, surrounded by tall grass, very tough and stringy. We were trudging through the leaves when *he* came into view. This rat humanoid—the first I had ever seen, wearing a type of military uniform. It was very old fashioned—as if it were made of burlap or something. He looked more like a janitor than an officer, and the translating device was set up in a way that made his language, whatever dialect he spoke, confusing. He had an accent, and his words were a little discombobulated, but nevertheless, he was immensely polite. He told us his name was Gradial.

"You men wait right here," Gradial said.

"I'm going to come back in a moment."

The officers around were quick to make jokes about Gradial, purely because of his accent and broken speech—which I thought was immature. It was more likely that our translators weren't prepared for his language than Gradial being deficient in some way.

Gradial returned in a type of flatbed truck, missing the front, but otherwise just like one of our trucks from Earth. He drove us to a camp, outside of a hut-looking dwelling. It could have maybe ten to fifteen people. There were also a couple of tents around, as well as black shipping containers. They were about eight feet tall, scattered amongst smaller barrels laying around.

Kronig stepped forward.

"I need a word with you," he said to Gradial.

Then the two of them walked off, in discussion. The Captain watched on. A few moments later, the

Captain looked over at me. He started in my direction. Another officer handed me a device.

"You know how to use that thing?" he asked, looking down at a lazering device I'd been given.

"I'm not actually sure, sir. I've never used one before," I replied.

"All the software is preloaded," he assured.

"All you need to do is point the device at the cargo, and that's it. It will record the length, width, and height. Gradial will tell us the weight, and then all you need to do is calculate how much we can take back onboard the ship."

I eventually came up with the numbers, and my job was done in five minutes flat. The whole week prior to this mission that I'd spent preparing was for this duty only.

Two hundred of the shipping container boxes could fit aboard our ship, and Gradial had about twenty-four hundred of them. Inside the containers was a rare raw material—very hard to get. Gradial and his associates were doing this transaction purely to get rich, they didn't want to trade for technology or anything else. They wanted to be personally wealthy.

I was able to speak with Gradial several times. He came onboard the ship and we spoke. I liked the guy —he was neat, and had a humor about him. He seemed to be just like us, except that he was part rodent.

We got off the planet quickly. We loaded up our cargo, got the hovercraft back on, and actually made it back into our temporal time-space bubble on time to Ceres Colony.

I later learned just how badly the American Navy officers were picked on by the Deutsche crew. They would walk by, smack their groins, then tell them to shut the fuck up if they had a problem with it. Many times they would spit on the two guys.

"They may forget their mission, but they'll never forget how back they got with us," one officer bragged.

That multimillion dollar LCAC hovercraft was never used again, and it wasn't even returned to Diego Garcia—it was kept out at Ceres Colony.

I learned on the ride back to the ship that it was all a front. We were on behalf of the Orion group to scope out their world for a future form of invasion. We were pretending to be friendly. I don't know what was done with the material in the crates. Nobody seemed to actually care about it. Gradial had given it as a free sample in hopes of future purchases.

I was so eager to go and tell Marie what had happened and where I had been, but when I turned up at Krums, it was being remodeled. And an entirely new train route was being built nearby.

It took less than two weeks for the entire remodeling to be complete at Krums. Everything had changed—the tables, the foyer, the microgravity artwork, the stage areas, fancy oak wood panelling—it was nice. The tables were actually made taller in size because so many ET's complained about how small the 'human size' tables were. The new ones were sleek. They were made of a   glass-like material that couldn't be scratched or broken.

Finally, I saw Marie. It was as if no time had passed. We had missed each other over those few weeks, and once we were back together, we picked up from where we left off. She wanted to hear about everything, and as I spoke to her about our last mission to the far-away planet and the encounter with Gradial, I could see her thoughts turn towards one thing.

"Did you see the sun?" She asked me.

"Was the sun out when you got to that planet?"

"No!" I laughed.

"It was dark."

"Well, I mean could you see the sky?" she pressed eagerly.

"No, it was cloudy."

"Well, next time you see the sun," she said, "Let me know about that!"

It had been so many years since Marie had felt the sun on her skin, one couldn't blame her for the persistent questioning.

A few weeks after the Krums remodel, I learned that the Ceres Colony had installed the first of the 'moving sky' ceilings. Ceres Colony is a place of huge caverns, so for the first time, there was going to be a moving sky that would be blue with clouds, and mimic the sunrise and sunset from that of Earth. It was only in one area at the time, but eventually, all the caverns would be covered in the moving sky.

The first time I saw the moving sky, I wasn't overly impressed. It was not as high or bright as the initial painted one. They had it lowered, in order for the transportation above the sky to move freely along.

Airborne taxis would use the space above the sky to travel through the cavern. This was around 1998.

19

KRONIG'S REVENGE

Many of our trips had great cosmic scenery. If we were traversing throughout space, the officers started opening the windows to let us see where we were. At the end of the C Deck, there was an observation window that could be turned on or off. Sometimes it was fully transparent, and sometimes it was fully opaque, set to match the colors of the adjacent walls of the ship.

I was still with my routine of going up around 11:00am, and I started to get in trouble for sitting on the toilet too long again.

Officer Kronig, who already hated me and was determined to make my life hell, would bring this up in the morning meetings.

"Just hurry up and get your business finished quicker," was the answer from the Superiors.

But Kronig would keep bringing this up. "I think he needs reconditioning," he suggested adamantly.

Thankfully everybody laughed this off.

"We hardly think he needs reconditioning for taking too long to use the bathroom," a superior noted.

We kept such a tight time schedule and were usually designated to be at our stations. But sometimes, if the scenery was majestically beautiful, we were permitted, without penalty, to go and observe at the windows. There was a time when our ship was headed to Ganymede and we passed a moon called Enceladus where hundreds of geysers were erupting. After the ship flew through the geysers, it was all anybody talked about for the next few weeks afterward. Ganymede is a moon of Jupiter, and Enceladus is a moon of Saturn. There was an inhabited planet near Ganymede, but the Germans were not permitted to visit or make contact with it.

Everyone boasted about how beautiful the geysers were, and that it was a once in a lifetime opportunity. Unfortunately, I never saw the geysers, as I chose to stay at my station. "Well, that was the dumbest thing ever!" one colleague said of my choice. "You'll never see anything more beautiful again!"

It was a battle for me to take a leap sometimes and do something different, even when I really wanted to.

Several months later, the geyser on Ceres Colony erupted inside the Occator crater. This time, I decided I would get out of my comfort zone and go and have a look. The main observation window was crammed with officers, so I couldn't see it there. But I knew a smaller porthole window. There were two other people there—one of them was a ranking Deutsche officer, that I had never seen in the meetings, donning the full uniform, hat and all.

It was an incredible sight. This geyser was spraying water over ten kilometers into the vacuum of space around it. The water would evaporate before reaching the surface, and left the remnants of what appeared to be snow in the air. It would funnel down in a type of 'cone-like' formation. This "snow" was actually salt with a little magnesium, and piles and piles of it were left all around this geyser. It was beautiful. The geyser was surrounded by mountains, and it all looked like it was part of a grey desert.

"There's gotta be something we can do with all that mineral" I said, pondering out the porthole beside the officer.

"Like what?" he retorted.

"Why don't you go out there without your suit and take a nice bath in it."

He was rude to me because he knew that I was a slave. But I've never forgotten how beautiful that experience was.

I was assigned on another mission, to another new planet, which actually wasn't that far away from our solar system. It was inhabited by a new species that we had not yet made contact with. We made the first initial contact, and all was fine, but then when we went back again, there was some type of glitch with the time-space temporal and the ship *jumped* too far away from the planet.

The progress officer came up to me.

"What's going on?" I asked.

"You're not gonna believe what's happened—the whole solar system has been quarantined!"

I was flabbergasted.

"How's that even possible? How much power would that take to even do something like *that?*"

He shoved the glass i-pad device he had in his hands in front of me.

"Take a look at this."

It was a graphic of a type of wire grid that was placed around the entire solar system. No way in and no way out. Other ships had tried to enter and found that they could not, and began making circles around the system. Some advanced species, more likely in charge of this sector of space, had performed this restriction. None of the super advanced species that we encountered during my twenty year term were ever human, though there were more advanced humans than us.

"So how much power would that even take? Who has that kind of power?" I stammered.

He never gave me any answers.

Everything in the cosmos, or at least from my perspective being on Ceres Colony, was about power.

I went and told Marie about this latest situation and she seemed less than impressed.

"You gotta try and get off of these away missions so we can be together more."

"Well, I gotta get promoted!" I replied. "That's the only way I can get off of these missions."

"I'm worried about you dying on these things," she expressed with concern.

"You're just a filler for them! You are too expendable."

I knew she was right. I requested this from my superiors, that I be removed from so many high risk missions. I was advised that I had one more high risk mission and I could then be taken off the list. And that's what happened.

I did one more away mission, and this time we went to an oil planet—a planet, whose main industry focused on oil and refinement. It was a reptoid or reptilian race. Rumor had it that their oil had a potency five hundred times that of Earth oil, which was attractive to Ceres Colony. We had a lot of training for this mission, and the objective was to try and reverse engineer their refining process, so that we could potentially synthesize our own.

We made use of a ship that was a 'double disc' craft. It was your expected UFO disc shape craft, but it had another exactly the same underneath it. This was the craft chosen to get there. It was a heavy-gravity, desert-like planet with dark blue skies, purple in the evening, and we went there and lifted countless barrels of oil—we stole it. And then we left. They were never able to replicate the process.

So that was the last mission away, and I settled into life on Ceres, taking no more away missions. It was nice—I got into a good routine, spent more time with Marie, and things were relatively comfortable. I had even made some friends, one friend in particular—a short and skinny Italian guy who was quite abrasive in character. He would always speak to us in Italian, calling us bad names. We would corner him on his way out and insist he repeated what he was saying, because the translators kicked in right near the exit doors.

"I was calling you a dumb cock-sucker," he'd say in jest.

It was funny, but there was something serious about it. Like he meant it, and he was angry, but he was so consistently that way that we learned to not take it too seriously. He was a unique character that I remember fondly. He was fun to me.

Things with Kronig went from bad to worse. He really had a vendetta against me and was adamant about making my life hell.

"I'm watching you," he would tell me. "I've always got eyes on you!"

He would take any opportunity that he could find to get me into trouble or try to make me slip up. Sometimes it was *he* who would get a ribbing from the other officers. Then something really bad happened.

It was a Friday and we had a short day at work.

"What are you gonna do later, Gerry?" an officer asked me as all sat around the table for the morning's briefing.

Gerry was my nickname, shortened from Gerostet, pronounced like 'Jerry' .

"Today's mission is cancelled, you got some easy time up your sleeve."

It was very lighthearted. I moved around towards a friend of mine from Cargo Bay.

"So, Gerry—what are you doing?" the officer asked again.

"He's gonna go and see his girlfriend!" my friend interjected.

Everyone started laughing around the table. Kronig was there. He was the last person I wanted to know that I had a girlfriend.

"Is this true?" an officer asked with a smile.

"Yes it is," I answered.

"—Oh and she's the most beautiful one there!" my friend went on.

I was feeling increasingly uncomfortable. When the meeting broke up, Kronig looked at me.

"Maybe I'll see you later," he said, looking smug.

I knew right then, something bad was going to go down.

It was payday. I went immediately to the trade window and got my pay and got on the overcrowded morning train. It was rush hour. If the train was full, I would be taken off, and would have to wait for the next one—and if that one was full, I would be taken off again, and this went on all morning. I finally got to stay on the third train.

By this time, a new military train line had been completed and was in full use. It would get me anywhere much faster than the civilian train line. But I wasn't allowed on it. I actually took a longer, cheaper route to Marie on a train that took more stops.

By the time I finally got to the red light district that day, it was already early evening. I walked in and Lynne greeted me.

"You're gonna want to sit down," she said to me soberly.

"Where's Marie?" I looked at her.

I could feel it. It was something very bad.

"What's going on? Tell her I'm here!"

She got up and left. Then Kronig walked up to me.

"Hey, I met your girlfriend," he smirked. "She's not that great looking! Especially not now."

He rubbed his stomach.

"Boy, my stomach is sure upset from all that."

He laughed and walked away. I had no idea what he meant by it.

About twenty minutes later, Marie finally came out. Her hair was wet from the shower. I knew something bad had just happened to her. She sat down, wouldn't look at me, didn't want to touch me—nothing.

"Are you okay?" I looked at her, trying to console her.

"What happened to you? What did he do to you?"

"I don't want to talk about it," she said in a small quiet voice.

I glared at her with her pained face, her wet hair around her shoulders. I was desperate to find out, but didn't push it. We just sat there the rest of the night and she was told by Krum that she could have thirty minutes in between rounds. We talked very little and I just sat with my arm around her.

She just kept saying "I hate this place," over and over. When she had to get up for a round after a few hours, she told me, "You should probably get going, come and see me tomorrow"

I have never felt so responsible for someone suffering than I did on the train ride home that night. I just had no way to process it. I had never been in a position to hurt someone, yet here it was. The brightest and happiest person I'd ever known had been devastated and it was by someone that really just wanted to hurt me. I couldn't believe that someone could be that cruel to someone so beautiful as Marie. After everything I'd been through to this point, I was still shocked by a new low—worse than anything I could have ever imagined.

I don't know what Kronig did, but he was a senior officer and had authority over local businesses. This meant he could do whatever he liked at Krums, and there were no rules with Marie. And she had to do whatever he said. She refused to tell me what went down, but she was fucked up by it.

I anticipated more terrible things would happen the next morning at the mission brief. But he was normal, and everything went normal. He slipped in one remark towards the end, when the translators were on and I could understand him.

"Yeah, I'm looking forward to an easier day. I had a rough night."

He didn't look at me, but he said it *to* me.

The next few weeks were hard with Marie. She had begun to see me as a real threat. She maintained that she loved me, she started to really coach me on keeping my mouth shut and telling no one that I visited her, or Krums, or even the red light district. She was right. I really never totally let go of my guilt for what I had caused.

Over time, we were able to put it behind us. It turned it into a reason to be closer. She let me start consoling her. She was the kind of woman that made the choice to process things and look for the positive—and she handled this experience, dealt with it.

A thing that really should have torn us apart, only made us closer. I thought at the time that it was just an easy effect of loving someone, but life since then has shown me that this isn't always the case. Weaker relationships would have failed, and they did for me. Not everyone has the strength of Marie—to handle a trauma with her determination towards optimism.

20

THE CAVALIER

Kronig continued to make his point. He had an eye on my every move and I needed to watch my step.

"Someone in your position shouldn't be so arrogant." he would sputter.

I hated him for what he'd done to Marie. I would glare at him when he wasn't looking at me, and in my mind, I would dismantle him. It was the worst feeling knowing there was nothing I could actually do to him. But the feeling of hate I had towards him was enormous. I would think back to Peru and things I had learned from Manuel about how what comes around goes around.

Kronig was a relentless force. Over time, I could feel the other officers beginning to side with Kronig's opinion of me.

I learned that a study of me was being conducted— everything about my entire life in Ceres Colony was under heavy scrutiny.

"We can even hear your thoughts," Kronig once taunted me.

A few weeks later, at the morning's mission briefing, Kronig presented my study file.

"On the grounds of this study report, Gerostet is displaying cavalier behavior. Therefore, I am recommending he undergo *reconditioning*."

"No," the Captain was adamant in protest.

"I do not support it."

Then the first officer jumped in.

"Don't even stick up for him this time," he retorted.

"Kronig's got plenty of information on the table to support this case."

The Captain was visibly upset.

"I'm the one that will determine the production of my crew."

Kronig reread the report.

"It is determined that this unit has cavalier tendencies and is recommended for reconditioning."

They began to talk over each other.

"I am the one that determines the policy of my crew," the Captain demanded, yet again.

"Stop trying to protect your lap dog. He's begun to slip into singular thinking and any other unit would have been reconditioned long ago"

The Captain responded, "His performance is well above expectation and I will not have it stunted by these procedures."

Others began to chime in, everyone speaking loudly.

"He's not special."

"You're going to have a stain on your record by defending a slave to this degree."

Kronig began to yell and the Captain spoke even louder.

"He has become cavalier and will be reconditioned."

"This is not your ship, you are a trade officer and will not dictate my…"

Kronig stood and shoved his chair out behind him.

"He has become cavalier!"

Another officer said in horror, "Stop what you're doing."

"HE HAS BECOME CAVALIER!" Kronig demanded.

Everyone froze. You could heat a pin drop. I had started out proud that the captain was defending me, but now I just wanted this whole thing to stop. I blamed myself for this huge disruption.

Truthfully, I still had no idea what I had done wrong. I didn't really know what cavalier behavior meant, but I could take a guess. I believe it was because I was enjoying my life. I had started to have fun joking with everyone all the time, even officers. And I guess I had a little hop in my step the days after I had quality time with Marie. Love will do that. I thought it was ok to behave like that, because I had seen so many others like me getting along the same way. It seemed like it helped production.

But they didn't have a Kronig breathing down their necks, I suppose, and they probably knew when to put the fun on a shelf. I think in many ways, I still don't know when to pipe down.

Kronig collected himself and the Captain looked away, disgusted.

"He will be reconditioned, effective immediately. The report will provide results and a three day observation period after, along with a monthly probationary assessment, made by the Captain."

What Kronig had presented was considered conclusive proof that I needed reconditioning. The Captain's efforts were futile and he knew it.

They went to the next order of business and finished the morning briefing. The Captain acted as if nothing out of the ordinary had happened. We all went on about our day.

Later that day when the mission was over and we had docked, I was escorted to a doctor. I had the feeling of dread all day. and it was all too real and too soon. It was a tiny office in the school area. There was an older, heavier set doctor. He looked at me with disgust at first. He told me to come in and do exactly as I was told. First order was to sit down, which he reinforced with a split second shock on my collar— just to let me know he could. I told him I was nervous but that I would cooperate. His demeanor changed when I said that, and he seemed to let down his guard.

"Well, I can see what you did to get in here. I have the report. You're barely someone that requires this"

I asked him, "Do you do this a lot?"

He laughed and shook his head yes.

"Some slaves are just criminals and the tendencies keep coming back after many sessions. There's no cure for personality defects on a generational, genetic level. We don't exactly acquire slaves like you from the cream of the crop."

I wanted to keep asking questions to try and delay what was about to happen, but nothing came to mind. I was terrified. I knew that there was no chance of this not being extremely unpleasant. Otherwise the Captain would not have made such a commotion.

I was strapped down to a table where he shaved my head, covered me in ECG-type electrodes, injected me with who knows what, and then placed a movie screen in front of me. Once the screen started playing, needles were stuck into me through the electrodes. I was receiving electric shocks continually. The screen was showing static mostly, but every now and then, imagery of insects eating people and crawling all over them came on. Gory, sickening images.

After a while, I could *feel* the insects on me and I would kind of cave. There was a threshold where I couldn't take it anymore, but I was powerless to stop it. I would break to the point of complete surrender, just like the cage in Inyokern when I completely gave up. And it would just keep going. It started to not hurt, but instead feel like a dream. At that point it would stop. He would check my eyes and sometimes wipe my face clean of the snot and tears. And then start it all over again. It would take me less and less time to get to the breaking point, but it was just as horrible to cross that line each time.

The sessions lasted for about six hours and I had two or three sessions in a row that week. I went back to my room each night and was not required to report for duty until the process was over. Just back to the Doctor's office each morning. I had no desire to visit Marie those nights. I was in a daze after the session. I remember walking around with no real awareness of my surroundings. I was impressed by how effective this new treatment was compared to the mind control I had experienced in the past. This was pure, concentrated mind control. Absolutely dense with trauma. *Improved.*

After a few visits, the Doctor said casually, "There, you're all finished. You may leave, I don't think I will be seeing you again."

I was afraid of my own shadow after the reconditioning. I questioned every decision I made, with complete fear. I was constantly asking others, 'what should I do?' or for their help with how to make a decision about something. Even the small decisions—like inputting data into the computer at my job. It was awful. Anything presented to me was met with a fear-based reaction.

I don't know how long it was, maybe a week or two after that one of the guys from C Bay came to talk to me at my post. He didn't have a nickname, he just went by his number. It was something like 572. Apparently he had a girlfriend in the red light district as well. Not at Krums, but some other place just like it. All the girls had contact with each other.

He said, "Hey, how are you doing man? We all heard about your treatment."

I just looked at him blank faced, mumbling, "I'm fine."

Then he went on to explain how his girlfriend had told him that Marie was asking about me and wanted me to know that she loves me and to come see her when I felt better. At that moment, I was totally numb emotionally. I had forgotten that I was in love with anyone. My memories of her were, for lack of better expression, blurry. And the feeling of love was somehow perverted into a secondary thought.

"Thanks for the message," I said, ignoring him further.

I simply went back to work. But throughout the day, I started to think more and more about her. I asked my coworker, nicknamed Renault, what I should do. He was my closest friend on the ship, mostly because we worked side by side all day.

He kept telling me what a poor bastard I was and that he felt sorry for me for what they had done. I had become a pale shadow of myself. He said that no matter what, I should go visit her and *try* to remember the person I was before the treatments.

I chickened out the first few days. I would get off the MVL and head to the train, but then I'd just stand there and watch them go. One train took me to the barracks and the other to the trade window to get money, where I could buy a train ticket to Krums. I would just stand there, indecisive, and watch them come and go until security would yell at me to move along. So, I would go to the barracks.

After three days of Renault asking me if I'd gone to see her, he started to get angry at me.

I would always say, "Well, I don't even know if she's working. We used to sync our schedules. She could be there or not and I don't want to throw time and money away."

He dropped it. He quit asking me if I'd gone to see her.

I would say in the morning, "Aren't you going to bug me to go to Krums?"

Deep inside, I wanted to see her badly and I wanted help because I was frozen by terror of making the wrong decision.

He just said, "Nope," and that was it.

The next day, Renault and 572 were waiting for me at the ship exit after we docked.

"Here you're going with him. Here's the money for a ticket, you can pay me back."

I didn't show it, but I was happy someone had made the choice for me. When we got to the entrance to Krums, 572 stopped.

"Ok—I'm not going in with you. They will charge me and you get in for free. For that reason alone, you should be happy to not be in the barracks and get stuck doing laundry. So just go in and relax, she's in there. I checked. Good Luck"

I went in and sat down. It was a daze. I could sense the familiarity of the place, but I was somehow completely detached. I started to have a panic attack. I started feeling like I was doing something wrong and I was going to get in severe trouble. Lynne came running up and hugged me as I sat in the booth.

"GERRY! What did they do to you?? Don't move!"

Then she left to find Marie. Luckily, it wasn't very busy at Krums. There were just a handful of other people there. Marie rushed over and hugged me. She didn't ask me anything. She knew. She was supportive, and helped me.

"Don't worry, you'll get past this, you'll see. Other's have come through it," she assured me.
I couldn't believe what I was hearing.

"Yeah? How do you know?"

Marie and Lynne talked among themselves, then Lynne walked off.

"She's going to get you a drink, trust me—it helps. Over time, what they did to you will wear off and you will be more yourself."

I asked, "Can you tell I'm not myself?"

She laughed, "Oh yes."

Lynne came back with a drink for me. They both said at the same time, "Drink this!"

Looking back, it was the first alcoholic drink of my life. I didn't really care for it, and couldn't understand how it could possibly help me. Marie explained that others had come into Krums that they knew were put through the same treatment. And they felt better after drinking alcohol.

When I was done with the drink, it was true. I did feel much better. It was like the fear went away and I felt more comfortable in my own skin. I asked for another, but they used a favor to get me that one. And that was it. I would have bought another if I had brought money with me, but I didn't go to the trade window that trip. I just had the "borrowed" day pass for the train from the guys in my crew.

Marie made a round and came back to sit with me. I told her I felt better and that I was really sorry for putting us through everything. I had a real moment where it all kind of came back to me. The emotions all came back, and the fear immediately began again. I started to cry and she just held me. She wouldn't let me speak, just told me over and over that it was going to be alright.

In that moment, we weren't lovers—it was as if she was my mother, and I was her child.

That night was the beginning of recovery from what I had gone through. The underlying fear and indecision was always there, but it continued to lessen over time. Just allowing the emotions of our conversation and having her as an anchor was what I needed to begin to dispel the whole process.

Kronig was happy that he got what he wanted. For the most part, I simply ignored him at the morning's briefings. My entire existence was overshadowed by a subconscious fear, permeating everything that I did. And he was thrilled about it. I actually think he moved on to someone else after me, because I fell out of his radar.

21

THE DEMOTION

There was always talk about the Pleiades. Not just on Ceres, but everywhere. It was synonymous with "shut up about it."

"Where are these boxes from?" I might ask.

"From the Pleiades now load them and fuck off," an officer might snark.

Anytime someone asked where we were going on a mission, the answer was always, "We're going to the Pleiades."

We knew that the beings within the Pleiades system were extremely advanced—both culturally and technologically speaking, much more so than that of

Ceres Colony. We were always told that we were not allowed there.

The Pleiades star cluster is roughly four hundred and forty-four light years from the sun and is one of the nearest open clusters to Earth. It is visible in the night sky most months of the year, and thus a relatively known cluster for Earth dwellers. It was just as common and well-known on Ceres. We were told there were hundreds of thousands of stars there, with thousands of civilizations—none of which were willing to do business with the Ceres Colony Corporation.

One day, it was mentioned that there were representatives on Ceres Colony from the Pleiades. They were there requesting pharmaceuticals to help combat a disease that had wreaked havoc on a civilization that they were taking care of.

It was a major deal, and people of the Ceres Colony tried to trade anything and everything we could with them, in exchange for classified technology. The Captain, who had fought so hard for a deal, was thrilled to learn that our ship was the one assigned to visit the Pleiades. This would be going down in the history books. The first trade agreement that Ceres Colony Corp had secured with members of the Pleiades system. It was huge.

When it was time to go, the Max Von Laue ship was packed to the brim. I remember going back to my work space with my coffee, and even *my space* was filled with cargo. We were making three or four trips per day to the Pleiades.

During the Pleiades runs, I had one of my first encounters with what would be termed within the Ceres Colony as an *ultra-human*. They had their own 'grading' system according to the level of advancement a certain human species has developed to. These were terms such as *beta-human* or *uber-human*, for example. Anyway, I got on the train one morning, and I saw *her*. She was no ordinary being—she would be what we might currently refer to as a sixth-density being, meaning extremely advanced. She was dark blue, with a bulbous head, a 'grey looking' female being. She had three fingers on each hand and three toes per foot —and every bit of fourteen feet tall. She was so tall that she had to lay down to be on the seat of the train. She wore a long, silky gown with sandals. When I looked at her, there was a shimmering 3D effect within the air. It was coming from the jewelry that she wore.

I sat there, completely blown away by this female being—she was beautiful. I couldn't keep my eyes off her.

You could help me, I thought to myself, looking at her. *You could help me out of this situation.*

She turned and looked up at me and smiled. I swear it was like seeing a unicorn. I lit up at her expression. It was an honor that she had even acknowledged me.

"Hey!" I heard someone shouting from the back of the train cart.

I turned around. It was an officer glaring at me.

"You're not supposed to be interacting with them!"

"Yes, sir," I replied quickly, making my way to the back of the train.

"Sorry, sir."

I knew she was someone who had the ability to fix me, and all the torment that had followed since the reconditioning I had experienced. She had somehow filled me with a hope that I hadn't felt in some time.

We continued our daily supply missions to a specific planet within the Pleiades. When we landed, we were amongst a dense, tropical forest on a landing pad built out of seamless megalithic stone tiles, perfectly positioned, and at least a mile wide.

We would offload the cargo on this platform, then the Command Crew would walk along a stone road towards pyramids in the distance. They would meet with other beings to go over the manifest and what was delivered for that day.

The beings of the Pleiadian planet *chose,* by name, officers from the Command Crew that were permitted to meet with them (and the ones that weren't). They literally scanned us—upon entering the planetary atmosphere, and decided who was 'suitable' for their meetings. Their scan list determined who could land with the cargo and who had to stay aboard the craft.

Our work effort became devoted entirely to this one trade agreement. Usually, under normal circumstances, we would do a drop off at one planet, then go to another, then maybe do a couple of inter-solar system runs. But now, we were dropping off cargo for about six weeks straight. And we continued to haul massive amounts of cargo to them. We weren't returning with any goods in return at this stage.

We kept doing these massive drop offs, several times a day, until one day, the deal was broken off. We arrived with our load as usual, but the entire area had been deserted. Everything we had dropped off was gone, the base was gone, and only the pyramids remained. There was not a soul to be found. We were robbed. They hadn't given us anything in return for all the goods we delivered.

One day, not long after, during a morning briefing, I was called to do a mission to Jupiter. It was connected to what had gone down on the Pleiadian world.

"You're coming with us," a superior officer informed me. "You're required."

"—But I'm not even on the away missions anymore!" I replied.

"No—" the officer was adamant. "We've all been ordered. You have to come."

We entered one of the temporal bubbles surrounding Jupiter where I learned that there was a Draco base. This base was this species' home within our solar system. It was made of brown and black steel with appendages extending from the central dome unit. We docked along one of the appendages. There were no stars around this base. Everything was just black.

We exited our ship through an umbilical. Once inside, there was a seven foot tall reptilian with a snake looking face waiting to meet us. He was wearing a long robe.

"You'll come with me," he said loud and telepathically, escorting us along the hallway.

His tone meant we were in trouble. To amplify this, we felt like children walking through the hallway. The viewing windows were about ten feet from the ground and it made us feel small and insignificant. The floors were an epoxy red color, and it was obvious that the hallway was made for someone who was at least fourteen feet tall.

As we walked, Kronig came alongside me.

"You know why we brought you here?" he said to me.

"You are filler. We brought you here to die in case anything goes wrong."

That scared the shit out of me. I knew he would.

The reptilian stopped outside a set of doors.

"Aren't you coming in with us?" one of our officers looked at him.

"No, these others stay here—just you three," he answered, referring to the Captain, the Korvetten Captain, and the next high ranking Officer in charge.

The rest of us stayed outside. We stood at attention outside the doors. We could hear the discussion because the translators were turned on.

"They have swords," an officer spoke.

You could hear that they were scared of the Draco Reptilians. When the doors fully sealed, we could no longer pick up the conversation.

After about thirty minutes, the two officers came through the doors carrying the Captain out. The Captain, who I have never seen so damaged and disturbed, had rows of snot coming from his nose. He was crying hysterically, had pissed himself, and looked like he had been beaten. He was in complete shambles, as if he'd just had a nervous breakdown.

"Get to the ship!" the officers shouted hurriedly. "Now!"

Everyone ran as fast as we could back to the ship. I was already scared, but to see our Captain, who was such a strong man, become broken like that, absolutely shook me to my core.

The Ceres Colony was essentially sponsored by this group of Draco Reptilians. It was by their measure, their personal goods that were stolen by the Pleiades.

When we returned, the Captain took a leave of absence for about a week. During this time, the Max Von Laue and crew had no missions. When the Captain finally returned, he was not himself. We met for the morning mission briefing.

"You've been ordered from now on, to take matters into your own hands to ensure that this never happens again," the Captain advised.

"We lost a lot of material, and if it ever happens again, we will face worse disciplinary action than what we already have."

The Captain never went into the specifics of what had happened, but nothing at our meetings was ever the same. Everything was back in German, and nobody knew what was talked about between the superior Officers. Sometimes they raised their voices amongst each other, but the Captain just sat there, his eyes glazed over looking down at the table. He used to be engaging, would look at people, laugh and whatever, but he was never the same.

I had entered the phase where I knew I was going to be going home very soon. I had about eight months left of service, nearing the end of my twenty years.

A couple of days later, we took a mission to Diego Garcia in the dead of the night to wait on a Russian ship. Most of the guys down in cargo thought it was simply business as usual, but I knew otherwise because I had sat in on the meetings.

When we went to Diego Garcia, there was a running joke amongst the cargo guys.

"We're going to pick up Russian cargo off of a Chinese boat at an American Airbase with an Italian first name and a Spanish second name in the Indian ocean—for a German Colony."

We loaded up the cargo from the Russian ship, and it went straight into the C Bay. Whatever it was, was extremely heavy. It was completely covered in tarps, but you could make out that there were round drum type objects; thirty feet tall and about twelve feet in width. After that load-up, I got another three days off.

Krums became extremely busy, and I kept missing Marie during my visits. Every time I went, it was packed and there were people sitting at my table, so I couldn't stay. I went three or four times and missed her every time.

I bumped into Lynne once, and gave her a big hug before she had to get back to work.

"Tell Marie I said hi!"

She smiled, "I will!"

They were celebrating something like Oktoberfest— the girls were wearing corsets and dressed in all green. I didn't realize it at the time, but this would be my last visit to Krum's. It was too busy for me and I wasn't going to participate in the holiday with anyone. I planned to return when it settled back down. That belief would come to haunt me for the rest of my tour.

The next time I returned to the hangar for a mission, someone was handing out flyers and pamphlets about radiation protocols.

"Hand these out to your guys," the worker said.

I glanced over the information. It was a refresher of training I had already done. My colleagues and I began to wonder what was going on. This was unusual. Then we were called in for a briefing by our superiors.

"Because you are the only one certified on your side of the bay to use the old crystal cranes, your system is now adapted to a missile cassette," the officer spoke.

"So, you'll get the order, the missiles will be deployed out of the side of the bay on the cranes, and then you get the order to rotate the cassette after one missile is fired."

I was dumbfounded. *What?*

"Don't worry," the officer assured me.

"We're gonna go back to that Pleaidian planet and give them a show of force. Let's see if they come clean and follow through on their part of the bargain."

"Why do we even bother with these Earthling type nuclear missiles?" another officer spoke up next to me.

"You know we can do way better than this, even with smaller ones."

The Captain answered, "Because we've already lost too much material. We don't want to commit any more material to this deal than we have to. Cheap weapons are the order."

The rumor mill really went crazy amongst the crew aboard the ship. Everyone that I knew admired the beings in the Pleiades system. They were fourth to fifth density beings who were very peaceful. Everyone that I spoke to—at least twenty people, swore they were going to refuse to fire on this planet.

I voiced my concerns to the Superiors, "Everybody's concerned about this, and nobody wants to participate."

"Don't worry," an officer said to me.

"This isn't your business to be concerned with. It is simply a show of force. This is how business is done."

We returned to the Pleiadian planet and you could feel that shit was about to go down. The engineers had placed a wall where the crane was inside the cargo bay, and almost as soon as we entered the planetary atmosphere, the missiles were fired. It was deafeningly loud. I was totally shell shocked from it. When I got the order to rotate the cassette, I didn't—I hesitated and just sat there. Partially because I was in shock and partially because the magnitude of mass murder was heavy on my shoulders. It was my way of abstaining from being party to something I didn't agree with: firing nuclear missiles on people. I couldn't stop thinking about how many people could die from this. I thought that other crew members would join me in protest. But it seemed to be just me.

Suddenly, I got a shock from my collar and the programming kicked in. I went into a daze.

"Now, rotate the cassette!" came the order.

I did, and all six of the missiles fired. Then they continually shocked me on low voltage for a while thereafter. I just lay on the floor.

When we got back to Ceres Colony, I was demoted and told that I was going to receive immediate discipline. I was stripped of the small rank that I had acquired, while still being required to do my same job. After I completed my day duties, I had another shift of manually unpacking boxes. I lost my bank account and the money I had in it. I couldn't take the train anywhere, and had to work a sixteen-hour day for the rest of my time in Ceres Colony. I never again sat in on another mission briefing meeting, either. It was all over.

I was made to attend classes as well, extending my day even further. And the content was stupid—it was merely another form of punishment. But it was a requirement, and there was no getting out of it.

My days were so full that there was no going to Krums anymore, and I was totally devastated. I tried to get messages to Marie through a friend, to explain to her what had happened, and continually had thoughts of how I could escape and get out of my situation. I even asked friends for money.

"Where are you gonna go?" the friend replied.

"You've only got a couple of hours, you will never make it back in time!"

My day was so overloaded—and done purposely—there was no time to do anything, even to rest. At the end of my late shift, I would walk from the hangar to the giant elevator with a bunch of kids that were attending classes also. They were part of the bridge crew on the Max Von Laue.

Every time I got on the elevator, there were the same two girls. I remember one's name was Nicky, and she would always tell people what was on her mind. She was heavy on respect. I stayed on the elevator when all the other guys had gotten off, for the remaining seven levels. One day, Nicky and her friend got into an argument. The taller friend became nasty with Nicky.

"I'm done with you!" she shouted. "I don't ever want to talk to you again!"

The girl pressed the nearest level and got off.

When the doors closed, it was just Nicky and me. She started to cry. She turned and looked at me, and I gave her a hug. No words, no talking, just a big hug. She got off the elevator, and the next day, her ex-friend didn't even ride with us. When the ride finally emptied, Nicky turned to me.

"Thank you," she said.

"I know about you. You had a girlfriend. And your time is almost up."

"Yes, that's right."

Over the next few days on the elevator, Nicky and I would talk a lot. Eventually, she invited me over to her apartment.

"I can't come," I said, "I don't have any money."

"I'll give you the money."

And then Nicky gave me money to go and visit her at her apartment. It was far down within the Ceres planet. Originally, the Deutsche found caverns, with triangular stone doors that must have weighed tons. The caverns were massive, and they converted them into apartments.

It was a ten minute train ride, followed by a thirty minute elevator ride down. I never saw the bottom of the elevator and I took it at least a few miles down. There were catwalks meeting the elevator at each floor, enabling access to the apartments.

Whatever was living on Ceres Colony before could either fly, or was some type of aquatic species. Urban legend had it that the caverns could have once been filled with water.

I went to Nicky's apartment often and spent time with her. I almost never slept. Before long, we became lovers. I was still madly in love with Marie, but I felt a bit of entitlement wash over me. I figured, well she was having sex with multiple people all the time— why couldn't I? In retrospect, it was a coping mechanism.

Nicky and I didn't have a deep, mental connection. But she was very beautiful, and we had a nice physical attraction. When we had finished being intimate, she would say to me "Don't talk to me," or

"Just lay there." But we both filled a void for that time in our lives, and we both needed each other. This went on for about a month. Then Nicky quit giving me money and didn't want to see me anymore. I craved Marie again. I really missed her.

22

THE RETURN

Then came the day. My time on Ceres Colony was up. I was walking to my morning shift on the ship when the Bridge Officer in charge of cargo approached me.

"Today's your day," he said to me.

"You're gonna come with me."

We walked together for a good thirty minutes from the big hangar towards the little ones.

"You know, you were basically a good guy. We liked you. Up until the very end," he surmised.

"It was no business of yours to interfere—none whatsoever. You didn't know what we were doing— we could've been putting warning shots in the air!

You had no idea what we were shooting at, and that decision was not yours to make. You could have cost people their lives by doing that. I hope you learn a lesson from all of this."

"Well, if it's any consolation," I replied, "I'm gonna remember all of this."

"—Don't even bother!" the officer interjected.

"You will not remember anything. You stood out from your peers most of the time, and because of that, you have qualified for a breeding program. But don't worry—we will keep an eye on your children. Your offspring could qualify to become personnel on Ceres Colony. Forget all about this and go back to your little Earth life and marry a good German girl. Don't be trying to make big decisions."

We had been walking down a hallway, where we then exited and he walked me to a metal catwalk. It led to one of the old chrome colored discs.

"Don't worry about the Captain," he called out.

"Go back to your life and forget about all of us."

The walk down the catwalk to the ship door was devastating to me. Even to that moment, I still had hope that I would see Marie again. As if something magical would happen and I would be gifted a trip to see her. The reality of my leaving forever set in and I paused halfway. In my mind I was crushed with grief.

Someone from the door of the disc yelled, "Come on, don't be shy."

I broke my thought and walked in. When I got inside the disc, the motor compartment was shrouded in some type of black cover. I passed it by and proceeded to the left, where I found a staircase leading to the top deck. To the left of the stairwell and down a little was the cockpit. There sat a reptilian pilot, as well as a human one.

"Welcome aboard," they said.

"Do not try to cause us any trouble—just go on up there beside the rest of them. We are going to be taking you to the Moon. The duration of this trip will be approximately six hours."

I went up the stairs to a rounded room with a built-in rounded sofa. There was disgusting carpet. Five people were already there, and I was told that we were awaiting a few others. This was actually the first time that I had seen a black man on Ceres Colony.

"Don't talk to me you stink ass motherfucker," the black man seethed at the reptilian.

"Yeah! That's right, you piece of shit asshole."

I couldn't believe how disrespectful he was to this reptilian pilot.

"Hey man—" I intervened. "Just chill out, they gotta get us back there yet!"

"Oh really, whatta they gonna do, huh?" The black man mouthed.

"They can't do shit now. They got our travel time down to a 'T', without a second to spare. Whatta they gonna do, put us in jail? They gotta get us back and put us in our original lives—and they time it to the last five minutes. They don't have time to discipline me, so I can do or say whatever the fuck I want."

He glanced back over to the pilots. "Ain't that right you stupid fuck faces?"

Finally, he and everyone else got settled. There were eight or nine of us occupants, journeying to the Moon. Nothing eventful happened—it was a boring flight. I found myself pacing back and forth, watching while everybody else lay back and got comfortable. All I could think about was Marie. I was desperate to see her. It killed me that I couldn't say goodbye to her.

I'm not ever going to forget her. I'm gonna find her one day. I'm gonna remember all of this. I'm gonna remember, I'm gonna remember, I'm gonna remember, I'm gonna remember. For hours I made this vow to myself.

This went on through my mind over and over and over again. The psychic told me that I was gonna find *1 of the 3... 1 of the 3...* I remembered these words like my life depended on it.

At last, we arrived on the moon. We were taken to a part of the base that I'd never seen before. There was a quick intake by very robotic greys, then we were lined up and chaperoned into a medical-type doctor's room. I tested my luck.

"This isn't going to work, I'm going to remember all of this," I blurted out. "You'll see."

"Do not worry about it," one of the tall, white greys replied.

"We have to do a thorough assessment. Sit on the table."

"No!" I retorted, "So what are you gonna do about it?"

The grey looked at me. He had absolutely no idea of what to do. He was so overwhelmed and confused that he left to get help from two co-workers.

"You need to cooperate with us, because otherwise the process could go very wrong and you could end up crippled," the grey advised.

"And if we have to do it, we will terminate you. So please get up on the table."

I did what they asked, I got up on the table, but I was adamant.

"I'm still going to remember all of this. You won't be able to erase my memory."

They then wheeled me into another room that resembled an arcade. They started a series of injections. They told us straight up what they were doing. One injection for forgetting faces, flashing of hypnotic lights, and then came movies with images to make you forget more faces. Then followed a brain scan to see if their efforts were successful.

"Well that doesn't matter," I said to the grey, "because I'm still gonna remember you."

I was wheeled around six or so different booths in the arcade room, all with more processes of erasing memories. I remember one of these processes involved the use of 'flying ship' imagery from Peter Pan, so that anytime I would recall a craft in my memory, my brain would see the flying ship of Peter Pan instead. I laughed at how ridiculous this all seemed.

"Do you really think I'm gonna remember seeing this Peter Pan ship?" I laughed.

"This is so ludicrous, what kind of fool do you take me for?"

After the memory erasing procedures, they took me to a surgical area where I continued on with my nasty rants. They ended up bringing in a reptile, just in case I did anything wrong. He would handle me. I believe they were removing something from me in this surgery, but what it was, I am not sure. I could hear them setting little items into a pan.

Then they laid me down on a table and peered down at me.

"You are going to be here for a few weeks," they advised me.

"During this time, you cannot move your spine. If you do, it could cause you permanent damage."

Then they injected me with immobilizing muscle relaxants, so I couldn't move anyway. My body was surrounded by a bed of soft black foam, and a feeding line was inserted in my arm. There were several other tubes inserted in me to facilitate normal bodily functions. The muscle relaxants were administered regularly—everyday I'd guess, to stop my muscles from moving. They would come in, say hello to me telepathically, and then get on with it.

"How long is this going to take?" I asked them repeatedly.

"Don't worry about it," the tall, whitish grey would blow me off.

"I bet you would love to remember this part of your experiences."

I had lost all sense of time around me. It could've been weeks. My desire to move a limb was unfathomable. After some time, they stopped giving me injections, but I still couldn't move. Eventually, the black foam surrounding me was pulled off and I was put on a gurney.

"Well? What's next" I wondered, looking at them as they wheeled me inside a big tube.

No one answered. Suddenly a bright purple light filled the tube, and I remember the pain that began to flood my body, first in my legs. It felt like golf ball sized areas of pain, just pulsating throughout. It felt like I was being incinerated, the pain was torturous.

When I woke up, I found myself on another table. My body was ten years old. I was surrounded by greys, a tall white, and a reptilian. We were in a brightly lit surgical room.

But this time, I knew I was myself. I was my Earth self again. I was a ten year old boy from the 1980's again. I hadn't a clue what was going on.

They looked at me.

"Do you remember?" one asked me.

"Do you remember where you just came from?"

"I just came from my house!" I answered them.

"I'm from Willis, Michigan!"

The Reptilian and one of the greys started laughing.

"After all the talk, you're not going to remember a thing, are you?"

"I am going to remember this!" I stammered

They continued laughing. "No, you're not."

I could feel my cheeks burning with anger. I was so mad at them. Here I was sitting on the table, naked, feeling myself become livid.

All these memories of my mother, my sisters and my life in Michigan flooded back into me. It was as if I was in a completely different body. I remembered a conversation from the week before with my mother.

She was telling me about God and Jesus, as she was quite religious at the time.

"If you believe in Jesus enough, you can ask him for anything, and he will help you," she had assured me.

I sat there looking at all these ET's.

"In the name of Jesus—I am going to remember ALL OF THIS." I shouted at the top of my lungs.

The tall white who was looking at a computer screen, called a Chronovisor, snapped at the others.

"Quit what you're doing to him. I see here that he does remember," he scolded them.

"You've just caused an anomaly. So quit it now! You're all going to be reported for this."

The room became dead silent. Every one of them became still. The tall white was observing my probable timelines, since I told him I was going to remember everything. That's what the Chronovisor did—it scanned your timelines. At the moment I became super angry, I literally changed the probable timelines of the course of my life.

They stopped everything and one of them made a call, most likely to the administration. Finally he turned to the others.

"He is going to be taken for another round of programming."

The reptilian escorted me down another hallway to another type of medical room full of ET's and a few humans. I was then taken to yet another room— a corner office with windows that I could see out to the lunar surface.

I sat down for another procedure. Another grey being came beside me, but he looked older and had darker skin. There was a certain look about him, more robotic.

"The sun comes up in another eighteen hours," he turned to me.

"Then it's much better looking out there."

He then put something on my head, and hooked in some electrodes.

"You need to cooperate with me," he advised carefully. "I need to get your percentage down to under twenty-five percent. If not—you will receive a lobotomy."

"Ok, well I guess I can," I said, not knowing what he was talking about.

In between procedures, the reptilian talked to me, and made me laugh. I almost want to say he is the original reptilian from my first initial abduction. The Bruce Lee lover.

"It's good to see you again!" he said warmly.

He was the muscle in the room this time—there as security, just in case I didn't cooperate. The darker robotic grey, who was also the one in front of the Chronovisor, was disappointed. He kept repeating the procedure over and over because he was not satisfied with the results.

Eventually he called someone else in, and I was injected again. Next, I was wheeled into another area in front of another computer monitor to my right. There was a second monitor, about the size of a clipboard and it was displaying static.

I was injected again and then plugged into this clipboard computer device. I was given a shock and then the screen responded as if it were alive, as if it were responding to me.

The computer to the right of me came closer, and out of nowhere, I heard words through my mind.

"I am your God! And I am angry with you!"

I wasn't in awe, but I was dumbfounded. The clipboard sized screen, still full of static, then moved and forced me to look at it. It was like he'd Zoomed in an evil reptilian. I was shown imagery inside my head of a first contact type scenario in a village that looked like it was in Vietnam or Cambodia. I was seeing everything through the eyes of one of the men in the scene, as if I was there, experiencing it. There were six men going into this village, hacking these village people to pieces. Women and children included, and I was completely shocked by witnessing this. It is still the most horrific thing I'd ever seen in all of the programming.

"You are *not* my God!" I retaliated.

I felt the volts of electricity burn through my body. They had shocked me again.

"I am your God and I am angry with you!" the voice bellowed through my mind again.

I kept saying to myself over and over again: *You are not my God, you are not my God.*

Suddenly I lost consciousness, and when I came to, the grey tested me again.

"It didn't work," he responded to the reptilian. "Take him down, he's gonna have to get surgery."

Now the reptilian, who was originally funny and friendly with me, turned cold and despondent towards me.

"Come on," he said, chaperoning me out.

I don't remember walking from one office to the next, as I was completely catatonic at this point. When I snapped back to focus in the next office, there were two greys sitting there.

"He's here for the lobotomy," the reptilian said, "I'm here to drop him off—he's all yours."

The two greys scanned me.

"There's no record of his service," one replied.

"He hasn't completed his time, so there is nothing to lobotomize."

"Is that so?" the reptilian replied stupefied.

"Well, he's going to remember everything."

"Well he's got no record to sign," the grey answered. "We need to sign something in order to proceed. And besides, if there is no record, and he does remember, there's nothing he can do to us anyway. So technically, there's no record of him ever being up here, so just put him back!"

"Oh!" the reptilian replied, looking surprised.

He looked at me, "Well! It's your lucky day."

Suddenly, I went catatonic again.

And this time, I woke up in my bed. My bed, back at my house, on Earth.
It was April of 1982 again. I woke up and glimpsed around my room, looking at all my stuffed animals. I saw my messy floor, with a pile of toys laying there.

I was totally shocked. I felt like I hadn't been there in twenty years. I was happy. It was a nice day outside, sunny, slightly cool.

"Tony!" my mom called out from downstairs.

"Get down here! It's breakfast time!"

I went downstairs, and my mom had set the table. She was being weird that day. She hardly ever made breakfast.

"Oh, I should be making breakfast for you everyday," she said.

My dad was also acting a bit weird, and he sat to the right of me. My sister was across from me. We weren't even sitting at the normal dining table, we were all sitting at a fold-out card table. It was so weird. I looked at each of them.

"I feel like I haven't seen any of you in years," I said, almost in tears, giving my mom a big hug.

"Don't be stupid!" my sister scoffed at me.

"We only had dinner together last night."

I felt my mom looking down at my head.

"Michael! He's got a mark on him!" she gasped, looking behind my head.

"Here! Behind his ear."

On the left of my head, behind my ear, was a mark.

"Natalie, knock it off!" Dad answered, making no big deal out of it.

"You're making a big deal out of nothing."

"—Did you see those bright lights last night?" my sister chimed in.

"—Don't worry about it," my dad said quickly. "Nothing happened."

"But he's got a mark on him!" My mother was adamant.

"You know, I've just been working for twenty years, and that's all I'm gonna keep doing forever!"

My mom looked at dad.
"It's all your fault, too," he said, looking at me.

"Michael, what's got into you? You've always loved your job."

My dad was talking weirdly, super depressing.

We finished breakfast, then my sister and I walked down our long driveway to catch the bus. She got on hers first, and then I got on mine. Like every other Earth day, I rode the bus into town to get to school.

Later on in the day, around 1:00pm, I raised my hand in class to use the bathroom.

"Can I go to the bathroom?" I asked the teacher at the front.

"Yeah, you can go."

"Well, where is it?" I asked.

Suddenly the class erupted into hysterical laughter. I honestly had forgotten where the bathrooms were and had a hard time remembering the layout of the school. Everything was different. I even looked at everyone differently. To my own confusion, I began to see adult women differently. I was totally spooked.

And that was that.

I was taken on a Thursday, lived for twenty years in this program, and was then slipped back into earthly reality—waking up Friday morning. I would remember almost nothing of this experience for the next thirty-three years of my life.

That is, until I got headaches in my early forties and was sent for an MRI. Within a few weeks of the scan, everything came flooding back in.

Later that Friday night, when I was a boy back home, there was a huge rain, and I went out to play in the mud puddles. My dad took a picture of me. I remember it so clearly because I remember the sense of shame that I had felt, and how much shame I felt for my father. I felt shameful for what had transpired. I could not understand anything about my feelings, let alone process them. I was never really the same after that.

They were half right. At that point, I didn't remember. Just felt something.

Not long after came the end of the school year. In 5th grade, I completely withdrew from school, from everything. I couldn't care less about being good at anything. I just wanted to be alone.

And then, I started searching...

MY 20 YEAR TOUR TIMELINE

1972
- Birth

1981 - 82
- Attended 4th grade
- Started classes for Talented and Gifted, TAG, at Lincoln Elementary School on Wednesdays in the library
- Had contact with self proclaimed son of an Illuminati
- Sometime around April, had the school science fair and met student's father, who was volunteering as a judge for the science fair
- A day or two later, woke up with grey alien in my face and was taken for twenty years

April of 1982 - Jan of 1983
- MK-Ultra programming
- Woke up near China Lake at Inyokern airstrip buildings and put through MK-Ultra style trauma based mind control
- During that time, taken on TR3B style craft to moon base for medical procedures and returned to Inyokern base

- Then shipped via underground high speed rail to near Helena, Montana and picked up woman to be driven to island near Seattle
- Kept for about 2 weeks and witnessed Satanic ritual human sacrifice.

Jan of 1983

- Flown via private plane to Puerto Tahuantinsuyo, Peru
- Did intuitive missions on shipments of cocaine, monthly, from there to Santa Marta, Colombia.

1985

- Lost intuitive ability and became sick from the drugs used and flown via cargo plane back to Northern California and picked up by same woman and driven back to island

Fall 1985 - Summer 1988

- Used as sex slave for private parties with political guests

Summer of 1988

- Became allergic to medication given to the boys there and sold to military
- Taken to moon trapezoid base and trained for suicide missions - possibly 3 months
- Taken to seperate moon base with an arena and tested against giant insectoid with a dozen other boys.

1989

- For a month or so, taken to Mars Colony Corporation and used for 3 combat missions as a bounding maneuver - bait - forced to engage indigenous bugs on mars - 3rd mission failed and project was cancelled
- 3rd mission had contact with an advanced mantoid

Summer of 1989

- Taken to Aries Prime and trained in starship repair procedures and then shipped via portal train system to Ceres Colony Corp on planetoid Ceres for the German Breakaway colony there.

1990-1997

- Served on the Blitzbus ship as repair slave

1997

- Pipe incident and ship was decommissioned and was reassigned to a new ship still under construction and promoted to cargo engineer

1998-2001

- Cargo engineer position, had income and was able to travel thru the colony and met Marie - working sex slave in the red light district at Krums bar.

2001

- Last 6 months of service had a nuclear incident on the Pleiadian world and demoted and lost income and was unable to see Marie again, had a brief month or so affair with a coworker from communications on the bridge crew.
- Taken via disc back to the moon and age regressed and returned to 1982 and put back in life the same night I was taken

Made in the USA
Columbia, SC
30 January 2025

52984670R00263